Marie S. Beddoe-Talbot

Ave.

Scranton, Pa. 1854

WIDOW'S WALK

PAMELA CUMING

WIDOW'S WALK

A Personal Journey Through Loss, Fear, Anger, and Love

Crown Publishers, Inc.   *New York*

Printed in the United States of America
Published simultaneously in Canada
by General Publishing Company Limited
Library of Congress Cataloging in Publication Data
Cuming, Pamela, 1944–
Widow's walk.
I. Title.
PS3553.U437W5 1981   813'.54   80-27461
Book design by Camilla Filancia
ISBN: 0-517-54332X
10 9 8 7 6 5 4 3 2 1
First Edition

SPECIAL THANKS TO

*Clyde . . . for being there
when I needed him, and for making me laugh at myself
even during moments of keen despair.*

*Joy . . . friend and critic,
for adding color and texture to both my life
and the pages of this book.*

*Kaye and Bill . . . for their unending devotion
to me and my children, and for their cabin in Maine,
without which I might never have completed
this book.*

*Margaret . . . for her continuous positive regard,
and for her encouragement even as my need to write
added to the burden she herself bore.*

*Marilyn . . . for caring enough
to look after me throughout my long journey
back to peace.*

*Monica and Melissa . . . my children,
for being simply themselves, and for loving me and encouraging me
to write even when it meant sacrificing some of our time together.*

*Phil . . . my new friend,
for helping me gain valuable insight into myself.*

*Vic . . . for convincing me
that I could and should undertake the writing of this book.*

*My friends and family . . . for picking me up
each time I fell during the long and often
treacherous widow's walk.*

Part I

THE FIRST WEEK

Death and Its Aftermath

1

Trauma

We were having a family barbecue on the porch. Bill was obviously delighted that the three children—his son and my two little girls— were vying for his attention. Seated comfortably on the chaise longue, he held court. While he let Monica pour out her troubles, he held Melissa's hand. Then it was Pete's turn. Melissa interrupted and was lovingly chastised. And on it went as words poured out in an effort to express the love that had been bottled up in each of them during "Daddy Bill's" hospitalization. I had to content myself with frequent loving glances. Princess, our malamute puppy, had to settle for only an occasional pat on the head. The king was home.

Just that afternoon we had taken him from the hospital. His heart, after two attacks, seemed strong. His medication had been adjusted, and after months of worry we allowed ourselves to hope. Bill had been something of a gourmet cook and had to content himself with supervising our efforts to cook hamburgers and corn on the barbecue. He seemed pleased enough and vigorously ate several burgers. I let the little girls sit to his right and left, and I determined to have my time with him after they were in bed.

I felt at peace for the first time in months. The threat that had loomed over all of us seemed to have vanished as thoroughly as the clouds after a summer shower. I sat and quietly thought of the small pleasures that give life substance and meaning, and looked forward to crawling into bed next to him at night. I mused over how nice it was going to be to share again—to share thoughts and feelings and the burden of keeping us all safe. I had been brave during his illness and looked forward to dropping the pretense of being the invulnerable, independent woman. I wanted to lean a little for a change and knew that he looked forward to that, too. Being constantly cared for and waited on, Bill had begun to lose self-respect. He needed to be needed, and I needed him desperately. Just a few hours, I thought, and I'll be able to be me, fully me—with my weaknesses showing along with my strengths, with my love showing as well as my perseverance. If I had known what was to happen within a few moments, I could not have survived.

We had all finished eating. The children were busy clearing the table. Bill said that he felt a little light-headed and thought he should lie down for a few minutes. I helped him to the bedroom and sat with him briefly as he closed his eyes. I wasn't too concerned—it had been an active day, a thousand times more active than had been his days in the hospital. Seeing him resting, I returned to the porch to help the children. They were singing as they worked. Any concern I had was immediately outweighed by the way I felt at being a family again. I sang along and worked with them.

Suddenly I heard Bill shouting my name over and over with an urgency I had never before heard. I dropped the dishes and ran. As I bent over him, he grabbed my wrist, grabbed it with such force that I can still feel the pressure. My hand went numb and, as suddenly, his grasp relaxed. The light went from his eyes. I screamed to Pete to get an ambulance. Six-year-old Melissa ran into the bedroom and simply stood there and stared. I don't believe I felt anything at the time. I was unaware of everything except the need to save him—to bring back the light in his eyes and the fight in his body.

I pulled him off the bed. He seemed very light, though he was a big man. I felt for his carotid pulse. There was none. I became a machine, all my energies devoted to applying the steps I had learned in the coronary-pulmonary resuscitation course I had taken. Breathe four times. Follow with fifteen chest compressions. Push hard. So what if you break a rib or two. Make sure he doesn't choke on his own vomit. Clear his mouth. Keep his head back. Remember that. Do it again. And again. And again. Nothing was happening and I knew it. The air was coming from him and still the same blank stare. I panicked. I started to cry and then stopped. Keep going. Keep going. Suddenly the bedroom was filled with people, and they pulled me away from him. They wanted me to leave the room, and I did not resist. There was a policeman and he started asking questions, questions that made me angry. He asked for Bill's name and then asked if I was any relation of his. Any relation! Then my children were around me, and Melissa wanted me to tell her it would be all right. I couldn't lie to her. I didn't think it would be all right. I *knew* it was all wrong. Everything was wrong. I sat on the kitchen floor with her and we cried.

I caught a glimpse of the stretcher being carried out of the house. They were still working on him. I began to hope. Maybe they had gotten a reaction. Why else would they still be working so hard? Getting up from the floor, I forgot my children, forgot everything but my new surge of hope. The policeman took me in his car, and we followed the ambulance. I talked constantly. I didn't want to think. I said I knew it would be all right and waited for the policeman to agree with me. He didn't. He started talking about his own life, about the time when his mother had a heart attack and about how he had suffered.

I really didn't want to listen—how could he compare the loss of a parent to the loss of my husband! After all, we are taught to expect that our parents will die before we do. Loving a parent is different from loving a spouse. By the time we are adults, I thought, although we love our parents, we no longer need them—need them and depend on them in the way that I needed and depended on Bill. He made me angry, but he was also my only hope, my only way to get to the hospital and to my Bill. I said, "That must have been very hard for you." He answered, "Yes, and I guess that's why I really feel close to this case."

This case! Suddenly I had a vision of the report he would file—case number, name, address, time of call. My trauma would be reduced to a line on a call sheet. So, that's the way it would be. That confirmed it. No one in the world really cared about me the way Bill did, and no one cared about him the way I did. He just couldn't die. My strength vanished, and I managed to say only, "We've got to get there when the ambulance does. Bill needs me. If I'm not there, he'll give up. He's got to fight his way out of this one. I know he can do it, but only if I'm near him. It's that way between us." I wanted to cry, but I would not. I had had only a few hours respite from being the invulnerable, indomitable one and found the script of Miss Independence, Miss Cool, to be a familiar one. I knew the lines. I started acting.

After what seemed like an hour (it was only ten minutes), we arrived at the emergency room of the hospital. The ambulance was parked at the entrance, but no one was around. Running in, I went right past the nurse sitting in the waiting room. I knew all too well where I was going. I had been there before. Suddenly I was inside the emergency room itself. There is a large nurses' station in the middle of the room, surrounded on all sides by a string of small rooms, closed off from view only by yellow curtains. It was a Sunday evening and the hospital was quiet. I sensed that there was activity behind only two of the closed curtains. I knew where Bill was because of all the feet under one curtain. No one was talking. But they were still working. That was a good sign, I thought. Suddenly I felt very faint. I hoped that one of the nurses would impose hospital regulations and take me to the place where I was supposed to be. I knew I looked composed and in control of myself. I also knew that was just part of the act, and that the real me was a very frightened child.

Within moments, my wish came true. The nurse and, with her, the cop, came over to me and guided me to the back of the emergency room. I had never been there before. It was a small room, with a couch and four chairs and no room for anything else—the right size for a single family. I wondered why they hadn't taken me back to the larger waiting room. I hoped it was because I looked different, more "special" than the people who had been in that room.

Asking for a cup of coffee, I kept trying to block out the idea that I had been taken to the room reserved for the family who is about to be told that a death has occurred. I noticed for the first time that my skirt was soiled, my blouse was no longer tucked in, and the bottom button was missing. I cried a little then, thinking of how I had chosen my best silk blouse to wear that day—that special day when, after all those weeks, I was to make the three-hour drive to get Bill out of the hospital. I had wanted to look so nice and to have everything perfect for him. The house was clean. His car was waxed. The refrigerator was fully stocked with his favorite foods. I had even installed the filter on the kitchen sink. He had wanted to do that for a long time. With the thought of the filter, my tears came harder. Bill hadn't even seen the filter. He didn't even know I had done that for him. He hadn't seen most of the house either. I tried to make myself believe that he would see it in the weeks to come. With that, my despair was rekindled. The weeks to come! I didn't think I could take any more of that.

Self-pity began to mix with the fear and the love that I was feeling. For five months I had been running the house and the consulting business that Bill and I had started together. Twelve-hour workdays had become the norm as I struggled to bring in enough money so that his salary, as well as mine, could continue. Our obligations to our own family as well as to his prior family were such that we needed every penny.

Bill had often said that he didn't understand why I loved him so much. He was seventeen years older than I, and after his first attack, he had been unable to do things that required sudden physical exertion. That hadn't mattered to me. In fact, it had triggered a role reversal that I enjoyed. I have never been very fond of the sedentary activities that go along with running a house. He was a fine cook and preferred indoor activities to outdoor work. He ran the kitchen and I split the wood. He drove the car up the icy driveway while I spread the sand. He did the painting and I lugged the ladders. He hosed down the screens while I washed the windows. He was the ultimate supervisor; I was the worker. I looked up to him, and he respected me.

For the first several years, the age difference hadn't mattered at all. It had only started to matter a few months before his death. His illness began to take a toll on his appearance. He had gotten very thin. His arms had begun to look old. His skin had lost its rosy tint. Despite all my efforts to convince myself that none of that mattered, it did matter. At fifty he had looked as if he were forty. At fifty-one he looked sixty. At the same time I was going through the transition of the middle thirties. I was still getting used to being called "ma'am" instead of "miss." I had enjoyed the role of professional ingenue, but that role was slipping, and I was unsure of what would be next. When Bill looked forty, I looked twenty-five by comparison, and I liked that. When he looked sixty, I figured people must assume that I was at least forty. I didn't like that. It added to my confusion. The age difference had begun to matter.

And Bill's children made a difference, and further challenged my sense of self. In marrying Bill, I became a stepmother to a grown son and daughter and to an adolescent boy. Pete was seventeen when he moved in with us. The adjustments we all had to make were difficult, and at times I bitterly resented the situation.

Bill's other two children did not have a daily impact on our lives. Edward, his oldest son, was married and involved in his own life. His visits were infrequent, and when they did occur, father and son were typically fully engrossed in chess. He came for dinner once or twice a year.

Cathy, Bill's daughter, visited us more often. During her visits we talked a lot. She conscientiously helped me with the household chores and spent time with my children, her young stepsisters. We learned to enjoy each other's company.

As I sat in the emergency room, engaging in self-pity over having to carry Bill's baggage along with my own, I began to think of Bill's family. I wondered whether I should call them. I worried about Pete. He had called the ambulance. I had seen him talking with the policemen in the house. I remembered asking him if he thought he could drive our car to the hospital. He had said that he could. I believed he had had an accident on the way, so great was my general feeling of pessimism and defeat.

Finally, as I sat wondering what to do about Pete, he ran into the waiting room. He looked so vulnerable. We held onto each other, and in the clinging we both lost our resolve not to cry. The tears flowed hard and fast for both of us. And then, as suddenly, we stopped. He sat down. I sat down. We were silent, each in our own private hells. Now and again he would reach out or I would reach out and we would grasp hands. No words were spoken.

We were silent and apart when a doctor, a stranger to me, entered our small room. Standing and looking down at me, he said very simply, "I'm sorry. There is nothing we can do for your husband. He never regained consciousness. I'm sorry." With that, he walked out. Pete moved over and sat next to me on the couch. We held each other, and he screamed, "Oh, God!" and cried. I held his head; I didn't cry. Not then. I felt nothing. It was as though nothing existed beyond that little room. We were cut off from the rest of the universe, floating. I felt dizzy and nauseated and realized that I needed to use the bathroom. When Pete was quiet, I got up and walked across the hall to the ladies' room. When I came out, a nurse was waiting for me and asked if I wanted her to call Dr. Wilson. I replied that I did and sat down again.

Dr. Wilson had been Bill's doctor for five years. He is a kind and approachable man. Bill had liked and respected him. I think he felt the same way about Bill. I didn't know him as well, having seen him only once a year for standard physicals. And yet, I needed to see him that night. I didn't know why. I needed to be taken care of, and he was elected.

Shortly after the nurse left to call Dr. Wilson, my friend Amy walked into what had become "my room." I had not called her, but I wasn't surprised to see her. We had shared so much over the years that it seemed only natural for her to simply sense when I was in trouble. She had been watching my children for the past several weekends while I was at the hospital with Bill. Only four hours earlier, she had brought the girls home for dinner. As I later discovered, when I had suddenly left the children at home and gone to the hospital, Monica, then eleven, had called Amy and asked her to pick them up again. Whenever I think of Monica's courage that night, I am saddened. She took it upon herself to make sure she and her younger sister, Melissa, were safe. Amy had picked them up, taken them to her house, and left them with her teen-age daughter to join me at the hospital. Amy knew Bill had had another attack. That is all she knew, until she walked into that room.

Amy sat down and looked at me. For a few seconds I couldn't meet her eyes. I couldn't bring myself to say what had to be said. Somehow, things don't become facts until they are verbalized. Bill was not yet dead to me. I didn't want to say it, for the saying of it would make it real. And yet Amy had to know. She had to know so that she could break the frightening loneliness that enveloped me. Finally I looked at her and said, "He died." And she responded, "I know." She stood and motioned for Pete and me to do the same. We found ourselves in the center of the tiny room, clutching one another as hard as we could, as if to form a barrier against the terror that was all around us. Pete and I cried again. Amy wouldn't cry, not yet. She had become our protector. She had to be the strong one, in spite of the deep affection she herself had for Bill. Her loss couldn't count, not then.

Our tears spent once again, we sat quietly, separately, each alone with private thoughts. Dr. Wilson came in. He moved a chair so that he could sit directly opposite me. I tried to introduce Pete and Amy, but he seemed interested only in me. Taking my hand, he said some things that helped me tremendously that night and during the difficult times that were to follow.

"Pam, I have never known a man to be so happy in his marriage as was Bill. At times, I envied him that. You made his last years very happy. Never forget that."

Dr. Wilson's words made me weep, but they also made me smile inside, for I knew that what he said was true. After giving me a minute to reflect, the doctor continued.

"The nightmare you're living now had to happen someday. Bill's heart was terribly scarred. His first attack should have killed him. That it did not is testimony to his will to live. That, and that alone, saved him. But he couldn't deny his damaged heart forever. We hoped to buy time, Pam, first with medication and then possibly with a tightening of the mitral valve. We had not discounted the possibility of a heart transplant. Bill was in serious trouble, Pam, over these last few years. That his illness did not dominate your lives is wonderful. It surely would have been allowed to dominate the life of a less happy man. In time, Pam, you will learn to value the memory of the love you and Bill shared."

They were trying to buy time. We didn't know that, and I am glad that we didn't. Dr. Wilson said that Bill and I had had four years that, according to medical science, we shouldn't have had. He reminded me that they had been four wonderful years, and that far too many people never in their lifetime know the kind of love we had shared. He made me momentarily glad for the years we had experienced. I began to focus on what had been ours and not on the loneliness that was to come. He also reminded me that I was a strong person and said that he didn't want to give me tranquilizers or other emotional pain-killers. I felt a twinge of self-pride and inwardly agreed with him that I was strong and could look my loss straight in the face. Then he stood, as if to leave, and that feeling of strength left me. I panicked, not at all sure I could handle my feelings without his support. Taking my hand again, he asked if I would like to see Bill for the last time.

The idea was horrifying. It was too real, too stark and naked. Recalling the blank stare I had seen only an hour or so before, I knew

I could never again look into those eyes and see no response. Something that resembled my Bill was lying on a table down the hall. Bill was not in the hospital. For the first time since I met him, I could not feel his presence. The hospital began to feel cold and desolate. It was not possible to see Bill once again. Bill was gone. To look at his corpse would have been to humiliate his memory. He had valued life and vigor, stamina and fitness. His lifeless body was a travesty, a mockery of what had been Bill. "No," I said to Dr. Wilson, "I don't want to see his body." Dr. Wilson then looked at Pete, and Pete simply shook his head and looked down at the floor. Putting his hand on my shoulder, Dr. Wilson left.

The head nurse hesitantly came in and asked me what funeral home I wanted to use. I responded that I really didn't know. The business of death was already making itself known, and I could not cope with it. All I could tell her was that Bill had wanted to be cremated. He had often told me that he didn't want a static monument or a gravestone that would recall more memories of his death than of his life. The nurse said they usually used the Gilbert Home in cases like these. Cases like these! There it was again. We were only one "case" among many.

I felt very, very tired. Too tired to stand up. And yet I knew that we couldn't stay where we were. As long as Bill lived, we had been invited guests at the hospital. Suddenly I felt as though we had overstayed our welcome, that our little room was no longer ours. Check-out time had come and gone, and the owners were waiting to make the room ready for other visitors. It was not that the nurses were unfriendly or hostile; it was just that there was nothing more to be said or to be done. We got up and walked out into the emergency room itself. I had to struggle not to vomit as I walked past the closed curtain behind which I knew lay Bill's corpse. All I could do was to walk fast. I walked too fast and lost my sense of direction. Turning, I looked at Amy and Pete. Amy understood and, taking my arm and Pete's, she led us out.

We had two cars at the hospital: Amy's and Bill's. Amy wanted me to leave his car in the parking lot. I was hesitant to drive, but I knew that I couldn't leave Bill's car in that place. The awful finality of Bill's death offered no solace other than its certainty. My life had been turned upside down; there were no knowns. Everything was going to change. There was only one indisputable fact: Bill was dead.

To leave his car in the hospital parking lot would have been to argue with the finality of it all. I couldn't do that. I said that I wanted to drive Bill's car and that I would follow Amy, letting her taillights guide me. Pete decided to go with Amy. That was the right decision. One man had died, but the loss Pete was experiencing was totally different from my own. We could not console each other at that point. Our grief was private and totally selfish. Somehow, we made it the five miles to Amy's house. It was only as we pulled into her driveway that I realized I was about to have to tell Monica and Melissa that Bill was dead.

As we walked into the house, I saw Amy look at her daughter and shake her head. They both disappeared, telling me only that Monica and Melissa were down in the playroom. Pete followed me down. Immediately upon seeing me, Melissa happily shouted, "Mommy!" and ran to me, putting out her arms as an invitation to me to pick her up. I knelt down and hugged her, and then took her hand. Sitting on the floor, I motioned for Pete and Monica to sit with us. Monica looked very frightened. She knew what I was about to tell her. The last time we had sat in a circle on the floor was the day Harvey died. Harvey had been her dog, and Bill's. But on that day Bill had sat with us. Pete cast his eyes to the ground. We put our arms around one another, and I said, "Bill isn't coming home. He died tonight." At my words Monica screamed "NO!" and started crying, loud and hard. Pete started sobbing, quietly, but with enough force to shake his body. Melissa looked from one to the other, held my hand for a moment, and then started methodically plucking fuzz off the carpet. I just sat there, holding onto Monica, rocking her. Melissa stood up, breaking what had become my almost trancelike state. Saying only, "Let's go home," I stumbled upstairs and asked Amy if she would guide us home. She already had her bag packed. It was ten-thirty at night. Pete, Monica, and Melissa all got into the car with me. This time we needed each other. No one wanted to ride with Amy. That possibility wasn't even discussed. We rode the ten miles to our home in complete silence.

Once home, the familiar surroundings created a pull toward normalcy of routine. Almost without thought, I told Monica to get into her pajamas and took Melissa into her room to put her to bed. After tucking her in, I kissed her good-night and promised to leave on the hall light just as I had done every night. She asked for several of her stuffed animals. I gave them to her, and we laughed at how there was hardly room left in the bed for her. Before I was out of the room, she had her thumb in her mouth. I did not tell her to remove it. She looked so small and so vulnerable that it was all I could do to get out of the room without breaking down. The enormity of raising the children without Bill washed over me like a tidal wave. By the time I got to the kitchen, I was shaking.

Amy gave me a hot cup of coffee, and we sat in silence at the kitchen table. The coffee tasted good, and I began to feel safer. Remembering Monica, I went into her room and found that she had put herself to bed. She was sobbing quietly and hugging a stuffed bear. Kissing her cheek, I told her that I loved her, and that we would be all right. I think my temporary feeling of safety reached her, and within a few minutes she was asleep.

I returned to the kitchen, in search of Amy. My feelings were at a low ebb; a strange combination of numbness and peace had replaced the earlier panic and fear. In a way, it felt like a normal night when Bill was out of town. The children were asleep, Pete was down in his room, Amy and I were having a cup of coffee. There was nothing unusual about any of that. For a few minutes, I focused on normal, mundane things. I remembered that Melissa should have taken a bath and recalled that Monica was supposed to be in a swim meet the next morning. Realizing for the first time that it was pouring rain outside, I walked across the family room to look outside. It was at that moment that my brief inner calm slipped away. The devastation on the porch made me confront and admit the devastation in our lives.

I was looking at the back porch, at the scene of our last family dinner together. Wet hamburger buns and soggy ears of corn were all over the floor. The barbecue cover was off and the charcoal was rain-soaked. The cotton cushions on the chairs and the chaise longue were soaked through and probably ruined. The rocking chair that belonged in Bill's and my bedroom was on the porch, moving with the wind, its cushions falling off with the weight of the water they had absorbed. The disarray of the porch rekindled feelings of panic and despair. Devastation seemed to be all around. It was not a normal night. It was the most terrifying night of my life. Nothing would ever be set right: not the cushions, not the rocking chair, and not my life. It all seemed to be of the same level of importance. The cushions were no more and no less of a disaster than what had happened.

What had happened? Bill had died. Died! The enormity of that word struck me. This was something that I couldn't fix. All my life I had been able to work things out the way I wanted them to be. Sometimes it had taken a lot of work, but that hadn't mattered. Where there's a will, there's a way. That had been our motto, and we had never been proven wrong. Bill had willed himself out of his first attack. And then, when his heart had stopped in the restaurant five months earlier, I had worked on him and helped him back to life. We didn't want him to die, and so he wouldn't; he couldn't. But he had. He had died tonight, and I hadn't been able to do anything about it. He hadn't been able to do anything about it. I recalled with horror the sound of his cries for help and rubbed my arm where he had grasped me as if to say, "I'll hold onto you so tightly that death won't be able to wrench me free from life." My arm hurt. It was red and slightly swollen. Oh yes, Bill had fought as hard as he could. I wondered if he realized what was happening—that he was about to die—and knew the answer was yes. I wondered if he had been frightened and knew that the answer to that, too, was yes. I knew, too, that he had been angry. Bill hadn't wanted to die.

My thoughts were broken by the sound of Pete entering the room. I turned and saw that his eyes were red and swollen, but that he had pulled himself together and had something on his mind. I looked at him, and he asked me if I wanted him to call Cathy and Ed. He wondered whether this was the right time to tell his mother. Decisions had to be made. I had to make them. I felt angry at Pete for making me aware that people had to be told. I didn't want anyone else to know. First I had to face the reality of death in my own mind and heart. I wanted to return to that feeling of calm and peace and deny the whole thing. I wanted to believe that like other difficult times, this too would pass.

It would never pass; I would never awake from this nightmare if I had to tell someone else what had happened. But I knew that Pete was right. Bill's family had a right to know. I asked Pete if he felt he could tell Ed. He said yes, he could, and agreed that would be the best thing to do. He would ask Ed to tell his mother. Ed lived near her and could do so in person. I wanted to call Cathy myself. She would expect to hear it from me.

We had become friends and had shared confidences.

Taking my address book out of the desk drawer, I looked up Cathy's number. Sitting down at the kitchen table, with Amy opposite me, I hesitantly dialed. Cathy answered, her voice heavy with sleep. "Cathy, this is Pam." She said nothing, nothing at all. I continued, "Cathy, your father died tonight." For a few moments, we were both silent. Then she said, "But I thought he was just released from the hospital today." Trying to explain, I managed to say, "He was, Cathy. He was. He felt a little dizzy after dinner, and the next thing we knew he was in trouble." Again, we were both silent. Cathy didn't cry. Eventually, she said, "I don't know what to say. I can't say anything. I don't know what to say." Interrupting her, I said, "I'm sorry, Cathy." She answered, "Pam, are you all right?" "Yes, I think so, Cathy," was all the reassurance I could offer. She offered to call her uncles, Bill's brothers, and, after a few more moments of silence, hung up.

I looked at Amy and told her that I couldn't say those words again. I couldn't tell anyone else that Bill had died. And yet suddenly, I wanted all the people who cared about him and about me to know. On that evening, Bill had taken the biggest step of his life. He had died. That was more important than getting married, having a fiftieth birthday, or fathering a child. It was momentous. It had to be announced. I asked Amy if she would make the rest of the calls. She looked frightened, but said of course she would. We looked at the clock. It was almost one in the morning.

Amy asked me whom she should call. I felt confused. While I couldn't think of a single name, I knew that there were a lot of people who needed to know. My eye fell on the bulletin board. Only days before, Monica had recopied our lists of telephone numbers. It bothered her that the pages were dirty and that corners had been torn off. She had thought that Bill would be pleased to see a tidy bulletin board when he got out of the hospital. I picked out a name on our list, and asked Amy to call.

Amy stood up and went to the phone. She looked at the number and started to dial. When Brooks answered, Amy turned her back to me and said simply, "Hello. Is this Brooks Winter? This is Amy Peterson. I am calling for Pam Miller. Pam asked me to call to tell you that Bill died tonight. . . . Yes, he was home . . . at around eight-thirty. . . . Yes, she is sitting right here . . . she seems to be all right. . . . Yes, I'm staying with her tonight. . . . Thank you."

Amy sat down. She was flushed. After taking a sip of coffee, she looked at me and asked who should be called next. She had begun to regard the calls as an unpleasant job that would tolerate no delay. I looked again at the list on the bulletin board and said that she should call Tom and Mary Jansen. The conversation was little different from the one that had preceded it. The system was working. The announcement was being made. Amy had her script and, through the first several calls, no one challenged it. No one made her say more. She seemed to be handling it fine. There was a job to be done and we were doing it.

It was after the fourth or fifth call that the reality of Amy's script struck me. She was systematically and methodically telling people that my husband had died. The realization made me feel weak and vulnerable. I wanted to be protected. I needed the next call to be to someone whose concern for me would be greater than their personal grief over their loss of Bill. I needed my own family to know. Most particularly, I wanted my brother near me.

My brother, Clyde, and I had always been very close. He was seventeen years old when my parents decided to leave the New York area and emigrate to Australia. Because Clyde chose to go to college in Connecticut, it was only natural that he would begin to regard my home as his home. Eight years his senior, I was both able and more than willing to share my home with him.

Over the years, Clyde and I experienced a lot of life together. He was there during the painful months preceding my divorce from Jim and gave me the courage to allow Melissa to be born in spite of the fears and insecurities that accompanied the breakup of my marriage. He was there, too, the day that Bill and I were married. It was Clyde who was summoned out of bed in the middle of the night to care for the children the night Bill woke up with his first chest pains. It was he who held my hand when the doctors said that Bill would most likely never recover from that first attack, and that if he did, he would almost certainly be little more than a vegetable. Clyde and I had enjoyed the highs and made it through the lows together. Our relationship had been one of solid mutual support.

In the beginning, Bill seemed to resent our closeness and to feel left out when Clyde and I read each other's thoughts without having exchanged a single word. While Clyde and I treated each other as peers, as friends, Bill persisted in treating Clyde as a son. We all understood why; after all, Clyde was twenty-five years Bill's junior. While understandable, Bill's attitude toward Clyde created problems. In working through these problems, Clyde and Bill gained an enormous respect for each other. Clyde learned to love Bill, as Bill came to regard Clyde as a friend. Bill cried the day we put Clyde on the plane to Australia more than three years before the night of Bill's death.

Communication with Clyde during those years had been at best sporadic. Clyde never wrote a letter. It just wasn't his style. Periodically, he would telephone and we would all find it easy to reconnect no matter how much time had elapsed. It was Clyde whom I needed now.

I didn't know whether Clyde could come. While he wasn't married, he had his own apartment and a job in Australia. I did know that if there were any way to join me, he would. I had to ask. But that wasn't an easy thing to do. I didn't know his latest telephone number. Even if I had known it, the time differential posed a problem. Western Australia is thirteen hours ahead of the East Coast of the United States, which meant it was now the middle of the day, Monday. Clyde would be at work. His work involved extensive travel. I decided to call my parents. I wanted to share my pain with them and be comforted, and knew they would get hold of Clyde as soon as they could. I had begun to dial when I realized that only my mother would be at home; my father would be at work. I was afraid to blurt out the news to my mother because she is chronically hypertensive, and I feared triggering a stroke. I sat down again, overwhelmed by the fact that half a world divided me from my family. I wanted to cry out to Mother as I had as a child, and found it impossible to do so. Amy seemed to know that I was struggling and put a comforting arm around my shoulder.

After a few minutes, I calmed down a little, and decided that the best thing to do was to call my sister Gay. Gay also lived in Western Australia, with her husband and two children. I didn't know quite how I would approach Gay. When we were children, I had always functioned as the "big sister," braver, more worldly, more assertively adventuresome than she. In turn, she had reluctantly accepted the role of the more passive, kinder, less selfish, put-upon younger sister. I knew that it was important on this night that I not pretend to be stronger than I was; I had to resist that perpetual temptation to put forth false bravado when talking with her. I needed her to comfort me and to help me. I had never asked that of her before.

Finding it too difficult to actually go through the motions required to get Western Australia by telephone, I asked Amy to try to get Gay for me. Amy was more than a little nonplussed by my request. She was not in the habit of making long-distance calls of any kind, and the remoteness of Australia intimidated her. She looked actually surprised when the call was answered and Gay identified herself. Amy then handed the telephone to me.

Gay immediately knew that something was very much the matter. I had called her only once during the six years that they had been in Australia. This time, it was a friend of mine, whom Gay had never met, who was placing the call. Gay began with, "Pam? What's wrong? Is something wrong?" Her concern and her affection for me were so apparent that I couldn't stop myself from weeping. At that moment, I knew family was a very special thing, and I was so grateful I had Gay for a sister. Finally, I was able to blurt out, "Gay, Bill died tonight. His heart just stopped." At first, Gay didn't say anything. Eventually she said, "Oh Pam . . . Pam . . . Pam . . . I don't know what to say! I'll come be with you. Oh, you're alone. You're all alone!"

She was beside herself. I pulled myself together enough to request that she go over to Mom and Dad's house and tell them what had happened. "Be careful, Gay, I'm worried about Mom. You'll break it to her gently, won't you?"

"Pam, please don't worry, I'll go over there right now. It's you I'm worried about. You're all alone over there. I want to be with you."

"Gay, you're so good, and so kind, but I can't let you do that. I mean, Dick and the kids, and your business. I'll be all right, really. I thought maybe, just maybe, Clyde could come be with me for a while."

Gay was silent. When she finally spoke, her words were discouraging. "Pam, there is no way for me to find Clyde. I don't even know where he is today. Oh, I'll try, but I doubt I'll be able to find him immediately. Sometimes we don't see him for days at a time."

Sensing that Gay's reluctance to contact Clyde was more than a matter of locating him, I asked, "Gay, what is it? What are you trying to say?"

"Pam, I know that you need someone with you, and I understand that you and Clyde are especially close. It's just that, well, I wish it could be me."

"But, Gay, your kids and Dick. That would never work."

"Oh, I know that. It's just that, well, Joy and Clyde were about to sign a lease on a house together."

"Can't Joy find another housemate?"

After a pause, she said, "Sure, no problem. I'll find Clyde for you."

"Gay, there's something else. What is it?"

"Nothing, Pam, really. I guess I'm just upset by your news. I'm not helping you very much, am I? I'll go over to Mom and Dad's right now."

Only later was I to learn the reason for Gay's reluctance to contact Clyde and tell him that I very much wanted him with me. Both Joy, my youngest sister, and he had been having a very difficult time. Joy's love had just left for a year-long trip to New Zealand. She was lonely and unhappy, and anxious as well about her first job as a practicing architect. She needed Clyde in much the same way that I did. Clyde himself had only just begun to build a meaningful life in Australia. After years of loneliness and uncertainty about his job, he had finally begun to make friends and to enjoy a professional momentum. To wrench him free was potentially to undermine his newly found social and professional self-confidence. But I understood none of that, and Gay, anxious to soothe and not further upset me, did not speak of her concerns.

My own parents would soon be grieving. Because their child was hurt, they would also hurt. I thought about that, and then began to consider my own children. They had been hurt. They had suffered a trauma, and part of my pain was a result of their pain. I realized then that my ex-husband, Jim, needed to be told. Monica and Melissa were his children, too. I needed to call Jim. I *wanted* to call Jim. We had lived together for eight years. At one point we had been in love. But we were not compatible. He was solid, predictable, and rational. I was volatile, unpredictable, and a romantic. He stifled my energies, and I made him nervous. But we still cared for each other. We were friends, not adversaries. I trusted that Jim would suffer not just because his children were hurt but because I, too, was hurt. I dialed his number. "Jim, Bill died tonight."

Jim's response was immediate and sympathetic. "Oh, you poor child. I'll do anything I can to help you. You know that, don't you?" I did know that, and it helped.

After the calls to Gay and Jim, I was emotionally spent. I had no more tears, and not enough energy to feel frightened. I told Amy that we had better get back to the business of calling people. She agreed and suggested that Ann and Phil would want to know. Once, Ann and Phil, Amy, and Bill and I had been neighbors, residing in the three houses at the end of a dead end. We had gotten very close, as compatible neighbors living on one-third-acre lots are likely to do. Since then, Ann and Phil had moved into a larger home on four acres, and Bill and I had subsequently moved to the next town. Only Amy still lived in the old neighborhood. Putting fifteen miles between us had made little difference in the affection we felt for Ann and Phil. It had, however, drastically reduced the amount of time we spent together. We had no mutual friends other than Amy and tended to go our separate ways socially. Still, Ann and Phil remained special people to me, and I knew that they had truly cared for Bill and would regard his death as a very great personal loss.

It was difficult for Amy to call Ann. Amy and Ann were too close; her comfortable script wouldn't work. While I could sense Amy's pain, the conversation they had did surprise me. "Ann, this is Amy. . . . I'm with Pam. . . . Yes, he died tonight. . . . She wanted you to know. . . . No, I don't think she expected it. . . . I'm sure she'd like to see you. . . . We haven't given any thought to tomorrow. . . . Yes, I think that would be a good idea. . . . No, I don't think she wants to talk right now. . . . I'll give her your love. . . . Yes, I know. . . ."

It sounded almost as though they had talked about Bill's condition before. When Amy got off the phone, I asked her if that was true. She told me that she and Ann had been very worried about Bill for the past several months. He hadn't bounced back from his last heart attack the way he had from the first one. Each time Amy had seen Bill, he had looked worse. The old fighting spirit seemed to be slipping away from him day by day. Even his music lacked the zest it once had. I listened to her until I couldn't listen anymore. I knew that she was right, that Bill had been dying right before my eyes, and that I had refused to see the slow but certain progression of his illness. I no longer expected friends to be shocked by the news of Bill's death; I began to expect only sadness and concern on the part of those who had seen him during the last weeks of his life.

But not all the special people in our lives had seen Bill's deterioration. Shelley, in fact, did not even know he had been ill again, and Shelley was one of my closest friends. We had been roommates in college and still shared the affinity that growing up together brings. We were so close, in fact, that maintaining our friendship did not require frequent, planned visits. Shelley was my foul-weather friend. I saw her only when times were rough for either of us. She had kept a key to our house as she went through the emotional trauma of a divorce. I had been her source of support when her father died. She had stayed with me when Bill had his first attack, arriving at the hospital in the middle of the night in a long dinner dress and staying that way throughout the next day. In between foul-weather episodes, Shelley led her own life and I led mine.

She lived in New York City; I was in the suburbs. She dated different men; I preferred to be married. She focused on her career; I spent a lot of time with my children. Our differences seemed to magnify our closeness. We had a lot to give to each other. I needed her now. Amy tried calling Shelley's apartment, but to no avail. She tried periodically all through the night and the next several days. Shelley had vanished. I was angry at her. She should have sensed my trouble. She was letting me down.

Amy continued to call friends until about three in the morning. Each time I heard her say that Bill had died, my stomach turned over, my heart sank a little more, and my mind began to accept Bill's death as a reality. Periodically, Amy would ask me if she sounded too mechanical. The precision and sameness of the script was beginning to wear her down. I assured her that she didn't sound mechanical, amazed that she had the strength to repeatedly say those words to people whom, for the most part, she had never met. She said that made it easier. Not knowing them, she couldn't visualize the pain that her words created. Calls to mutual friends and to my relatives in the United States were more difficult.

Finally, Amy sat down to recompose herself. The telephone lines were free for the first time in hours. Within seconds, the phone rang.

Amy answered. It was Clyde. The things he said and the scene he described made me feel more hopeful and less lonely than I had felt all night.

Clyde was calling from my parents' home. The entire family was there: Gay and Dick and their two children, my youngest sister, Joy, and, of course, Mom and Dad. The events of the last several hours had convinced all of them that the power of love can bridge even thirteen thousand miles. Gay had gone directly to my parents' home after hearing from me. She had been there only a few minutes, and had said nothing of what had happened, when my father came home unexpectedly early from the university. He had sensed that something was wrong, perhaps with my mother, and cut short his planned research for the day. Clyde, too, had been preoccupied all day with a feeling that something was amiss, and had canceled one of his appointments in order to check in at my parents' home. He had never done that before. Joy had been home, ill. Was this just a series of coincidences? I don't believe so, and neither do they. Gay had said only, "Pam called." Clyde said, "Bill has died, hasn't he?" Gay said, "Yes." They were quiet for a while. Clyde announced, "I've got to go over there." In spite of the turmoil this would create, no one disagreed. Within minutes, the entire family had decided that the best thing they could do for me and the children was to work together to attend to the myriad of details that had to be accomplished before Clyde could make the trip. His apartment had to be let. His car had to be sold. Hundreds of pages of job-related reports had to be written and typed. Reservations had to be booked.

In the midst of their discussion about the complicated logistics of the trip, they decided that Clyde should call and reassure me that he was coming. Listening to him then, telling me he was on his way, I felt overcome with relief. I should have known Clyde would never let me down.

"I'm coming over there, Pam. There is no question about that. It's going to take me a little time, though. I'm afraid it might take as long as ten days or two weeks. Will you be all right that long? Can you cope?"

"Oh, Clyde, I can cope a lot better knowing that you're on your way. I hope I'm not really throwing a monkey wrench into your life."

"Come on. Don't worry about my life, at least not right now.

Anyway, you're not really changing my life. You're just escalating things a little. I had planned to return to the States sometime in the next two years to go back to graduate school. So I'll just get to it a little sooner than planned. Like I said, don't worry about me now."

"Thank you, Clyde. I guess we both knew that someday this would happen."

"We did, but that doesn't make it any easier. Everyone would like to talk with you, but we'll save that for another time. Try to get some sleep, huh? I'll see you soon."

The talk with Clyde calmed me. I had something positive to anticipate in the midst of a general feeling of pessimism and despair.

Seeing that I had regained some composure, Amy reminded me that in a few short hours it would be Monday morning. Reluctantly, I began to think about our company. My husband had died. The president of the company had also died, and neither his employees nor his clients knew anything about it. I did not think Amy's script would be suitable, but neither of us had the strength to write an appropriate one. I suggested that Amy call Meg, a professional on our staff whom I both trusted and liked very much. I knew that Meg would be very concerned about me, but that she had the presence of mind to handle client calls and to tell the other employees in the best possible way. Meg had not known Bill very well. Hired only shortly before the onset of his illness, she would be able to handle her own feelings of grief, and knew our clients well enough to help them handle their reactions. Amy called Meg, who in turn asked Amy to assure me that everything would be done that needed to be done, and that I should not worry about the business.

Thoughts of the company brought to my mind the business of death. I realized that I didn't have a great deal of liquid cash, and wondered about life insurance. Only a few months before, we had changed insurance agents, and all our policies had been reviewed and modified. I was somewhat vague as to their status and the amounts involved, recollecting only that it had been Bill's intent to provide enough money that I would have at least a period of readjustment, and some life options. Neither of us had believed it was either necessary or appropriate to make us insurance-poor during our lives in order to make me financially independent upon his death.

Thoughts about insurance triggered thoughts about other legal ramifications. I realized that Joel, our attorney and our friend, had not been notified. It was critical that he know, both as a professional and as someone who cared. I asked Amy to call Joel. The conversation was brief. Joel announced that he would be at the house early that morning, and that Amy was to take all calls, making sure that I made no decisions about *anything* until he got there. He urged Amy to try to get me to go to sleep.

At about four o'clock in the morning, Amy suggested that I lie down. I was tired, more tired than I ever remember being, but I did not want to go to sleep. I was afraid to sleep, fearing the morning: the children waking, having to face the first full day without Bill. I was coping, and believed that in sleep I would lose whatever strength was keeping me going. The coffee that I had been drinking all night did not help. My nerves were frayed, and my hands were shaking. In spite of the warmth of the summer night, my body felt cold all over. Amy poured me a glass of white wine. It tasted good, and I finished it quickly. Then she poured me another, and yet another. The wine made fuzzy the discrete events of the last several hours. I couldn't dwell on a single thought or a single person for very long. Thoughts kept intermingling with other thoughts, the boundaries of each indistinct. I wondered briefly about Pete, but didn't check on him. I pictured the stuffed animals surrounding Melissa, but it was Monica's face that I envisioned.

Telling Amy that I thought I could sleep, I walked to my bedroom. Opening the door, I entered the room and felt a force, a presence like nothing I had ever before experienced. I had not been in the bedroom since the emergency medical crew had pulled me away from Bill. That seemed like an eternity ago. Bill's down pillow still showed the imprint of his head. The throw that had covered him was still in a heap on the floor. His slippers were positioned neatly beside the bed where he had placed them when he lay down. The essence of Bill was very much in that room. I could smell him, sense him, and wanted to touch him. Oh, I so very much wanted to touch him. I couldn't stay there, unable to lie down on my side of the bed, unable even to open the dresser drawer to get my nightgown. I couldn't change anything about that room. I had to shut the door tight, as if to capture the presence that existed therein. I knew at that moment that I could allow no one else in the bedroom. I had to keep Bill locked up in there until I could enter, sit down, and let him envelop me. To let another person enter would be to weaken the spirit that I felt resided there. Closing the door, I told Amy that I was going to lie down in the guest room.

I took off my skirt, blouse, and shoes and crept under the covers. The weight of the blankets felt good, so good that I pulled the heavy spread over me too. Amy sat on the other bed and watched me. Within a few minutes, I fell into a sound, dreamless sleep.

2

In Memoriam

Awaking at around nine in the morning, I was confused and disoriented, not realizing at first that I was in the guest room. Unwelcome thoughts began to consume me.

I tried to fight them back by clinging to the semiconsciousness of the first few minutes of waking. Pulling the covers up tighter, I refused to open my eyes. I must have lain that way for an hour or so, but sleep would not return. The sound of voices in the kitchen began to take on a reality that demanded attention. My mind began working. To whom did the voices belong? Most were women's voices. One had to be Amy's, but there were others, two others. And I heard male voices, too. One was Pete's, of that I was sure. The other was loud and commanding. I liked the sound of that voice.

I wondered what they were doing. It sounded as though breakfast preparations were under way. I heard the bell on the microwave oven. Then the teakettle whistled. Someone urged the group to keep their voices down so as to avoid waking me. The door to the bedroom wing was shut quietly. They, whoever they were, wanted me to keep sleeping.

The intercom buzzed. They were calling Melissa. I smiled, realizing that they didn't know the intercom blasted in the bedrooms. Melissa must be down in the playroom, watching her early-morning television shows. Monica must still be sleeping. I wanted to go into the kitchen, but I was afraid. They had become a group; I was an outsider. I had company in my home; that made me a hostess. But the company was taking care of itself. I felt lonely and a little angry. Getting up, I walked down the hall to the children's bathroom. Signs of Melissa's morning routine were everywhere. Her nightgown was on the floor. Toothpaste oozed out of the tube onto the counter. A soggy washcloth was draped sloppily over a towel.

Looking in the mirror, I didn't at first recognize the person who stared back at me. I was attractive; the person in the mirror was a mess with greasy, streaked hair, swollen eyes, lips looking unpleasantly fat, eye-liner smeared, accentuating the lines under the eyes. I started crying, quietly so as to encourage my guests to continue believing that I was sleeping. Then I heard the door to the bedroom wing open, and that frightened me. They were looking for me. I didn't want anyone to see me. I quickly turned on the shower, closed the curtain and got in. I was safe again. No one would venture in. I had given up the safety of apparent sleep for the safety of the bathroom.

The shower felt good. When I finished, I liked the look of the person in the mirror. Putting a towel around me, I returned to the guest room. The telephone rang and gave me a start. Someone picked it up by the second ring. I couldn't hear what was being said. I didn't want to know what was said, or even who had called. I had to get dressed. It wouldn't do to walk into the kitchen with only a towel wrapped around me. I got up and walked toward Bill's and my bedroom. The door was still tightly shut. I couldn't find the courage to open it. Returning to the guest room, I sat down on the bed. I felt naked and exposed. The guest room was anybody's turf. I needed to be in my own space, in my own bedroom.

Suddenly I wanted very much to be inside that room. I hastened back and opened the door quickly, and shut it as quickly, locking it behind me. The sight of Bill's slippers made me feel dizzy, and I sat in the large comfortable chair that had been his favorite thinking place and tucked my feet under me. I stared at the bed. The pillow on which Bill had rested his head was still indented. I could almost see the outline of his body.

Images of Bill's face passed before me. I saw his broad smile; I pictured his soft, full, curly gray hair and heard his laugh. Bill had had a wonderful laugh, solid, honest, and contagious. I remembered his eyes, warm, and caring and beautiful. I thought about his arms. I remembered how sexy I had thought them to be when I first met him. They had been strong and muscular, with just the right amount of hair on them. They had held a magic for me. No matter what trouble we were facing, I had felt safe and secure when his arms were around me. But something had happened to them. I couldn't stop myself from picturing how thin and weak he had finally become.

Suddenly I couldn't stand the sight of those slippers. I got up and kicked them under the bed. As I did so, I hit my foot on the bed frame, and cursed. The cursing felt good, and I did it again, and again. I didn't care if anyone heard me. "Damn! Damn! Damn!" I screamed. I picked up Bill's pillow and threw it down again as hard as I could. I punched it over and over. I felt angry, angrier than ever in my life. How could he do this to me? We had been married only five years. This was July 2. July 6 would have been our anniversary. Bill had promised me that on the morning of our anniversary, he would get up and say to me, "I feel good today." He had promised! He had no right to leave me now. I didn't deserve it.

Self-pity took over. I cried so hard that I had to vomit. I ran into the bathroom, but nothing would happen. I sat on the floor and hung my head over the toilet bowl. Nothing would happen. My stomach ached; my head ached. I cried until I couldn't cry anymore. Someone knocked on the door. It was Amy. "Pam, are you all right?" I didn't answer. I couldn't answer. I just wanted her to go away. She called again, "Pam!" This time, I tried to make my voice sound even and answered, "It's all right. I'm getting dressed. I'll be out soon." I sensed that she stood by the door for a while. Then I heard her footsteps and knew that I was alone again.

The exercise of composing my voice had done me good. I grabbed the edge of the toilet bowl and pulled myself up, and walked back into the bedroom. I had no more feeling. I opened the dresser drawer and took out my underwear. I found my blue jeans and a T-shirt. Dressed, I looked around for a comb. My hair had almost dried into a tangled mess. I looked for my lipstick and realized that my purse was in the kitchen. That did it. The time had come. Taking a deep breath, I walked out of the bedroom, careful to shut the door tightly behind me.

On my way to the kitchen, I ran into Jennifer, the children's baby-sitter. Immediately upon seeing her, I realized she had not been telephoned the night before. I felt sorry for her, for how she must have felt when she arrived that morning ready for a normal day's work, to be confronted with what had happened. For a minute, we just stood there, looking at each other. Then, her eyes filled with tears, and she said, "I'm so sorry." I held her then and said nothing. She asked me what she could do. Hearing the sound of voices in the kitchen, I asked her if she would take Melissa and go to the grocery store. She agreed and quickly disappeared downstairs.

Taking another deep breath, I walked into the kitchen. The voices suddenly made sense. Joel, our attorney, was sitting at the kitchen table, talking with Amy. Jackie, Joel's wife, was talking on the telephone. Pete was at the sink, doing dishes, and Ann was wiping the counters. I said simply, "Good morning." They all stopped what they were doing and looked at me. Joel broke the silence, commenting on my hair, "You look like you got caught in the clothes washer." I remembered that I had not yet found a comb, and smiled. Catching a glimpse of my purse on the counter, I walked over to it and took out a comb.

Joel had set the tone. Everybody had something to say about my hair. Ann changed the subject but kept it light. "It figures that you wouldn't have any sponges. I brought the cleanser, the least you could do is to supply the sponges." Over the years, Ann and I had enjoyed teasing each other about the differences in our life-styles. I was Miss Liberated, Miss Career Girl, Miss Working Mother. She, on the other hand, devoted her energies to her home, her husband, and her three young children. Her house was always clean; mine was clean when I was lucky enough to find someone to clean it. Her children were always pressed and neat; my children's clothes looked pressed only when they wore their permanent-press garments.

In spite of the difference in our life-styles, Ann and I had been very close. Two of her children were the same ages as Monica and Melissa, and that gave us an important common denominator. Ann was generally laid-back and relaxed; I was generally so busy as to be frenetic. Ann had a calming effect on me, and I an invigorating effect on her. The relationship worked. Her comment about the sponges was perfect. In those few words, she had managed to capture the relationship. I teased her in return. "When you've finished with the kitchen, you might work on the bathrooms. They're a disaster."

I sat down at the table. Amy brought me a cup of coffee. Joel took my hand. I smiled and told him that he should be at work. He responded with something like, "You know me, I'll use anything as an excuse to stay out of the office." Jackie got off the phone and sat with us. She, too, took my hand for a minute. She cocked her head slightly to one side, letting her lush brown hair fall over one shoulder. Her warm brown eyes said it all; she needed no words. Joel broke the silence with a greeting that he had so often used with me, "So . . . how are ya' doin, kiddo?" The question was, as always, followed by a twist of his plentiful mustache. I answered him honestly: "I don't know."

Throughout the day, that question would be asked of me dozens of times. It would make me wonder about how, in fact, I was doing. Was I more composed than people normally are? Was I feeling enough, or too much? Was I acting rationally, irrationally? What does normal grief look like? Feel like? Within days, I would learn to hate that question because it defied a comfortable answer. The response "I'm fine, thank you" didn't quite fit. "I'm really lousy, thank you" was unnecessarily hostile. I wanted to respond, "I am. That's all; I just am."

Finally Joel summoned the courage to begin to address the business of death with me. He mentioned that certain legal documents had to be signed and official papers collected. Signing documents didn't trouble me; assisting Joel in locating our official papers would be painful. I found it hard to control my tears even as I told him that he'd find most of the papers in Bill's personal file in the office.

Sorting through Bill's file would have been impossible for me, and would be painful for Joel. Bill had been a saver, and interspersed among official papers were terribly intimate letters and heartfelt greeting cards.

As he had often done over the years, Joel was going to have to act at once as both attorney and friend. I could tell from the look on his face that retrieving Bill's personal memories was going to be very painful for him. For an instant, I was able to focus on Joel's hurt. Here he was having to expedite the business of death while, inside, he was consumed with the loss of his friend. Only by relying on his somewhat sarcastic sense of humor could Joel mask his feelings sufficiently to function as the attorney.

"Now to more important things. I've got to leave for a few hours, but I'm leaving Jackie to baby-sit. She'll make sure you don't go and sell the house out from under all of us. How's the scotch supply? I'll be back this afternoon, and plan to sit here and drink my dinner. This is Monday, and the start of my diet. If you're going to keep me in scotch this week, we'd better make sure you've got some cash on hand. How's the money situation? How much do you have in your checking account?"

After checking my wallet, I told Joel that I had seventy-five dollars in cash, but that I was giving all that to Jennifer for the groceries. After looking at my checkbook, I realized that I hadn't been subtracting the check amounts and had no idea as to the balance. Joel took it from me and, after doing some calculations on a paper towel, told me that I was overdrawn. The look on his face was one of paternal exasperation. Smiling, I told him that, after all, today was to have been payday, and I hadn't been paid. What could he expect?

We both realized simultaneously that if I hadn't been paid, then neither had any of our employees. Joel asked if anyone else at the office could be trusted to act as alternate check signatory, and I immediately thought of Meg. Joel said that he would talk with Meg when he got to the office. He then handed me a hundred dollars and said he would see us all later. A minute later, he was back in the kitchen, asking whether the insurance companies had been notified. Shaking my head, I gave him the name of our agent. He assured me that he would contact him and brief me later as to the status of Bill's insurance.

Things were happening; a strange momentum had begun. People were scurrying around, taking care of problems before I even realized they existed. Over the past few months, I had been functioning as head of the business and head of the household. I had gotten accustomed to teasing out incredibly complicated logistics on both fronts and then issuing directives to everyone in sight. I think I had begun to assume that, without my directives, the universe would have broken apart. Now, suddenly, I was not the boss-lady, but the weakened child who had to be guided through the day. For a moment, my contempt for the ability of others surfaced, and I panicked at the thought of losing control of things. As if in an attempt to regain control, I found a piece of paper and started making an extensive shopping list for Jennifer. I remembered that Bill's car was supposed to be serviced that day, and asked Pete to call and cancel the appointment and make another for later in the week. I made a mental note to stock up on sponges so that Ann, and others, would not find the organization of my household lacking.

I remembered that the gardens needed weeding, and worried about that. My head began spinning with the myriad of details that, in my mind, all required immediate attention. I wished everyone who was idly sitting around the kitchen would either do something productive or else leave me alone so that I could get some work done. The sliding glass doors needed washing. The filter on the stove needed to be replaced. If I didn't spray the fungicide on the dogwoods, I would surely lose them. The garage needed to be swept. The vet was waiting for a stool sample in order to make sure the dog was healthy. The cat was due for a shot.

My mind began to whirl so fast that I made myself dizzy. I lay down on the sofa, turning my head away from the people in the kitchen. I couldn't do any of the things on the endless list. My husband had died, and no amount of work or frenetic activity on my part would set that straight. Things were totally out of control. Neither the best planner nor the most effective logistical expert could regain control. I gave up and just lay there. Amy, Pete, and Ann were quiet.

I expect I might have lain there all day if Melissa and Monica hadn't come into the room. Melissa wasn't used to seeing me lie down on the couch and feared that I was ill. I reassured her by sitting up. She asked me if I was going into the office that day. When I told her no, she said, "Oh, goody! Then, you can take Monica and me to the swimming club." I realized then that she did not yet understand what had happened. That was not surprising, I told myself. After all, Bill had been in the hospital for several weeks, and, on the surface, nothing had changed. I was concerned, though, since I knew she had witnessed his death and my reaction. I wondered whether she had suffered such a trauma that she would be unable to grieve and would suffer in years to come because of her inability to confront her feelings. I decided to be honest and open with her, and to invite her to share in my grief, hoping that then she could face her own. "Melissa, Mommy is far too sad to go to the swimming club. Our Bill died last night, and I'm feeling very frightened. I don't have the strength to tell people at the club that Bill died, and I can't laugh and swim and pretend that it didn't happen. It's going to be a long time before I'll be able to go down there with you."

Melissa's reaction both frightened me and made me smile. Putting her tiny hand on her hip, and cocking her head to one side, she said, "Mommy, you're going to have to get over this. I'll go into the club ahead of you and tell everybody what happened. Then, you can come in. Okay?" I had neither the heart nor the strength to explain why her idea was very much not okay. I could only say, "Not today. We're not going swimming today." She seemed to hear the determination in my voice, for she simply shrugged her shoulders and said she was going to watch some more television.

Not long after that, Jim called. He said that he and his wife, Sara, had temporarily moved in with his parents in the next town, and he wanted me to know that he was available to help in any way that he could. All I had to do was ask. He wanted to come and take Monica and Melissa. That unnerved me. I realized then how much I needed them to be with me. I needed to be forced to continue to look after their needs, and I needed their love. On the other hand, I was very concerned about them and had to think about what would be best for them. For a fleeting instant, it occurred to me that Jim was now remarried. I was alone. He could perhaps provide a more integrated home for the children than I. I panicked. Would I lose my children? Unable to think straight, I told Jim I would call him back.

I found it very difficult to separate my needs from those of the children. Would it be better for Monica and Melissa to get away from the house, to go swimming and forget the sadness of our home for a while? Should Jim take them for the week? Would it help if he talked with them about what had happened? Would it frighten them unnecessarily to see me upset? What impact would it have on the children to see people coming and going all week? Should Melissa be forced to talk about what had happened, about what she had seen? Monica had been extremely upset the night before, but this morning she seemed to be very much in control of things. How deep did that control go? Was she, too, blocking out her feelings?

I desperately wished that I could talk it over with Bill. I was sure that together we would have arrived at the best answer. I was very unsure that, alone, I could sort it out. I did something then that I was to repeat many times in the months to come. I went into my bedroom, shut the door, and spoke out loud, as if to problem-solve with Bill. A very strange and wonderful thing seemed to happen. Within moments, I was very sure of the right thing to do with the children. It seemed that Bill had heard and provided me with the answer. I decided to keep the children home most of the time, asking Jim to take them for an outing for only a few hours each afternoon. It would have been artificial to pretend that only I had suffered a loss. Whether they were able to openly admit it or not, Melissa and Monica shared my loss.

Monica would never again have a chance to compete at the pool table or the game board with her "Daddy Bill." I knew she would miss that challenge; he had been a strong believer in putting forth his best effort, regardless of the age of his opponent. To win in play against Bill was to effect a great victory. Nor would Monica benefit again from Bill's urging her to openly express her feelings, from his assurances that she had a right to her feelings and to her opinions. Monica had tended to be secretive and somewhat withdrawn before Bill entered our lives. I believe that it was largely due to his influence that she had become outgoing, freer in her expression, and a leader among her friends.

A strong-willed child, Melissa would miss the structure and sense of order that Bill, as disciplinarian, imposed on the household. Melissa and Bill had often locked horns, engaging in a loving battle as to whose will would prevail. The contest seemed to be good for Melissa. She gained a sense of security as Bill's openness left her with no doubt as to where she stood. I feared that, in time, Melissa's loss would be the greatest. She was so young to lose such a strong model.

The children had lost. I believed then and still believe that to deny and thereby repress that loss would have been unhealthy. They had to grieve, as I had to grieve. To remove them from the house would have been like giving them tranquilizers, encouraging them to postpone facing their loss or to deny it altogether.

At the same time, I felt that it was important to remind them that they were fortunate in having not just one parent remaining, but three. Over the years, Bill, Jim, and I had taken pains to create and sustain a healthy relationship between Jim and Monica and Melissa. Later, when Jim married Sara, we were pleased to see that the girls rapidly learned to love and respect her. Now, with Jim and Sara, the children could perhaps find a sense of solace and security. I couldn't share that with them, but to deprive them of it would have been cruel. In the weeks to come, they would need both a time for grief and a time for comfort. I hoped Jim would understand that.

Any concerns I had had about Jim's reaction were totally unfounded. He agreed with me that they had to have a chance to grieve. He shared my concern that Melissa was repressing all that she had seen and felt, and wanted to help her talk about it. We agreed that he would take the children out each day for a few hours. That our decision was right was confirmed by Monica and Melissa's elation at the prospect of having some time out of the house. Both, however, expressed concern about leaving me alone, and said that they wanted to be home for dinner.

Jim arrived within the hour. After the children left, Jackie took me aside and said that she thought we should talk about placing Bill's obituary in the newspapers. Jackie handled me perfectly. She brought pad and pen and treated the whole episode very matter-of-factly. She triggered my officelike behavior and gently cajoled me into a dictating mode. It was not difficult to begin.

William Miller died on July 1, 1979, in Warren, Connecticut. Beloved husband of Pamela. Devoted father of Edward, Cathryn, and Peter Miller. Loving stepfather of Monica and Melissa Sanderson. Brother of Kevin and Michael Miller. . . .

When I paused, Jackie answered, "And what about the funeral? Do you want people to visit you at the funeral home? We have to think about that, too. Is there a particular church you want to use?" I couldn't answer her right away. There seemed to be so many things to decide. The things Jackie was pointing out were not surprises, and yet I had not given any consideration to them. I appreciated for the second time that, in dying, Bill had done something monumentally important, and that the ceremony had to be right. Not just any type of service would do; not just any church would do. Both had to be in keeping with all that Bill had represented.

Amy came into the room at that point and sat down on the floor beside me. She quickly grasped what we were doing and suggested that I consider the Congregational Church, of which she was a member. While Bill and I had been married at home, the minister from Amy's church had performed the ceremony. Because it had been one of his first nontraditional ceremonies, he had not forgotten it. Amy assured me that she thought the minister had developed a special feeling for Bill and me as a couple and would want to be part of Bill's service. It didn't take much reflection to realize that her suggestion was very appropriate.

Having made that decision, my thoughts flowed freely. Bill would not have wanted a funeral, a ceremony that marks the end of life. He would have chosen a ceremony that celebrates life. It had to be dynamic and vital. A funeral procession accompanied by melancholy and solemnity would be so completely wrong. The final testament to Bill needed to be a memorial service designed to make people remember Bill at his best, not conjuring up images of his last months.

Amy asked me what day I would like to hold the service. I thought about the people who had loved Bill and about his brothers, who would have to come from distant states, and suggested that Thursday evening would be the best. To hold the service sooner would have pushed me faster than I thought I could be pushed. But it had to happen before Friday. Friday would have been the anniversary of our marriage. That day loomed in my mind as an emotional mountain that I doubted I could climb. And I didn't want the two events confused. Our marriage had been a wonderful turning point in both our lives. It required its own day, as did the service in memory of Bill's dying. Amy said that she would call the church and see if arrangements could be made for a Thursday evening service.

Within a few moments, she returned and told me that she had arranged for the assistant minister to perform the service at seven Thursday evening. Watching my expression change, Amy explained that the minister himself was away on vacation and couldn't be reached. She said that she knew the assistant minister well and believed that he would represent Bill as I wanted him represented. She said that John had asked to come over the following day to talk with me in order to understand the kind of man Bill had been.

Jackie brought up the subject of flowers. That one was easy. Bill had been a pragmatist. I suggested that Bill would have wanted donations made to the American Heart Association instead of a bunch of flowers that wouldn't last the week.

That was all I could handle. Excusing myself, I went out to the porch to be alone. Amy and Jackie left me in peace. Through the closed door, I heard Ann starting the vacuum cleaner.

When I went back into the house, Jackie said she had finished writing the announcement and wanted to check it with me before telephoning the newspapers. I couldn't add anything to what she had written.

A Memorial Service will be held at the Congregational Church in Turner on Thursday, July 5, 1979, at 7 P.M. In lieu of flowers, donations to the American Heart Association would be appreciated.

She then listed a number of papers she felt should carry the announcement. To her list, I added one or two western Connecticut papers so that the news would reach people whom Bill had known during his prior marriage.

Jackie left the room in order to begin telephoning the papers, leaving Amy and me alone for the first time since the night before. We sat for a while in silence, but the silence was comfortable. My thoughts were consumed with the unreality of everything that was happening around me. It was as though I were taking drugs that make dreams and nightmares seem real and endless. Ann was cleaning my house. My attorney's wife was calling the local papers to announce that my husband was dead. My friend was sitting opposite me, her shoulders atypically slumped and her eyes uncharacteristically droopy. I said, "It's amazing; it's all amazing. Yesterday at this time, I was driving to Philadelphia. I sang along with the radio all the way there. I was so happy. Things were finally going to be better. That was less than twenty-four hours ago! It can't be real." Amy simply nodded.

I was beginning to flounder in self-pity when Brooks came through the front door. Brooks never simply entered a room. She always bounded into a room, her blond ponytail flapping at her back. The fact that she was several months pregnant didn't affect her entrance at all. She plopped herself down on the floor next to me and opened with, "I wanted to be here first thing this morning, but decided that if anybody in this house is going to eat, I'd better concentrate on making some casseroles. I just put six casseroles in your refrigerator. You don't need food poisoning from your own cooking on top of everything else!"

37

Anybody who didn't know Brooks would have thought she was unnecessarily sarcastic at a time when sarcasm wasn't warranted. I didn't feel that way at all. I gave her a long hug and thanked her for coming over. She got serious for a minute. "I called the office and told them that I wouldn't be in for a few days. I want to be available to you when you need me." That's all the serious talk either of us could handle. Brooks then launched into a commentary far more typical of her outgoing and effervescent self. Pulling out her knitting, she said, "Bill wouldn't have believed this. Miss Compulsive Executive, sitting in the middle of his living room knitting away on a Monday afternoon. He was always telling me that I should relax, but this is really going too far. He always did have a way of making a point."

Amy, who had not met Brooks before, didn't know what to think. That amused Brooks and encouraged more of the same behavior. "You know what else Bill wouldn't have believed? He wouldn't have believed that I finally have a bust! It's wonderful what pregnancy does for you. You know that last Christmas, Bill filled a Christmas stocking for Rob and myself. You'd never believe what he put in my stocking. He wrapped up a training bra, and the note he attached read, "When you wish upon a star. . . ." I guess he just couldn't take being wrong. He had to exit before he ever saw me in this glorious condition!"

At this, Amy allowed herself to smile. She was beginning to appreciate Brooks and what Brooks was doing. It was obvious that, in spite of her banter, Brooks had adored and respected Bill. Bill's wit had been every bit as sharp as hers, and they had spent many hours exchanging affectionate barbs. Not today, though. Today, Brooks had to go it alone. It was obviously painful for her. That she continued was nothing other than a courageous attempt to make me feel better.

Brooks couldn't keep it up very long, however. Within an hour, she said that she had to go home, but that her husband, Rob, had also made arrangements to take some time off work, and they would be in and out each day. Her parting comment was serious. "Rob just can't quite face you and the children yet. He has taken the news very hard and feels as though he lost his only friend. He asks you to understand; he will be here tomorrow." There were tears in her eyes when she left.

Shortly after Brooks left, Jackie came into the living room to say that she had to get home because her children would be returning from summer camp. Then it was Ann's turn to leave. She came in and, carrying on the script that we both found comfortable, said, "Ma'am, I finished the upstairs. Tomorrow I'll do the downstairs." I responded in kind: "I don't know. Seems to me I pay you an awful lot for an awful little work." Ann went on, "Well, Ma'am, you wouldn't want me to miss my soap opera in the morning. I can't get through the day 'less I knows what happened. You jus' made a mistake when you picked the mornin' 'stead of the aft'noon. If ye'll 'scuse me, I got to pick up my chillens." I pictured her picking up her "chillens" in her brand-new baby blue Mercedes and smiled. Ann then took Amy aside. I overheard their conversation, though I'm sure they did not intend that I should. Ann asked Amy if she should come back later so that Amy could go home for a while herself. Amy assured Ann that everything was all right at her house, but that she really had to go into the office the next day and would appreciate it if Ann could relieve her then.

I was both sorry and glad that I had overheard their conversation. Clearly they both cared deeply for me. Clearly, also, I had become a temporary burden on them. They had to help me make it through the day, while the demands on them continued without interruption. Amy's employer was not about to give her the week off because the husband of a friend had died. Ann's children were not about to cease needing her. The old saying "Life goes on" occurred to me. But it was not my life that was going on, but everyone else's. I felt incredibly lonely. No one in the world could really share this experience with me. It was mine, mine alone. Looking back, I am glad that I began to realize this early in the week. The shock of an empty house after a week or so of constant friends in attendance might have been too much. In a way, Amy and Ann's conversation began to make me face the reality that, in the end, I would have to go through the depths of grief by myself.

After Ann left, the house seemed ominously quiet. For the first time in hours, I wondered about Pete. Was he home? I buzzed the intercom, and after a few seconds a sleepy voice said, "Yes?" I said, "Pete, I was just wondering if you were all right." He seemed to be very happy that I asked. I felt guilty that I had not inquired earlier. He, too, was having to go it alone. I wanted to say more, to say something that would make him feel better, but I could find no words.

Amy suggested that I sit in the sun with her and think about the things I wanted to tell John, the minister, about Bill. That struck me as exactly what I most wanted to do, to think about Bill, about who he had been and about how good I had felt being with him. I didn't want Amy with me, however. I wanted to be alone with Bill. I found a pad and pen and went out to the porch.

For the first few minutes, the porch made me uneasy. I avoided the chaise longue on which Bill had sat only the day before. Only the day before! Time seemed to be playing cruel tricks on me. Never in my life had the clock moved so slowly. It seemed impossible that I could have traveled such an incredible distance in so short a period of time. I wondered what would happen if I sat in the chaise longue. I thought I might get sick; I also thought it might make me feel closer to Bill. I decided to take the risk and sat down slowly and gingerly, as if I were sitting in a car with vinyl upholstery that had been parked in the sun all day. Once down, I realized it wasn't bad at all. On the contrary, I felt quite comfortable. The mystery of things Bill had touched, places he had sat, began to slip away. The chaise longue was just a seat after all. In spite of the incredible things that had happened, the chair had not been imbued with surrealistic power. Placing the pad and pen on my lap, I tilted my head back and closed my eyes.

I may have fallen asleep. I don't know. When my mind finally refocused on where I was and what I was trying to do, the thoughts came rapidly. I was going to write the sermon for Bill's memorial service, and I had a strong sense that all I would have to do is open the pen, put my hand to the paper, and the words would write themselves. I had little need to stop and think. My mind was one with Bill's mind, and the values he held dear defined themselves easily. I began with thoughts of our marriage vows, and the days before when Bill had carefully selected pieces from books of Rod McKuen and Kahlil Gibran and then added his own words until he had just the right message. I wrote . . .

Bill followed in his life what he said to his children on the day of our marriage:

"I would like you to consider a new concept of family, not

as a bounded entity but a transcendent force that brings us close in times of joy and in times of need. I encourage you to be free, to find your own way, knowing that I will stand by you when you need me and will stand aside when it's time for you to seek your personal destinies.

"Live your life as though you have only one life to live. Give your love as though you have only one love to give. Above all, don't compromise, even in the spirit of charity.

"Remember, you must be responsible for you—your life, your love, your clarity."

Bill truly did pursue a new concept of family. If family is made up of persons whom we love unconditionally, whom we care for deeply, whom we struggle for in order to help them realize their full potential, then Bill's family is enormous.

He had few acquaintances; he had a number of friends with whom he had a deep bond that did not require structured socializing or even frequent meetings to maintain.

Bill made a positive impact on the lives of almost everyone he met. He was never too busy to listen, to empathize, to help.

He despised manipulation and told it like it was, regardless of the personal pain he often felt in doing so. He valued honesty and the straightforward expression of feelings.

Bill rarely confused his own needs with those of others. This was reflected in his statement to his children: "I will stand by you when you need me and will stand aside when it's time for you to seek your personal destinies."

Bill lived his life vigorously and with vitality. Obstacles were perceived as challenging opportunities. Even a massive heart attack four years ago, from which he was not expected to recover, did not stop him. He told afterward of entering a long velvety tunnel with a brilliant light at the end and deciding not to enter. He loved life, in all its aspects.

Compromise was something he refused to do. He firmly believed that, in the end, conflicts could always be resolved in such a way that there would be only winners, no losers.

His laughter was hearty and contagious.

Bill was not afraid to die, having come so close before. He simply did not want to die. Nor did he want to live if he had to be weak and dependent. He valued his vitality, interdependency, and mutuality of effort.

Bill took total responsibiity for his own life. He never cried, "Why me? It's not fair." Throughout, he showed occasional anger, but never self-pity. His focus of concern was for others whose lives were made more difficult by his illness.

Bill died in the way he lived—quickly and at a point of family joy and togetherness. He died with dignity.

The minister was later to take these sentences and turn them into an integrated, beautiful sermon. I felt no need to struggle with the ands, ifs, buts, and bridges. I felt extremely good about what Bill and I had written. The words captured Bill. But they did more than that. They reminded me of what it means to have courage and to live life as it should be lived. I had long ago fully embraced Bill's values. It is not that mine had been different; I don't believe they ever were. Somehow my relationship with Bill helped me both to clarify and to confirm those values. By the time I had finished writing, I was very sure that I, like Bill, had the strength to continue to love life even though Bill was gone.

I was aware that the ultimate monument I could offer in memory of Bill was to continue to live up to the values he had represented. I promised myself that I would continue to be responsible for my own life, and to avoid wasting life's energies on faultfinding and blame-placing. I vowed to be straightforward and courageous in my dealings with others. I decided that I would and could be happy again, and that the way to find peace within myself was to regard the grief that I felt as an emotional peak experience. I had experienced a lot of life during my years with Bill. Our relationship had been emotionally intense, and I had learned to relish the highs and to not fear the lows. To live is to feel. The deeper we feel, the more of life we experience. And now, Bill would guide me through yet another feeling and introduce me to yet another part of life. I determined that I would not hide from my grief, but learn from it. I was ready.

Going back into the house, I noticed that it was nearly five. The house was still quiet. Amy was sleeping on the sofa. I was glad to see that. My heart went out to her, and I felt enormously fortunate to have such a friend. I had reached a point of rediscovering my own strength and courage, but until that moment I had leaned almost totally on her. She had to be completely exhausted. I sat and watched her sleep for a while, enjoying the peace within me, the quiet around me, and the comfort of being in the company of someone whom I loved and trusted. My reverie was broken by the sound of a car in the driveway. Going to the window, I saw that Monica and Melissa were home.

Once out of the car, both children looked up at the windows. There was a mixture of concern and fear on their faces. I understood. They had had a few hours respite from sadness. It must have been extremely difficult for them to contemplate returning. I waved at them, and Melissa saw me. She smiled and turned to her older sister. Both came running up the path to the front door. I went to meet them, wanting desperately to hug them and to share with them my momentary certainty that we would, in the end, be happy again.

Within moments of the children's return, the household went mildly crazy. First Meg arrived, her arms full of loose papers that wouldn't fit in the several briefcases that she carried. She and I went down to the playroom in order to avoid interruptions. The strain of the day showed clearly on her face. We had a major client project due the following Wednesday, and she had struggled not only with that but also with the dozens of calls that had to be made to announce Bill's death. Her task was not only to tell people but also to assure them that the business would continue and that their various concerns would be addressed as if nothing had happened. She had come, in part, to reassure me that everything was in control. I sensed, though, that her greater need was to be reassured that she had done a good job. I found that easy to do, for indeed she had.

Meg asked me if I thought I would be able to discuss the client project for an hour or so the next day, as there were some methods involved with which she was unfamiliar. To reapproach the details of the business seemed almost an impossibility to me. I felt as one feels after a vacation or illness of several months. The momentum was entirely broken, and the idea of resuming the reigns of the business filled me with a slight panic. My focus was still very much on Bill and the feelings of the afternoon, and I recalled how much that business had meant to him. He had been so proud when the firm had finally turned a critical financial corner. If, through my own behavior, I was to do justice to Bill's memory, I would focus as necessary on the business. I told Meg that I would be happy to work with her for a few hours and suggested that she come first thing in the morning.

Before we had finished with the details of the business, Joel joined us. He already had a glass of scotch in his hand and immediately chastised me for the brand he had found in the liquor cabinet. He mentioned that I was lucky to have Meg, both as friend and as associate. His comment seemed to both embarrass and please Meg. I sensed that they had had quite a conversation that day, and that Joel had already learned to trust Meg as I did. He had no regrets about having made her an alternate signatory on the corporate account. In so doing, he had abruptly changed her status from a new employee to a fully trusted, senior member of the firm.

When Meg had gone, Joel and I returned upstairs to a bustling kitchen. Someone had set up a full-fledged bar, and Amy was busy at the stove, heating several of the casseroles that Brooks had brought over earlier in the day. Mary Jansen, an old friend whom I rarely saw, given the demands of both of our careers, was sitting on the floor attempting to keep Melissa occupied with a game of Candy Land. Pete was on the telephone. The noise level in the kitchen was incredible. What struck me first was that people were not only loud, but laughing. It looked and sounded like a typical weekend night at our home, except that the stereo was silent. Joel and I joined the group at the kitchen table. Mary's husband, Tom, asked me if he could fix me a drink. I asked for a glass of wine and sat and listened to them for a long while. I was happy to have the distraction. I felt as though I were watching a television show, a show that was good enough to capture my attention and yet removed from my own life situation. Tom and Joel began a dialogue that should have been recorded for television. Tom's sarcastic wit matched Joel's, and the two engaged vigorously in contests over the merits of various sports cars, politicians, and marketing approaches.

Pete got off the telephone, and I caught his eye. He managed to tell me over the noise in the room that Cathy would be arriving on the late train that night, and that he would meet her. Again, I asked him how he was doing, and he said that he felt surprisingly well. He had had a good nap that afternoon. He spoke of his concern for me. We enjoyed a very special communication at that moment. The kitchen was populated with people attempting to see us through our distress, and yet only we really knew the depths of our grief. I returned to my live show, and he went to his room to play his guitar. I knew then that he was all right. Pete and his guitar had a very special relationship. They were best friends. That he could summon the energy and the mental focus to spend time with that particular friend told me that he was confronting his grief in a healthy way.

Hours passed. I drank a lot of wine but never felt the effects. I watched plates come and go and never chose to eat. I put Melissa to bed and saw that Monica was settled in, and returned again to the kitchen. Sometime around ten, Pete returned with Cathy. I was nervous as she entered. I had gotten used to the people who had been around me all evening. There were no expectations. All that was asked was that everyone be themselves, saying whatever they wanted, whenever they wanted.

My concerns were short-lived. As Cathy walked into the kitchen, I got up to embrace her. She hugged me back firmly. That one gesture said it all. She was very much in control of herself. Looking at me, and then sizing up the situation in the kitchen, she said, "We'll talk later." She may have been my stepdaughter, but at that moment she was clearly the wiser. Once again, we were off to a good start as peers, as friends.

Sometime during the evening, Amy suggested that since Cathy was there, she would like to go home for the night. Her two girls were old enough to fend for themselves, but young enough to miss their mother. I was glad that Amy felt free to openly speak her mind. A less assertive friend might have reluctantly put her own family concerns aside and stayed with me. That would have been a shame. True, I needed someone around me, but I also needed a friend who felt her own life was in place. ,

After Amy left, Cathy and I talked until the wee hours of the morning.

I could not yet go to sleep in the bed that Bill and I had shared. As I had done the night before, I crawled into a bed in the guest room. Cathy lay down on the bed Amy had used. For a moment, my mother's dictum that beds must be changed for guests troubled me, and I shared my concern with Cathy. Once again she emerged as the more mature of the two of us, as she said, "For heaven's sake. You worry about the dumbest things at the dumbest times." I was glad that she had come.

When I awoke on Tuesday morning, Cathy was still asleep in the bed beside me. I did not fight the morning by attempting to cling to sleep. I was beginning to accept that my first thought of the day would be, "Bill is dead." Now I knew that the surge of fear and panic that accompanied my waking would subside as the day progressed. Nor was I surprised to hear the sound of several unidentified voices coming from the other side of the house. Today, unlike yesterday, I had a purpose. I remembered that I was to work with Meg this morning and faced the prospect of that meeting with some relief.

Entering my bedroom to get my clothes, I immediately realized that the benevolent, caring, warm presence that had been part of the room the day before was slowly ebbing away. Hastening to close the door behind me, I thought about the conversations Bill and I had had after his first heart attack. He had described dying as entering a long velvety tunnel and, at the same time, seeing those persons he loved and was about to leave. Perhaps, as my strength grew, Bill's presence would fade in kind; perhaps, too, my courage would allow him to be free of this world.

The activity in the kitchen was much like it had been the day before. Brooks was there and with her, Rob. Seeing me was hard on Rob. His smile was stiff, as was his kiss. As usual, Brooks broke the silence. "My God, you look awful. Amy said you were looking better. If this is better, I'd hate to see worse!" We sat and talked about nothing in particular for an hour or so, until the lack of activity began to bother me. The inactivity was apparently troubling Rob also, for he asked me if there was anything around the house he could fix. Always the list maker, it didn't take me more than a moment to suggest that he might like to climb up into the attic and caulk the window. Each time it rained we had been getting water in the house and it was ruining Monica's ceiling. Rob greeted the idea with enthusiasm. He was even more elated at discovering that I had no caulking gun, and that he would have to go out to the hardware store to get one. Later, as he worked, Rob didn't even seem to mind the wasps that had made a home in the attic. It was his unique way of looking after his friend's widow and children.

Meg arrived while Rob was in the attic. Our work session went well. Meg's questions were thorough and organized, and I had only to answer them one at a time. She didn't put me in a position of having to conceptualize, to think of the questions as well as the answers. She left me confident that the client deadline would be met with a high-quality product.

Ann came back sometime in the middle of the morning and told me that she planned to work that day on putting together food and drink for people who might come to the house after the memorial service. We never even had to discuss whether or not people should be invited back to the house. Bill had been a very open, people-loving man, and it was only right that his home would be open to his friends on that of all nights.

Until the late afternoon, the day was largely uneventful. I remember the telephone ringing to the point of distraction. It became an unspoken policy that I would not answer it. I think many were relieved that they were able to express their condolences without having to speak with me directly. The calls were important, however. They reminded me that a lot of people cared. I accepted only a few calls myself that day. For the first time in years, my mother telephoned. We had long ago decided that the cost of frequent calls was prohibitive. Somehow, having to watch the clock during a conversation led to stilted, unsatisfactory talks. Letters were better. Our decision had pleased my father enormously. Hard of hearing, he could not enjoy the calls. A Scotsman by heritage, he chafed at paying over a hundred dollars for a casual conversation. On this day, though, he had agreed with my mother that she should call. She had to hear my voice for herself. Only in that way would she know that I was coping. It felt so very good to hear her voice. She told me how much she wanted to be with me and that she and my father had learned to truly love Bill. She cried as she told me that the letter Bill had written to them from the hospital had arrived only that day. She read it to me, and we both cried.

Dear Rosemary and John,

I guess Pam has kept you posted on the events of the past few months. I only fear that I have put an enormous strain on Pam. Thankfully, that is nearing an end. We both look forward to a peaceful summer, and to long quiet summer nights together. Throughout these many weeks in the hospital, it has helped me enormously to know that I have found a new family, a wonderful family. It has been so many years since I felt truly loved by so many people. Having both of you in my life is wonderful. I love you.

Bill

The only other calls I accepted that day were from Franklin Samuelson and Bob Wilson. Franklin was both a client of ours and a longtime friend of Bill's. He had been Bill's best man at his first wedding and was godfather to Edward. Franklin, a leader of a major worldwide corporation, had many demands on his time. When he told me that he and his wife would be flying in for Bill's service, I smiled. Bill would have liked that.

Bob Wilson was a manager in a client organization. I chose to talk to him not for that reason but because I felt making the call had to be an extremely difficult thing for Bob to do. Bob is a brilliant man, and, as seems to be so often true of brilliant people, he often had a difficult time expressing his emotions. Our conversation, while brief, had a big impact on me. Bob simply said, "Pam, I . . . well, I . . . I am so very sorry. I hope I'm not disturbing you. I thought about you and Bill and about me and my family all night. . . . When I heard, all I could do was walk. I walked and I cried." Bill's death had clearly touched the very center of Bob's being.

Late in the afternoon, the minister arrived. I suddenly appreciated how awesome a job it would be to help him know Bill. I was thankful that Amy knew both the minister and myself as well as she did and would be able to make us at least somewhat comfortable with each other. An avid churchgoer, Amy would understand the minister's preference for the traditionally biblical. Amy would also understand my preference for a nontraditional sermon. Even as we began to select music for the service, our differences were apparent. John wanted me to select hymns from the hymnal. I tried, but nothing seemed to fit. He made several suggestions, but I found the hymns either too dismal and too depressing or too abstract and typically religious. Bill had been a musician, a lover of country-western music. The service we were discussing was for Bill. The music, too, had to be characteristic of Bill. I pulled a Kris Kristofferson songbook from Bill's music shelf and chose three or four of his favorite songs. I asked if the organist could learn to play those songs.

The minister seemed a little disturbed by my request. Taking the songbook from me, Amy looked at John and told him that she thought my selections were appropriate and that the organist would have little difficulty with them. The minister agreed. To show him my appreciation, I picked up the hymnal and selected "Morning Has Broken."

From that point on, the planning of the service was relatively easy. I suggested that we go downstairs to the playroom. The walls of the playroom were filled with pictures of the family and would, I hoped, provide John with a better portrayal of Bill's vitality. As we looked at the pictures, I talked freely about Bill and about our life together. The minister seemed to be very touched by what he heard. More than once, I saw there were tears in his eyes. When I could think of nothing more to say, I mentioned that I had written down some thoughts about Bill. John sat and read my notes and, having done so, excused himself for a few minutes. When he returned, he said that the notes wouldn't just help him write the sermon, they *were* the sermon. Pete walked in as we were finishing and, seeing him, I had an idea.

"Pete, we have been planning your father's service. We're going to ask the organist to play some of the songs Bill used to play. I wonder, would you like to play something during the service?"

Pete's shyness about performing was immediately apparent. "Oh, Pam, I don't know. I mean, I'd *like* to do it, but I just don't know if I can. I mean, there will be a lot of people there, and I . . . well, I don't know that I can handle it."

"Okay, Pete. Just think about it. You have a wonderful voice and it would have pleased your father to see you try to do this."

Pete didn't react immediately, but after a few minutes, he interrupted John and me. "Pam, I'd like to play a song or two at the service. I think you're right. Dad would have wanted it that way."

The feeling in Pete's voice was so great that the rest of us were silent. The minister left, saying little, touching my shoulder in lieu of any parting words.

Tuesday night remains very much a blur in my mind. Again, the house was filled with people. Somehow dinner was served, but it came and went without my eating. Someone bemoaned that the scotch was gone. Next, it was the bourbon. Someone turned on the stereo. Several people were playing pool. I recall Brooks asking

Monica what she should bring the next day. Monica amused me by answering, "Bourbon. Bring some bourbon for Mommy's coffee." Even I had to laugh out loud at that. Monica's comment was very loving; her concern was clearly for me and not for herself. I was amused at the way she had mixed up my favorite drinks: bourbon and ginger ale, Kahlua and coffee.

I drank as much as anyone Tuesday night. Rob later confessed that he had been making my drinks unusually strong. He was trying to make me sleep. Amy kept pushing food in my direction. It seems that underneath all of the pool playing, the joking, and the talk was an objective that was shared by all the people in the house: to get me to eat and to sleep. Convinced that I would not sleep on my own, they had apparently decided that the next best thing was to cause me to pass out. I fooled them all. I did not pass out. I did not even feel the effects of the liquor or of the lack of sleep. My sensitivities and emotions had become numb, but my body was infused with a kind of superhuman energy.

Unknown to me, Amy had decided that she would stay that night. It had become obvious that her presence was critical as the telephone calls came in with an ever increasing frequency. Only she knew me well enough to hand me the phone when it was appropriate and to take messages when the caller was other than a close friend. She had also become the constant in my life. While others came and went, Amy was there. While no one could fully share my grief, Amy had been with me from the start of the pain. Only she was able to track my emotional changes, my progressions, and my regressions. And the children felt safe and comfortable with her.

When, in the early hours of the morning, I finally decided to lie down, I was especially glad that Amy was there. I wanted to try to sleep in Bill's and my bedroom for the first time, and I was frightened. Amy understood my fears instantly, for she had seen my ambivalent approaches toward that room. Somehow, having Amy in the next room was a comfort, a hedge against my being over-whelmed by memories and by the still-lingering presence of Bill.

I pulled the spread down ever so carefully, wanting to avoid disturbing anything about Bill's side of the bed. Cautiously, I crept under the covers. I had no need for a light. The moon was shining through the uncurtained top of the cathedral window. Lying on my back and careful not to move, I looked up at the ceiling. Immediately I noticed a strange pattern of shadows on either side of the beam that runs across the center of the ceiling. The pattern resembled that of two large diamonds going out from either side of the beam. I tried to convince myself that the shadows were not a visible sign of Bill's presence but simply a function of the outdoor lights and the moon hitting the house at a peculiar angle.

The shadows had a spellbinding effect on me. I could not turn away from them. They seemed to be growing in size and in density, as if to dominate the room itself and everything and everyone in it. But I was not frightened; the shadows were benevolent and caring. They seemed to speak to me. My mind began to focus only on peaceful, sleepy words. Calm . . . Comfort . . . Warmth . . . Safety . . . Calm . . . Comfort . . . Warmth . . . Safety. I experienced the sensation of someone putting another cover over me. Still the shadows were unchanged. I didn't fight any longer. The shadows were Bill, of that I was convinced. They soothed me. I began to cry quietly. I suspect Amy heard me, though she never said so. Spent, I fell asleep.

Tuesday had been characterized by a blur of faces, as visitors came and went. On Wednesday, their activities became more focused, and I was drawn reluctantly into dealing with death. Amy was busy coordinating the memorial service and responding to the funeral home as best as she could. In spite of her efforts to shield me, in the end I had to deal with the funeral home directly. Their questions were painfully real. I had told them that Bill wanted to be cremated and that I was in no hurry for the ashes. Then, as suddenly, I changed my mind. Friday, the fifth anniversary of our marriage, began to assume an enormous symbolic importance.

Each year we had celebrated our anniversary by taking wine and cheese and riding our mopeds to a park some distance from the house. Year after year, we both found the day to be tremendously freeing, as we let the wind whip through our hair and the awesome view from the top of the mountain clear our heads of business concerns. I determined to spread Bill's ashes on Friday somewhere within that park. The day had to represent Bill's final freedom from this world.

At first, the funeral home said that there was no way they could accommodate my request to have the ashes by Friday. There simply was not enough time. Amy called the minister, and he intervened. Finally, the funeral home agreed to do their best. Amy arranged for the ashes to be delivered to the church so that I could pick them up after the service. Many tried to convince me to do otherwise. They were concerned that I would crack under the emotional strain of the service followed so directly by the anniversary and the spreading of the ashes. I would not be dissuaded. I believed that Bill had put the idea in my head. It had become his last wish.

Sometime in the late afternoon, I called my mother. While I had nothing in particular to say, I wanted to talk with her. I was beginning to feel the effects of lack of sleep. My emotions and sensitivities were awake once again, but my body was hurting. I had been an extremely strong-willed and stubborn child, but all independence used to disappear when I had the slightest ailment. I used to demand complete attention from my mother during those times, and she always responded. Now I felt similarly weakened in body and in spirit and wanted her to surround me with the tender loving care that only a mother can provide. The telephone call was painful. It is impossible to provide the kind of comfort I needed with thirteen thousand miles intervening.

Toward evening Pete and Cathy told me that Bill's brothers, Kevin and Michael, would be arriving that night. I began to worry about sleeping arrangements. Amy and Cathy had the guest room. All that remained were the extra beds in Monica's room and in Pete's room. There were the sofas, but I didn't like the idea of people sleeping in the living room and in the playroom. That would have disturbed the sense of order that I so desperately needed and Ann was so conscientiously providing. The thought of blankets and pillows spread throughout the rooms she so regularly dusted and vacuumed was upsetting. I discussed my problem with Cathy, and she assured me that neither brother had assumed he was going to stay at the house. Apparently they had already made arrangements to stay with relatives in another town.

By nine that night Kevin and Michael were part of the group in the kitchen. On entering, Kevin clung to me and cried. At first I found it painful to open myself to him. His physical resemblance to Bill was uncanny and terrifying. But within moments I began to derive a sense of peace from Kevin. I began to cry with him and to gain strength from the wordless sharing. By the time they left, an hour or so later, I felt a special bond with Kevin.

After Kevin and Michael left, the talking, eating, and drinking continued. Still I felt neither fatigue nor the effects of the drinks that were periodically placed before me. But I had grown impatient with loud voices and what seemed to be false gaiety. Saying nothing to anyone, I went into the bedroom and, as the night before, crept quietly into bed. Again I took pains not to disturb Bill's half of the bed. Lying on my back, I noticed that the shadows were very faint. But as I lay there, they gradually deepened in intensity, until their outlines were completely distinct. I opened myself to their influence, firmly believing that they were a sign that Bill's consciousness was fully with me. Again I let him soothe me to sleep.

I awoke Thursday morning to the sound of a light tapping on the bedroom door. In response to my question "Who is it?" a tiny voice answered, "It's Melissa, Mommy, Melissa." I paused for a moment and then urged her to enter. This was the first time she had needed permission to come into our room. I pained for her, realizing that she, like the visitors, had respected the sanctity of Mommy and Bill's bedroom. I had been largely unavailable to her. She must have missed our affectionate early-morning talks. Not wanting her to jump onto Bill's side of the bed, I got up and sat in the big lounge chair and motioned for her to come and sit on my lap. She smiled and snuggled against me. We sat there for a long time, comforting each other. When she could no longer sit there quietly, she began to ask me what she should wear to church.

I had given little thought to clothing all week. My uniform had been shorts or jeans and T-shirts. I didn't want to think about clothing, for to dress up was inevitably to leave the house. My stomach tightened at the thought of leaving the bounds of our property. I did not feel at all ready to venture out into the world and realized that, while I was coping, I was able to manage only in a very circumscribed universe.

Melissa broke my anxiety by suggesting that she would like to wear her light blue dress with the matching jacket. I immediately agreed, amazed that her selection was so appropriate. I began to consider what Monica would wear. Monica was difficult to dress. She always insisted that every detail be precisely right and seemed to be genuinely happy only in her khaki shorts and her faded jeans. To select an outfit for her was typically to initiate a major argument. To shop with her for clothes was to spend six or eight hours in purposeless meandering through the racks. I could think of only one outfit that was appropriate: the yellow skirt and jacket that we had managed to select for her elementary school graduation the month before. Melissa and I decided that, whether she liked it or not, Monica was going to wear that outfit.

I asked Melissa to help me select what I would wear. She pointed to three or four dresses, but none seemed right. I had decided not to wear the dark colors of mourning, since the service was to be a celebration in memory of Bill's life. Melissa's choices were not somber, but they were frivolous. The sundress with the sea horses on it wouldn't do. Neither would the dinner dress with the close-to-see-through top. I suggested to Melissa that perhaps I should wear one of the suits I wore on business trips. She was pleased with that idea, since it would mean I would be wearing a jacket similar to hers. Together we chose a peach-colored linen suit.

I stayed in my bedroom most of the day. At one point, Amy brought me some tea and toast. By the time people started arriving at the house, I was ready to talk with them. The Samuelsons were the first to arrive. They had flown in early so as to have time to talk privately with me. I enjoyed our quiet visit.

Shortly before we were to leave, Kevin and Michael arrived. Apparently Michael's plans had made it impossible for Kevin to get to the house as early as he had hoped. Sensing that Kevin wanted to spend as much time as possible at Bill's home, I asked if he wanted to share Pete's room for the remainder of his stay. He enthusiastically accepted the invitation.

The last to arrive were Rob and Brooks. Brooks had told me that it would mean a great deal to Rob to be able to drive the children and myself to the service. I accepted gratefully. I was reluctant to even leave the house and had no confidence at all that I could drive.

Arriving at the church, the children and I were shown to a private room reserved for family and invited friends of the family. Amy sat with me, as did Ann, Phil, Brooks, and Rob. Brooks was quiet and comforting. She said little; what she did say was spoken softly. Throughout, she held my hand. I expected no one else and was surprised when the door to the room opened and Shelley entered. Amy and Jim had failed in their efforts to contact her. Her office hadn't been able to tell us where she was. And yet, somehow, my foul-weather friend had managed to appear at the height of the storm.

Shelley ran across the room and embraced me. She cried and held me tightly. When she finally spoke, she said, "You didn't think your foul-weather friend would let you down, did you?" I smiled; it felt so very good to see her. I wanted to focus completely on Shelley. I sat and listened to the tale of the miraculous way in which Shelley had found out about Bill's death. She had run into a friend of a friend of a former client of Bill's on the street in New York City earlier that day. Even more incredible, Shelley had been vacationing in Acapulco and had not been due to return until the following weekend. She had been disappointed with her accommodations and so had decided to return early for a few days of rest and relaxation in her own apartment.

Shelley's buoyant conversation and her overwhelming concern for me, coupled with the wonderful feeling of a long-overdue reunion, kept me occupied until the sounds of organ music caught my attention. Someone said, "It must be time to go in." I was terribly nervous and forgot that the minister had promised to come and escort the children and me into the church. Taking Monica by one hand and Melissa by the other, I took a very deep breath and walked out of the family gathering place, around the corner, and directly up the aisle. My knees were weak, and I sensed hundreds of eyes on me. No one was speaking. Melissa walked so closely as to almost trip me. Walking toward the front of the church, I stopped only when I saw my aunt and two cousins in the second row.

I was incredibly glad to see them. Guiding Melissa into the third row, we sat directly behind them. They turned, and we grabbed hands. Somehow it didn't seem appropriate to speak. I was glad to be sitting down and out of the public gaze. Out of the periphery of my vision, I could see that the church was very full. I wanted to look around and see who had come, but I was afraid of catching someone's eye. I wanted to be invisible. This was to be Bill's show, not mine. I sensed that the children and I were capable of drawing attention away from Bill. I suspected that we looked pretty, and vulnerable, and young enough to inspire sympathy and divert attention. I didn't want that, not at this time.

Finally, looking up, I noticed how beautiful the church was. Utterly simple, it was adorned only with occasional stained glass and a simply carved wooden image of Christ. Beneath his image were two enormous baskets of flowers. They were wild flowers, simple, unpretentious, and abundant. I wondered who had thought of such a lovely thing. Only later was I to learn that the flowers were a gift from my parents.

I began to listen to what the organist was playing. It took my breath away. He was playing a song that Bill had loved and had often insisted on playing for me. I had stopped him more often than not. The lyrics spoke softly of love's joy and of its impermanence. The song reminded me that his heart was weak, and that he might leave me. As the organist played, I heard the sound of Bill's voice and his ukulele. I thought with great sadness that our story had ended; it had ended far sooner than I ever thought it would. Bill had tried to play that song for me in the hospital the weekend he was released, the day he had died. Again I had stopped him. I wished now that I hadn't.

My thoughts were still focused on the words of the song when the minister began his sermon. I noticed his beginning but was not affected by it. The words seemed predictable: "I am the resurrection and the life. . . ." Neither did the prayer that followed fully capture my attention. "We confess that we are children of dust." His lesson from the Scriptures was clearly carefully chosen and responsive to my request that the service be optimistic: "We are seeking a message of comfort and words which speak to the heart and the heart's need to celebrate the goodness of life."

I began to notice that the minister had a deep, melodious voice. That pleased me. Bill had had such a voice. During readings from the Book of John in which Jesus raises Lazarus from the dead, my attention wandered again. I noticed that Melissa was surprisingly quiet, apparently undisturbed by the tight grasp I had on her hand. Monica moved her hand in mine once or twice, but she let me hold on. I was beginning to feel comfortably small and insignificant. I refocused on the minister's words: "Life is a momentary affliction preparing us for a greater glory; things that are seen are transient; things that are unseen are eternal." I wanted to believe that there is a life after death. I wanted to believe in God.

Bill had been a fine Christian in his behavior but had given up attending formal religious services years before I met him. Was he a believer? I was not sure. We had often talked of an energy that passes between people, transcending both of them. That, I guess, had been Bill's concept of God. Yes, I decided, he had been a believer. Was Bill's soul still living? I remembered the presence in our bedroom, and the unspoken guidance I had been receiving, and knew he still lived, though in an unseen form.

"Things that are seen are transient." My stomach turned as I pictured the crematorium. I didn't like thinking about that. It frightened me and made me feel nauseated. I wondered briefly about the ashes. Were they in the church? The idea of my Bill reduced to a small container of ashes was something I could not comprehend. "Things that are unseen are eternal." I found a great deal more solace in those words.

I realized I had been looking down at my lap and had not heard the minister's most recent words. Suddenly, looking up, I saw Pete approaching the altar. He sat down, cleared his throat, and adjusted his guitar on his lap. He caught my eye and quickly looked away. Pete didn't begin right away, and I wondered whether he could do it. He was close to tears. My heart went out to him. I wanted to stand and comfort him and urge him to do what I knew he needed to do. I think I might have done just that had he not begun.

He sang about the painful end of a once-loving relationship. The words alone weakened me; the emotional intensity of Pete's voice was so great that I could no longer hold back my tears. I wept quietly and clutched the children's hands even more tightly. Neither tried to pull away. Pete began another song, and the message of warmth, tenderness, and love that once sustained Bill and me shook every fiber of my being. Pete couldn't make it all the way through. He began to cry. My own sobs went unnoticed. It was with relief that I heard the minister say, "Thank you, Pete. What you just heard was a gift from a member of Bill's family—a sign that love flows very deeply."

The minister then invited the congregation to share in a remembrance to Bill. I knew that he was about to deliver the thoughts and words I had given him earlier that week, and felt both embarrassed and proud at the same time. He elaborated the phrases and made them beautiful. Yes, the words did represent what Bill valued in life. I felt terribly proud of Bill, and thankful that I had shared in his life. The minister seemed to understand that feeling, closing the remembrance with, "We thank you for the gift of Bill's life."

It had been a gift, a beautiful, wonderful gift that had left me and my children more capable and more fulfilled than we would have been without him. I had a sense of things beginning, not ending, and joined happily in the singing of the hymn "Morning Has Broken." It was over. The minister announced that all were invited to a reception at Bill's home. He walked down the aisle and stopped next to the third row. I understood that it was time for the children and me to leave the church. Taking their hands, I hurried them down the aisle. Again, I avoided looking to the right or the left, feeling that all eyes were upon us. I wanted to get to the parking lot and into the car before anyone could stop us. Needing time to myself, I was not ready to break the spell of the service. I was glad that our home was a full half hour from the church.

By the time we arrived at the house cars were parked everywhere. Rob must have driven very slowly. I hadn't noticed. I braced myself for a difficult ordeal and marched directly into the living room. I claimed a permanent spot on the sofa, feeling no need to mill around and play hostess. This was Bill's party. He needed no hostess.

The time passed quickly as the house emptied and filled again in waves. The buffet was beautiful, and people were constantly milling around the table. Monica was later to tell me that she had to empty the kitchen garbage can three times; each time it was filled with empty liquor bottles and soda cans. I didn't find any individual conversation difficult, though some people said some very bizarre things: "Better to have loved and lost. . . ." "You'll find someone else." "Aren't you sorry you got divorced?" I understood why people said such things. Death is so frightening that it seems to strip away superficial courtesies. People don't know how to behave. The normal rules of the social game don't apply. To be a widow is painful; to offer condolences directly to a widow must be extremely difficult.

I remained on the sofa, receiving one person after another, not actively listening to what was said and not really caring. I smiled and nodded and pretended that I heard. The activity and noise level were so great that it overwhelmed me and made me numb. I didn't think and couldn't feel. I noticed that a few people stared at me, as if to study grief. I carefully avoided meeting their eyes.

After several hours, only family and good friends remained. I moved into the kitchen, seeking something indefinable. My aunt and cousins tried to fill the void in me, but they could not and eventually gave up trying. Brooks and Rob tried too, but again their words could not penetrate my shell. I could not find myself. Sights and sounds of a party breaking up were all around, and I had no role to fill. I was neither a hostess nor an invited guest.

Shelley brought me a glass of wine and sat with me. "Talk to me, Babe. Talk to me. You look so lost. Let me help."

"I don't have anything to say. It's all so unreal. I am lost, and that's scary. I'm tired of smiling, but I can't cry. I guess I'm just tired, really tired. I'm glad you came, but I can't talk about it, about me, right now. I guess I'd like to hear about you. Tell me about you."

Shelley did as I had asked, and before long Meg, Grant, Amy, Ann, Phil, Joel and Jackie were gathered around the kitchen table engrossed in a conversation about alternative life-styles. I cannot remember what was said. I did not participate; nor did I really listen. I simply sat and waited, a totally passive piece of driftwood stuck in a seemingly endless whirlpool. Pete, too, moved in and out of the conversation seemingly as lost as I.

It was Ed who finally provided me with a focus for my thoughts. Leaving Kevin, Michael, and Cathy, he sought me out and said that he wanted to talk about his father's ashes. Ed did not share my need to scatter the ashes at the site of our anniversary celebrations. He had other needs, other symbolisms, which required expression. We argued and we cried. We spoke first as adversaries and then finally as friends. In our shared love for Bill, we were able to overcome the distance that had existed between us.

Ed and I talked until dawn broke and agreed that he and his wife, Janice, were going to accompany me as I spread Bill's ashes. We agreed to leave for the park at one the next afternoon. That decided, Ed and his wife left to get a few hours of sleep. Meanwhile, Amy and Ann were talking at the kitchen table, trying hard to stay awake. They dared not sleep as long as I did not.

I asked Amy if she had Bill's ashes. She said yes, they were in the closet in the guest room, and that if I would go to my room, she would get them. I was sitting on my side of the bed when Amy entered. In her hand was a small box, wrapped in plain brown wrapping paper. Somehow, I had expected something different. She handed me the box, and I put it in my lap, asking her to leave. I sat, clutching the plain brown box, for a long time. I could not comprehend that I was holding all that physically remained of Bill. Thoughts of the crematorium kept intruding. I wanted to get sick but could not move to go into the bathroom. I began to rock back and forth, back and forth, clutching the box. My Bill was inside that box! I lifted it, and it felt heavy. Ashes are supposed to be light. Why was it so heavy? I began to visualize what lay inside the box, but stopped myself.

I needed Bill's help. I could not cope alone with that brown box. I turned off the light and, still sitting with the box on my lap, looked up at the ceiling. The shadows came and slowly deepened. They seemed to direct me to put the box on the desk on the other side of the room. I did as I was instructed, stripped to my underwear, and got under the covers. The message of warmth and comfort and security came again. Bill's soul was with me. What remained of his body was with me. Our anniversary had dawned, and for the last time, we were completely together. I dozed off, feeling loved and terrified at the same time.

3

Ashes to Ashes

I awoke refreshed an hour or two later, feeling as though I had had a full night's sleep. The house was quiet. I got up and picked up the box with the plain brown wrapping paper. I sat and held it, feeling a clear sense of purpose, of duty. Today, I would give Bill his final freedom. I would do something not only for him but with him. Picturing the park, I knew it would be beautiful on a day like this one. We would hike to the tower—the tallest point in the park. I would open the box and remove the beautiful urn. I would uncork the urn and tilt it slightly; the light gray ash would be caught on a breeze, and Bill would be carried to a wonderfully quiet and distant place, a place where no one could disturb him. It would be beautiful. It would be the most romantic day of my life. I would cry, but the tears would feel good, not bitter but sweet. And the group that would accompany me was perfect; it would be made up of all the people Bill loved most in the world. Kevin would be there, playing a part in this final drama of his beloved brother's life. Bill's children would be there, supporting and helping one another as Bill had always hoped they would. Amy and Ann would be there for me, and for Melissa and Monica. Ann would offer them all the tender loving care they needed as they witnessed their mother becoming one with Bill for the last time. Amy would be there to remind me of the strength and the courage that she knew I possessed. Monica and Melissa would begin to understand that death is not just dark, morbid, and scary, but a new beginning.

I held the box to my breast. It mystified me, and its mystery fueled my romantic thoughts. Turning it slowly, I began to try to understand it. I should not have done that. The mystery and the romance exploded as I turned the box. On the far side was a stark white label. Printed solidly in the middle of a vast white space was Bill's full name and an incredible series of numbers. The name of the crematorium was written in bolder letters. Again, I was confronted with the fact that to the outer world Bill's death was simply another case in a long list of cases. The beautiful visions I had enjoyed vanished. Death was not romantic; it was cold, sullen, and real.

I put the box down abruptly. I hated it. I hated my situation. I was angry again at Bill for leaving me. What kind of anniversary was this? It was lousy. It would be marked by nothing but pain on the part of all those who were going with me to the park. Bill wasn't the loser, we were. I walked to the window and looked out for a long time. My anger subsiding somewhat, I was flooded with guilt. Bill was still with me, and I had brusquely and without kind feeling slammed his ashes onto the desk. I returned and picked up the box, caressing it and apologizing out loud to Bill. I promised not to ruin his day, and to remain open to thoughts of him and messages from him. I prayed to Bill, not to God, for strength and asked him to surround me one more time with his love. I vowed not to look again at that label.

Walking to the closet, I searched for a shoulder bag in which to carry his ashes. I didn't want anyone else to see them, not even the box, until the moment they were cast to the wind. Nothing seemed right. Then I spotted the tennis bag Brooks and Rob had given Bill for his last birthday. It would be perfect. Taking it out, I was momentarily horrified to discover that it still contained Bill's tennis clothes from the last time we had played, some six months earlier. It took me a few minutes before I could remove the clothes and take them to the hamper. Having done so, it was not difficult to place the brown box inside the bag and to place the bag in the most secret corner of my closet.

That accomplished, I very much wanted to talk to my family. Without a thought as to the distance, the time, or the money, I dialed. It was past midnight on a Friday night, Australian time. My parents were home. So was Clyde. The connection was bad, and they could scarcely hear me. My mother answered.

"Mom? This is Pam. I just wanted to talk to you. I am going to spread Bill's ashes today, and I guess I just needed to hear your voice first."

"What? What did you say? Oh, honey, we love you. Just remember that we love you."

The next thing I knew, Clyde was speaking. "Pam, are you all right? I'm staying up nights trying to get on my way to you. I plan to leave on Monday."

"I'm all right, Clyde. This is Bill's and my anniversary, and I just needed to talk with all of you before I leave to spread his ashes."

"What? I couldn't hear, Pam. What did you say?"

"I'm going to spread Bill's ashes today, Clyde."

"I love you, Pam. Hold on, okay? I'll be there soon. Pam, Dad wants to try to talk to you, but we've got a really bad connection and I doubt he'll be able to hear anything."

"Hello, Pam. I'm with you, Pam. Remember that. Be strong."

"Thank you, Dad. Thank you for getting on the phone. I know that is painful for you, given your hearing."

"What? I didn't get that."

Giving up, I yelled at him. "I love you, Dad. That's all, I just love you."

"We love you, Pam."

And then, once again, my mother's voice. "I love you, honey, I love you."

They had heard almost nothing of what I had been trying to say. But they had been responsive to my needs. They loved me, each and every one of them. That was all I really wanted to hear.

Still in my nightgown and robe, I ventured into the kitchen and made a cup of coffee. I was glad that no one was around. This was the first time all week that I had been able to move freely around my own kitchen, and it felt good. I made English muffins for Melissa and Monica. Calling them up from the television room, I welcomed them to a long-overdue peaceful breakfast together. We talked of nothing in particular. The only mention of the day to come centered around clothing. I told both of them to wear long pants because we would be hiking. Monica complained that it was too hot for long pants, and Melissa echoed her complaint. My wishes prevailed.

We were just finishing breakfast when Cathy emerged from the bedroom. Shortly after, Pete joined us. Cathy suggested that we make a picnic with the remains of last night's buffet. I agreed, and together we began making sandwiches. Pete volunteered to go out for soda, beer, and extra ice. Melissa seemed a little puzzled that we would pick this of all days to have a picnic, but she was not about to suggest otherwise. On the contrary, she eagerly suggested that I make potato salad and deviled eggs. I don't think she was surprised when I said no, we would stick to the foods that were already prepared.

We had scarcely finished making the picnic when Kevin appeared, asking for towels. The stress he was feeling showed in spite of all his efforts to offer us a cheery "Good morning." He mentioned that he hoped we would have a chance to have a good long talk sometime during the day, and then disappeared.

By noon, Amy and Ann had arrived. Ed and Janice were due at one. I had an hour to shower and dress. So far, everything was working out fine. I selected my most comfortable blue jeans and a soft feminine blouse, and I felt pretty.

Shortly after one, we climbed into Ann's baby blue Mercedes and Ed's red Chevrolet. Amy, the children, and I went with Ann. The Miller children stuck together, going with Ed, Janice, and Kevin. I clutched the tennis bag tightly, not wanting anyone else to touch it. We rode mostly in silence broken only by occasional jokes about how Bill would have liked the thought of an expensive Mercedes taking him to the park. Occasionally I had to give Ann directions. The entire trip took no more than twenty minutes.

It was not until we were actually at the gate that I began to feel a little nervous. Sensing that the park officials would not take kindly to our errand, I was certain that the tale of what we had been through and were about to do showed on all our faces. It was extremely difficult to smile and pretend that we were just a bunch of mothers taking the children on a summer outing. We were all greatly relieved when the gate was behind us.

We had prearranged to meet at the parking lot at the base of the long trail that led to the fire tower. The road to the parking lot took us past several of the sites Bill and I had enjoyed during past anniversaries. I felt rushes of sadness at the thought that these days would never happen again. But I was in control and focused on the job I had to do that day. I was calmed by a feeling of certainty that the park was indeed the right place in which to give Bill his final freedom.

The sight of the parking lot and the adjoining playgrounds gave me my first real jolt of the day. Thousands of young children were screaming and running around. Parked busses indicated that a children's camp had chosen my park as the site for an outing. Feeling they had no right to be there, I resented them terribly. For a while, I could not bring myself to get out of the car. My sense of certainty was shaken. I wondered whether I should rent a boat and spread Bill's ashes over the water. I considered hiring a helicopter. The only thing I did not question was that the ashes needed to be dispersed before midnight. It had to be done on the day of our anniversary. I didn't care what I had to do to accomplish that.

Sensing my anxiety, Kevin got into the car and sat beside me. Once I had shared my feelings, he suggested that we walk awhile. He felt certain the place was right, and that as soon as we got on the trails, the feeling of being exposed in a public place would vanish. Kevin convinced me to get out of the car. We distributed the blankets and picnic gear among us and started up the trail.

The bag on my shoulder was light as we began our journey. For the first half hour or so, we passed no strangers. With Ed, Janice, and Pete in front of me, my children by my side, and Ann, Cathy, and Amy behind, I felt safe and secure. I noticed that the park was beautiful. The summer flowers were in bloom, and the mosquitoes were noticeably absent. It felt good to take a deep breath and to stretch my leg muscles as we climbed increasingly steep slopes. Periodically, Melissa looked up at me and smiled. She was enjoying her day with her mother. Her mother was enjoying the time with her children.

Halfway to the tower, we all noticed with dismay that a couple was coming down the trail toward us. Again, we feared that they would notice that something was amiss. As they passed, we all tried to smile. Apparently we got away with it, for they commented, "Beautiful day, isn't it?" Nodding, we kept walking until they were out of sight.

Once the couple had disappeared around a bend, I had to sit down. Again I resented what felt like an enormous intrusion into my most private life. The bag had begun to feel heavier on my shoulder. Changing it to the other side, I found no relief. Perhaps the park was not the right place. I considered the ocean. Bill had loved to sail. That, however, had been part of his earlier life and not part of our time together.

My concern was relieved this time by shouts from Ed and Pete. They had been moving at a somewhat faster pace than the rest of us and had come to a point from which they could see the tip of the fire tower in the distance. Enthusiastically, Pete shouted, "It's beautiful up there. It's perfect. I know it is." That was all I needed to hear. We were up and climbing again. The bag felt lighter.

Approximately an hour after we began our hike, we arrived at the site of the tower. Coming upon it suddenly, we were horrified to see that a young boy and his dog were seated at the base of the tower. The boy was eating his lunch. He looked at us, and then looked away. It appeared that he resented our presence almost as much as we did his. We moved to the far side of the clearing and sat in a tight circle. I asked if the others thought the boy would leave soon. Pete simply looked down at the ground. Ann tried to relieve the tension by saying, "Well, he's had two sandwiches, and a bag of potato chips. All I see now is a banana. How long can it take for someone to eat a banana?" Her comment summoned a round of weak, sickly smiles and then silence.

We sat without speaking for a while, each lost in private thought. Looking around, I noticed with disgust that there were wrappings and empty cans scattered here and there all over the clearing. The tower itself was not sparkling, clean, and majestic as I had envisioned, but squat and rusty. The platform on which it rested was cracked and filthy.

I didn't want to give up, but I could think of nowhere else in the park to go. The site had to be high, and this was the highest point in the park. Hoping against hope, I adjusted the bag on my shoulder and began climbing the tower. I prayed that, once at the top, the filth would disappear, and I would see the beauty I needed to see. Melissa started to follow me, and I impatiently told her to get down. She began to cry, but her tears simply made me angry. I didn't want to have to mother her then. I couldn't. I didn't have the energy. Sensing my dilemma, Ann came to the rescue. Taking Melissa down from the steps, she suggested they go and look for some wild flowers. I began to climb again.

I have always had a problem with heights. Once I am more than ten feet off the ground, I begin to get dizzy and my stomach tightens. I imagine falling, and my hands begin to sweat. At its worst, I panic so that I can neither continue upward nor come down again. As I climbed the tower, those feelings began to take hold. They reached a severe degree when I was about halfway up the steps. I stood there for a minute before deciding to climb down again. Pete looked at me, as if to inquire what I was going to do. I assured him that all I wanted to do was to go to the top and check it out. He volunteered to do that, and within a few minutes he was at the top. Taking pains to avoid my eyes, he called to Ed and Kevin to join him. I wondered what he saw but was reluctant to ask.

Kevin and Ed joined Pete, and I saw them look in the direction in which he had pointed. Within a few minutes, they had returned to the ground. I asked if they thought this was the right place. No one would answer me. Then Ed said, "I don't know. Let's give it a little while." Meanwhile, the young stranger seemed intent on intruding. Having finished his lunch, he lay down on the grass as if to take a nap. I wondered whether by concentrating my thoughts on him I could psychically propel him to leave. I tried, but nothing happened. Our eyes locked now and again, and I knew he had received my message. I thought how stubborn he was, and disliked him immensely. He squirmed around and seemed to be uncomfortable in our midst, and yet he persisted in staying. Why? I couldn't understand why. Then it occurred to me that perhaps this was a sign, a sign from Bill or from God that this was not the right place. Had it not been for the boy, I would have already tried to spread the ashes from the top of the tower.

Within a few moments, my feeling that the boy's presence may not have been accidental was confirmed, for around the bend and into the clearing came three arm-in-arm couples, talking and laughing. I knew then what Pete had seen from the top of the tower. Had I begun to spread the ashes from the tower, I would have been interrupted. The day would have been destroyed and perhaps I would have fallen apart along with it. The boy had prevented that from happening. I stood up and, with total conviction, said that I wanted to continue hiking.

No one challenged my request, and we set out along a different trail, leading away from the tower. We no longer had a specific destination. While we were still searching, we were optimistic that our search would end successfully.

Our optimism began to wane as the trail ended. The forest became so dense that it was impossible to continue. The idea of returning to the tower and retracing our steps to the parking lot was awful, and yet there seemed to be no other option. Pete introduced an element of hope as he said, "I noticed a small path branching off the main path as we climbed. I've got a good feeling about that path. It was very private and sloped upward. Let's go back and find it."

As we backtracked, we noticed a number of small paths leading off the main trail. In the beginning, we eagerly tried each one, certain that this was our destiny. After five or six such attempts, our enthusiasm began to fade again and be replaced by quiet despair. Melissa became impatient and broke out into a run. In spite of my shouts to the contrary, she continued to run. Ann urged me to let her go, saying that it would do her good to stretch her legs. I agreed, but I was worried.

That I had cause for worry was confirmed by the sound of her screams. Kevin, Ed, and Pete took off after her. Within a few moments, Kevin was carrying her back up the trail toward me. Her pant leg was badly torn and bloody. Seeing me, her cries redoubled. I took her and held her tight until her cries became quiet sobs. We sat down on a large rock, and for the first time, I removed the bag from my shoulder, placing it close to me. Checking Melissa's leg, I was relieved to find that in spite of the blood, the cut itself was small and shallow. Ann came up to us and suggested that we rub ice over the cut to clean it out. The attention seemed to heal Melissa's damaged pride. Shortly she was back on her feet. After a few steps, she forgot to limp. Within minutes, she was walking at a rapid clip. Monica took her hand, and they began to lead the rest of us down the trail to the parking lot.

We continued to spot occasional paths branching off from the main one. In only one instance did Pete declare he wanted to follow its course and would come let us know if he found anything worthwhile. He did not. And so it was that we found ourselves back at the cars. The bag was still on my shoulder. The ashes were still in the bag. We were all a little more fatigued and less confident than we had been. And it was getting late. That frightened me. I began to have visions of hiking through the park after dark. My resolve to spread the ashes before the day's end had not weakened. I spoke of my determination, triggering the idea that we get in the cars and explore the park for a while that way. Given our increasing weariness, that seemed to be the thing to do. Since I knew the park better than anyone else, Ann's car took the lead, with Ed following.

All the main trails emanated like spokes of a wheel from the center of the park. We chose one of them, following it until we came to a chain blocking our way. Getting out, we all looked at one another with dismay. Did we dare lift the chain and drive through? The sign hanging from the chain clearly indicated that such a move would incur the disfavor of the officials. We dared not risk that, desperately wanting to avoid calling attention to ourselves. We decided to leave the cars there and walk. The walk was not promising; the land was too open and too flat. But we kept going, hoping that just over the next knoll a sudden paradise would reveal itself to us. That never happened. The sun was beginning to fade when we finally had to admit that, once again, it would be necessary to return to the park's center and start over. I wondered out loud whether the park was indeed the right place. I shared my panic, and my willingness to rent a boat or a helicopter, or to do just about anything that had to be done. It was Ed who stated that he trusted my initial intuition about the park. He urged that we give it still another try. I was pleased, given his misgivings of the night before. I agreed to go along, but my heart was heavy and my spirits despondent. I was temporarily without hope.

This time Ed's car led the way. I paid little attention to where we were going. Ed took a route that was extremely rough, with large rocks jutting out everywhere from the dusty trail. I could tell that Ann was terribly worried about the car, but she said nothing. We bounced around on roads like that for what seemed like an eternity.

As we traveled, the trail got more and more promising as it became increasingly narrow and rugged. We had clearly left the public far behind. I began to have faith again. Then suddenly we found ourselves at the end of the road. There were only two choices: to turn around again or to continue up a path that was chained off and clearly marked NO ENTRANCE. OFFICIAL USE ONLY. We chose to ignore the sign. Pete raised the chain high enough that the cars could pass through. I was astounded that Ann went along with this. I knew her as someone who dared not challenge the word of an authority figure, particularly that of the police. She was now in a situation where she had to not only jeopardize their new car but to do so as a trespasser. When I thanked her, she admitted that she was extremely uneasy about what she was doing, but that somewhere in her being, she felt it was the right thing, the necessary thing to do.

Fortunately, the path was wide enough for a sufficient distance to permit both cars to get out of sight of the clearing. It became unlikely that the officials would spot us now. We all began to breathe a little easier. Eventually the path narrowed to such a degree that it became impossible to continue by car.

Getting out, we saw that a number of possibilities presented themselves. We decided to split up and explore them all. I opted to continue directly up the path alone. With the bag weighing heavily on my shoulder, I set out. As I walked, the voices of the others grew dimmer, until I could no longer hear any of them. The path grew narrower and the forest more dense. I was not afraid. The bag seemed to be getting lighter with every step I took. I had the distinct feeling that I was about to discover the site, the site we had been searching for all day. I began to walk faster. Then, as suddenly, I began to notice that the bag was getting measurably heavier. The leather strap seemed to be cutting into my shoulder. My hand that steadied the strap began to sweat profusely. The forest became ominous and threatening. The sounds of the wildlife became distinct and hinted of danger. I discovered my fear and worried that a snake would cross my path. Turning around, I began to run back, reaching the cars as the others did. The looks on their faces mirrored the despair I felt in my heart. Nothing. We had found nothing. The bag felt so heavy at this point that I had to sit down. Monica came and sat beside me in the dirt and took my hand. Melissa put her head on my lap, and her small hand rubbed the bag that held the ashes. I said, "We can't go on. This is not the right place. You're all tired. Let's go home. I will do whatever I have to do tonight. I won't ask all of you to continue with me in this madness."

No one seemed to be paying any attention to me or to my words. Looking up, I saw that Pete had taken off across the field in which we had parked the cars. Everyone was watching him. I couldn't understand him or their fascination. The field was the ugliest place we had seen all day. Garbage was everywhere. Bugs were abundant in the tall grass. Broken beer bottles were strewn about a wrecked foundation.

Then Pete was screaming, "I found it. Come look. This is the place. Oh, I know it. This is the place. Please, come. I'm sure." He sounded almost hysterical. Ed broke into a run. He was followed by Kevin and then Cathy and Janice. Amy and Ann looked after them and seemed to want to run and see what they had found. I was not interested. I could not stand. I would not stand. But the cries of discovery continued. Kevin returned to me and said, "Pam, I think Pete is right. Please, just come and look. If you do not feel this is right, then we will leave. Please, for me, just come and see." Reluctantly, I stood and began to walk across the field. Monica and Melissa ran ahead of me. Amy and Ann followed me, like two soldiers protecting their captain.

Halfway across the field, I noticed that the bag was once again becoming lighter on my shoulder. I began to walk faster. Finally I, too, broke into a run. Reaching the edge of the field, I saw what held the others spellbound. It was absolutely beautiful, a natural cathedral, set in the park in such a place that no one was likely to happen upon it.

The field ended abruptly in a rock ledge. The ledge dropped off suddenly and severely, creating a cavern of earth and rock. Pine and oak grew everywhere, towering above the top of the cavern and splitting the last rays of the sun into a dynamic pattern of flickering red and yellow light. Along the bottom of the cavern ran an actively bubbling brook, broken every ten feet or so by small waterfalls.

Awed, I sat down and, clutching the bag, dangled my feet over the ledge. I could not speak. Every fiber of my being shouted that, indeed, this was Bill's final resting place. It was not the wind that would carry his ashes, but the brook.

We gathered at the top of the cavern for a long time, enjoying the beauty and the peace that was slowly filling all of us. Steadied, I shouldered the bag and started making my way down the cliff. Melissa followed closely behind, with Monica taking her hand to prevent her from slipping. We reached the bottom without a single mishap. Once next to the brook, we remained speechless, everyone spreading out in search of the right point for our ceremony. This time it was Ed who happened upon the ideal spot. He had chosen one of the deepest parts of the brook, where the water swirled and bubbled before tumbling over a waterfall. A large oak had fallen just at that point, and it would become our pew. Pete, Cathy, Monica,

Melissa, and I sat on the tree trunk, and the others made a circle around us.

For several moments I could not bring myself to unzip the bag and remove the ashes. Having searched so long and hard to find this place, I was suddenly reluctant to give up my package. It had begun to feel like a critical part of my being. No one hurried me. I think they, too, were frightened by the thought of the drama in which we were about to participate.

Had darkness not been approaching, I suspect we would have remained that way for hours. But the yellow and red rays that lit our natural cathedral were dimming. We could not delay much longer. Slowly, I removed the box from the bag, careful to avoid looking at the white label. I opened the paper cautiously and dropped it on the ground. All our eyes were on the plain brown box. Pete offered his penknife, but I did not take it. The box opened easily. At first glance, all I could see was a mass of yellowed tissue paper. The paper gave us one last reprieve before we had to face the urn containing the ashes.

Finally, I reached in and removed the tissue paper. Scarcely able to stomach what I saw, I had to look away. It was all I could do to refrain from tossing the entire package into the river. It was disgusting. My love's ashes had been packaged in what appeared to be an unfinished coffee can. It was not an urn; it was a stark, silverish can. It had no beauty and no romance. It was cheap and cold to the touch. The seams were welded in a rough fashion. To touch it in the wrong place was to risk cutting your fingers. I hated the container at first sight. It was my enemy. It was Bill's prison. It had to be destroyed.

My anger kindled, I abruptly took the can from the box and threw the box to the ground. I began to tear at the lid with my fingers. My nails broke. My thumb began to bleed from the pressure of the seams. Pete gave me his knife, and I jabbed at the welding points. The lid would not give. I stuck the blade under the rim and pulled. The blade bent and came close to the point of snapping, but still the rim would not give. Kevin asked if I wanted him to open it. I shouted, "NO!" The can was my personal enemy, and I, alone, had to conquer it. Monica handed me a rock and told me to hit the can. I did, over and over and over. The can was scratched and dented, but still the lid would not give. I began to cry. Melissa wanted to try. I pushed her away. I set the can in my lap and huddled over it, as if to wish it open.

Finally, regaining some composure, I picked up Pete's knife again and inserted the bent blade under the rim. Before I had a chance to apply any pressure, there was a sudden snapping sound. The lid opened. All the welding joints broke simultaneously. It was a miracle. It was time.

Lifting the lid, I saw only more tissue paper. But this paper was different, pure white and heavy. I imagined that in opening the paper I would risk losing the powdery ashes. I bent over the brook. Tilting the can, I slowly lifted the paper and looked upon a sight that I will never be able to forget, try as I will.

Instead of the fine light gray powder I had expected to see, there were pure white, stonelike pieces. For a moment, I did not understand that the stonelike pieces were Bill's bones. I think it is as well that I did not comprehend, for if I had, I doubt that I could have continued. I shuddered at the thought of trying to cast this substance to the wind. With horror, I imagined being at the top of the tower, tilting the can, and having the contents pour sloppily down all over the clearing. The boy had been a gift from God. He had prevented a tragedy. The wind could not have borne these ashes. They were not ashes.

I began to pour the contents of the can into the water. I poured slowly, hoping the brook would carry them away as rapidly as I poured. It did not happen that way. The pieces sunk to the bottom and attracted a multitude of tiny fish. At first the sight of the fish horrified me. Then Melissa cried out, "Look, Mommy. They're picking up Bill and carrying him to the sea!"

Children are amazing. Melissa had managed to understand all that had escaped the rest of us. We did not have to fight nature and God. They were, in fact, helping us free Bill. Her words stifled my horror and triggered my faith and hope. I began to pour in a wider and wider circle. Some of the pieces got stuck on a mossy rock, and I bent down and brushed them off. I had touched the substance, I had touched my husband's bones. In the touching, I became no greater and no lesser than the tiny fish. Like them, I was simply an instrument of God, one element in a vast ceremony. I felt awe but no sorrow. Experiencing a kind of selflessness and calm, I wanted the feelings of the moment to linger forever.

Unhappily, the can was soon empty and its emptiness made it ugly once again. My bond with Bill, with God, and with nature was broken. Suddenly I rediscovered my anger toward the can. I noticed that the same white label as had been on the box was also on the can. With a vengeance, I scratched at the label, until my nails broke and my fingers began to ache and bleed. Melissa grabbed the can from my hand, dropped it to the ground, and began stomping on it. Her face was flushed, and she was breathing quickly before she stopped, picked up the mangled metal, and handed it back to me. It had become a despicable object. I lifted my arm back as far as it would go and violently threw the can to the other side of the cavern.

It was over. I glanced once again at the brook, and at the white substance that had been my love, and knew that I could no longer remain there. Without saying a word, I turned and began the climb to the top of the cavern. Melissa and Monica followed at my heels. We reached the top and sat together on the ledge. The others remained seated by the brook, speechless and staring, each trying to fathom what they had witnessed.

My strength slowly returned, and with it came a wonderful feeling of optimism and calm. I was happy and fully aware of that happiness. I had helped free Bill and in doing so had freed myself, at least temporarily, of sorrow and fear. I felt ravenously hungry for the first time all week. Remembering the picnic, I called down to the others that it was time to eat. Pete and Kevin joined us immediately, the expressions on their faces showing that they, too, had reached a point of peace and comfort. Ed and Cathy lingered by the brook. They were not yet ready. Janice remained sitting on a rock halfway up the cliff and silently watched her husband.

I noticed that Ann and Amy were walking around by the brook. At the time I did not appreciate what they were doing. I had given no thought to the debris I had left behind. They had decided to pick up the remains of our ceremony and, without calling it to my attention, hide away paper, labels, and the can in the trunk of Ann's car.

Eventually, we had all gathered on the ledge. Ann had retrieved the picnic basket. I was not alone in feeling extremely hungry. We had been hiking for six hours, and our bodies were making demands. The food tasted delicious. The people who had gathered together were wonderful. We felt a bond such as I had never felt before. We loved one another deeply that day. Everyone was open, honest, and caring. We talked a little and laughed a lot. Our laughter was not a defense against the expression of feeling but an honest accompaniment to a feeling of joy and well-being.

It was past eight o'clock in the evening when we reluctantly decided that it was time to go home. The lights in our cathedral were going out. Only a dim glow, as from an isolated streetlamp, lit our way. It, too, was fading. It was time to leave Bill, to leave him in peace in his new home. I lingered at the ledge for a few moments after the others had left to go to the cars, wanting to tell Bill one more time that I loved him.

The ride back was soothing. Ann breathed a sigh of relief once we were past the official's booth. Amy commented on the beauty of the evening. Other than that, we were quiet. Melissa quickly fell asleep in my arms. Putting my head back, I let my thoughts and feelings come and go. I was vaguely aware that I had become a different person, better, more fulfilled, and deeper. Because I had reached a level of self-insight and empathy, I was somehow set apart from others. Having experienced life's feelings in all their intensity, I had come out of it not only intact but enhanced. I had learned, and grown, and matured. The days to come promised to bring opportunities to put new self-discoveries and insights to work. Optimism had temporarily replaced grief.

Arriving at the house, everyone was reluctant to give up the feeling of togetherness we had found in the park. Gathering in the kitchen, we opened the bar and put on the coffee to brew. We relived the day time and time again in all its detail, as team players do after a particularly successful match. Extremely proud of ourselves and of one another, we applauded Pete for his discovery of the site and Melissa for her courage after her fall. We joked about what Phil, Ann's husband, would say when she returned the Mercedes dusty and full of debris. We teased Ann about her awe of authority figures and laughed at our cleverness in hiding our true purpose from the park officials.

And we talked of Bill. One after another, we recited his heroic acts. The others joined me in my belief that Bill's spirit was very much with us and that he had been aware of our moods as they changed during the day from elation to despair and back to elation again. We were convinced that he had enjoyed watching us search and search and hike until our legs could hardly move. Believing that we were pawns on a giant game board erected by Bill, we sensed that he had moved us about all day at his whim, very much enjoying the sport.

I continued to feel special and to regard everyone around me as special. Wanting to celebrate their specialness with gifts, I asked Ed if he would like to have Bill's electronic chess game; after all, chess had been their main common interest during the past few years. Ed was delighted with the game. Noticing Ann's interest in the children's mechanical puzzle that sat in the middle of the kitchen table, I asked her if she would like to have one of her own. It tickled me that I had purchased another in anticipation of Monica's birthday. Digging it out of my dresser, I presented it to Ann with great ceremony. Kevin said that if I was willing at any point to part with Bill's ukulele, he would like to have it. Without a moment's thought, I assured him it was his. I suggested to Cathy that Bill would have liked her to have his jade ring and that she might one day like to give it to the man she would marry.

Shortly before midnight, Ed and Janice left, promising to be back at the house early the next afternoon. Later, when Ann left, Amy and Cathy went to bed. Monica and Melissa were already in a deep sleep. Pete had excused himself earlier to go see his girl friend. For the first time since his arrival, Kevin and I found ourselves alone. We both had the feeling that we had a great deal to say to each other, in spite of the fact that we had spent only three days together in our lives.

We took turns describing our lives. I sympathized with what Kevin had been through, and he with the difficulties I had experienced. He had brought a picture album with him, and we pored over it together. I dug out my albums and introduced Kevin to all the people in my family. We compared careers and career goals. Bill entered our conversation frequently. With each mention, his greatness grew. If anyone had been listening to us, they might have thought we were describing a god; no man could have been so perfect. We remembered his singing, and attributed to him a great voice. We reflected on his laugh, and on his ability to make the whole world happy. We recounted the times when we had tried to fool Bill, and remembered that we could not. Through reminiscing, Bill became a king and we his most devoted subjects. Certain that Bill would have wanted us to become friends, we vowed a long-lasting loyalty to each other and promised to get our children together for long summer visits. The subjects would unite and, in their uniting, preserve the sacred memory of their lost king.

We talked until dawn. Periodically our voices rose to such a pitch that we woke people in the house. Eventually Cathy gave up trying to sleep and joined us. Her presence simply intensified our energy and desire to talk. We urged her to share her favorite memories, and so went back over Bill's life again through her eyes. We didn't permit mention of Bill's faults and shortcomings. She was drawn into our efforts to erect a verbal monument to her father's greatness. She joined in willingly and easily.

We had seen and touched Bill's physical remains. Even as we talked, his bones were being carried out to sea. I think, looking back, that our conversation that night protected us from focusing on the fact that we would never see Bill again, that he would never again walk through the door and join us at the kitchen table, that we would never again be able to sing along with him in front of a roaring winter fire. We helped one another focus instead on the memories, on the thoughts and feelings that were permanent, not subject to illness and death. In a way, we were beating death by not dwelling upon our loss. It was not that we were denying what had happened but simply that we were refusing to let it drag us down. We were building a psychological momentum that would allow us to live fully, as opposed to letting part of each of us die with Bill. We were staking our claim to life.

It was close to 6:00 A.M. when I finally went to bed. I had no difficulty being in the bedroom. The shadows on the ceiling were noticeably absent. I dozed off, believing that the absence of the shadows was a sign that Bill was now fully free from the pull of this world.

4

Birth of a Widow

Sleeping until close to noon, I did not see much of Saturday morning. I awoke to the sound of Jim and Sara coming to take Monica and Melissa to the beach and to Jim's mother's house for the weekend. Kevin was already up and dressed. Cathy was sitting in the kitchen having a cup of coffee. She told me that Amy had left a few hours before, planning to come back later that evening if I wanted her to do so. Pete was still asleep.

Signs of departure were everywhere. Kevin's suitcase was in the hall, and I noticed Cathy's train ticket on the table. Jim and Sara mentioned that they were moving back to New York City the following evening. Ann called to remind me that she was having a tag sale that afternoon and would be unable to visit with me. The magic of Friday was rapidly disappearing. I felt betrayed in a way. What had happened to the togetherness? Had that been a sham? A ploy to make me feel more secure than I was? A game to get me through the day?

Everyone was going their separate ways, anxious to begin picking up the pieces of their lives. I wasn't sure that I was ready to begin doing the same. I didn't know where to begin. It seemed as though everyone else's lives were partially completed jigsaw puzzles. The boundaries were all outlined, and all that remained was to fill in discrete segments. My life, on the other hand, was a brand-new puzzle. It had no clear shape. No two pieces were together.

I listened with disinterest as they made plans. Kevin and Michael's plane was to take off at eight o'clock that evening. Michael planned to arrive at the house around four-thirty. Ed and Janice were to drive them to the airport. Cathy's train was to leave at two in the afternoon. She had already asked Pete to take her to the station. I made a pretense of being interested and then excused myself to take a shower.

While I showered, I thought about my day; not about my life, but just about how to best get through the day. I knew waiting around for each person's departure was going to be difficult. There would be too many good-byes. I wanted the day to count. I needed to feel productive. It was important that I begin putting the pieces of my puzzle together.

I determined to set myself a goal, to carve out a project. Yard work struck me as the ideal thing. I could lose myself in gardening, in weeding. If anyone wanted to talk to me, they would have to come and find me. It seemed to be the perfect plan, providing both a focus and a way to avoid having to make senseless conversation all day.

I put on my oldest pair of shorts and a sleeveless T-shirt and returned to the kitchen to announce my plan. Everyone tried to dissuade me. They didn't understand and simply assumed that I was pushing myself too hard. I finally gave up trying to make them see that this was something that I was doing more out of choice than necessity and went into the yard.

The day was humid enough to bring out small beads of sweat on my forehead. Now and then a breeze would appear, cooling my brow and bringing relief. The flagstones by the garden were warm, but not so hot as to be uncomfortable. It was a nice summer day, the kind of day that fills the beaches, parks, playground, and tennis courts.

The gardens were thriving in the early summer sun. It pleased me to see that the pachysandra I had planted the previous summer was lush and multiplying. The azaleas were in bloom. Never an expert gardener, I felt a twinge of pride at having created such a potentially lovely garden. Only the weeds marred its beauty. I began tearing at them with a vengeance, seeking to resurrect at the same time the garden's beauty and my peace of mind.

With each weed I pulled, I felt a sense of progress and control over life. If I could weed all the gardens, that would serve as my private indication to myself that I could, in fact, put my life back in order. For the first time in what seemed like months, I had a meaningful goal, a goal I could meet, something I could fully control simply as a result of my own actions.

Eventually Kevin came out to join me. I sensed that he wanted to talk some more. Not trying to explain to him why I had to keep weeding, I simply invited him to join me. He hesitated for a while, standing and looking down at me in forlorn silence. After a while, he bent over and pulled the weeds that were growing between the flagstones. Apparently soothed by the project, he crouched down and began weeding with as much vigor as I. We did not speak much, our efforts broken only occasionally by small talk.

"My wife wouldn't believe this. I never pull a weed at home. The lawn is my job."

"I won't tell, Kevin."

"If the business brings you to the Coast, be sure to spend some time with us. Bring the kids."

"Okay. I'd like that, Kevin. You and your family are always welcome here, too."

For the most part, we quietly enjoyed each other's company and let our thoughts focus on the battle of the weeds. Time passed quickly.

With two gardens finished and only two to go, we decided to take a break. It was close to departure time for Cathy, and I wanted to give her a proper send-off. I no longer resented her leaving. On the contrary, I had begun to look forward to having the house to myself. I joined her in the guest room where she was putting the final touches to her makeup and packing a few last-minute things. We promised each other not to lose touch, and laughed as we had often done in the past about our stepmother and stepdaughter roles. We reconfirmed our friendship. When Cathy left, she had a smile on her face.

With Cathy gone, I thought about returning to the gardens but sensed Kevin's reluctance. He seemed to want to sit and talk, but I could not. I needed to be active. And yet, I did not want to leave Kevin, my new friend, alone. Suddenly, I had a thought: I would see if Kevin, who most resembled Bill, could wear Bill's clothes.

Kevin looked at me with disbelief. "Oh, Pam, it's too soon. I mean I couldn't, and you couldn't. Maybe in a few months." I interrupted his attempt to refuse. "Kevin, I think it will do me good to get Bill's things out of the closet soon. It's as though I can't even begin to start my life over until that is done. Bill's clothes will drag me down each time I open the closet door. No, I've got to force myself to get rid of his things soon. It would make me feel so much better if some of Bill's better clothes went back with you today. I can even give you one of his suitcases. Please, please, Kevin, just try on one of his jackets to see if it fits."

Kevin hesitated but was convinced when I reminded him that both of Bill's sons were far too tall to be able to wear his clothes. The jacket fit Kevin perfectly. Encouraged by that, we decided to try a full suit. Again the fit was perfect, so perfect that the suit looked as though it had been custom-tailored for him. I suggested to Kevin, and halfway believed, that the perfect fit was all part of the master plan. Kevin said something about clothes making the man, and we laughed. But it was not a heartfelt laugh. Handling Bill's clothing had made us both unhappy and melancholic.

We passed the rest of our time together with meaningless chatter and a lot of coffee. Then Michael arrived, and shortly after, Ed and Janice. Conversation was stilted and awkward. The comfort and intimacy of the day before was gone.

I found myself thrust into the role of hostess. Suggesting that everyone go sit on the porch, I brought out a pitcher of lemonade and some cold beer. My gesture did nothing to ease the tension. No one looked directly at anyone else, each of us preferring to stare at the backyard rather than risk making eye contact with one another. The occasional squeaks and squeals of the redwood furniture told of our discomfort.

We talked about airplanes until all aspects of flight fear, frustrating delays, and good and bad service had been exhausted. The dog began digging a hole in the back lawn, providing a welcome distraction and introducing the subject of home maintenance and yard work. Nobody really wanted to talk about either subject, but it was better than sitting in uncomfortable silence. I got up and went into the kitchen to make some hors d'oeuvres. I didn't really care whether people wanted them or not; I needed to get away, and that seemed like a gracious way of doing it.

Returning to the porch, I saw that Kevin had attempted to make everyone more comfortable by bringing out his camera. He wanted to include me in the pictures. I resisted, knowing that I looked awful. I was not only visibly tired but dirty from my work in the garden. And Kevin had taken dozens of shots of me throughout the week. He understood and didn't push.

Kevin's camera triggered the subject of photography in general. When Ed asked me if I still had all his father's slides, I told him I had thousands dating back to his infancy, and those of his brother and sister. We decided to get everyone together one rainy weekend in the fall to sort through them.

Somehow we managed to survive the afternoon. At six, Ed suggested that it was time to leave. I walked the group to the car, steeled myself for the good-byes, and prayed they wouldn't take too long. Only Kevin lingered, reluctant to leave. We had become each other's source of support. Grieving together, we had managed to blunt the pain. But his home and his loved ones were on the other side of the country. He had no choice but to leave, and I had no choice but to face my essential aloneness. Finally, Ed started his car, giving Kevin no choice but to leave.

I walked toward the house but did not want to enter. The departures had taken their toll, leaving me afraid, terribly afraid. It was Saturday evening. I was a mess. My house was a mess. The refrigerator was empty. I had not even completed the project I had set out to do that day. There was no order, only disorder. And no one was going to help me set it straight.

I wanted to be with Bill. I knew that he could make me feel better. He would hold me for a while, and take away the feeling of urgency. Together, we would sit at the kitchen table and have a Saturday evening cocktail. We would make a plan as to how to pick up the pieces. It wouldn't matter if we took our time doing it. Bill had a sense of priorities, and he knew how to relax. Left to my own devices, I would turn into a whirling dervish, attempting to accomplish everything at once. Bill slowed me down and put things in perspective. But he was gone. He was gone. I could not comprehend never seeing him again, never talking with him again. Nor could I imagine living life without his kisses and embraces. The world seemed so big, and I so small. Feeling inadequate and defenseless, I lay down on the grass and began to sob.

My despair was broken by the dog. She came up to me and began licking my face. Sitting up, I held on to her. She seemed to understand. Then she began whining, reminding me that she hadn't been fed all day. I felt sorry for her and decided to brave the loneliness of the house for her benefit. Going in, I went directly about the business of filling her bowl. Bringing it outside, I sat down on the grass and watched her eat.

Details came into incredibly sharp focus. As someone experiencing a marijuana high, I was alert to every sound and every texture: the sound of sandpaper as her tongue picked up morsels of the dry food, the sound of her teeth crunching, the sight of her saliva beginning to ooze from the sides of her mouth, the small sounds she made as she lapped up her water. I was fascinated and preoccupied with nothing else. Focused on these tiny aspects of the universe, I began to feel better.

After the dog finished her meal, we began walking the yard together. I checked the grounds and the gardens and began formulating a mental list. It would be good to focus my energies again. I started to regard beginning again as a challenge. A realtor had once said to me, during one of my house-hunting periods: "The next house I'm going to show you is owned by a widow. As usually happens in a case like that, the house has not been well maintained. But don't let that disturb you. In no time at all, you'd have it back in shape." No realtor was ever going to be able to say that about my house. Clyde was coming; he would help me. And Pete still lived with me. No, I wasn't really alone. While I would have to go it alone emotionally, I would have some help with the work that had to be done. I was still walking the yard and picking up odd twigs when Pete came home.

"What are your plans for tonight, Pam?"

"I don't have any plans, Pete. Amy said she'd come over, but I'm tired. I think I'll sleep."

"I had planned to spend the evening with my girl friend, but I'll cancel it and stay home with you."

"Thanks, Pete, but no thanks. I'll be fine. I'd like to be alone."

He didn't seem convinced but went into the house. I continued walking and picking up twigs. Unknown to me, Pete had called Amy and asked her to come over that night. He positively refused to leave until she got there. Pete was taking no chances. He had appointed himself my guardian, and that was that.

I was still in the yard when Amy's bright yellow car pulled into the driveway. Seeing me, the look of concern on her face changed to puzzlement. Pete's call had worried her. She had expected to find me distraught. The last thing she had expected was to see me picking up sticks, pulling weeds, and playing with the dog.

As it turns out, Pete was a better judge of my emotional state than I was. I had staunchly avoided the house and would have found myself in real trouble as night approached. With Amy by my side, I did not find it difficult to go in. That night, we began a tradition that was to continue every Saturday night for months. We sat in the kitchen and talked about what it means to be uncoupled and the differences in feelings that occur when the uncoupling is voluntary, as was Amy's divorce, and involuntary, as was my widowhood.

During our conversation that night, I passed an important hurdle. We had been talking about Saturday nights, and about the culture that teaches us to regard the weekend as the time for intimacy, fun, and coupling. It was more difficult to be alone on Saturday night than any other night of the week. The work that consumes the week ceases to demand attention. The expectation is to have fun. When fun doesn't happen, we feel a keen sense of disappointment. The hope is to see a friend, preferably a friend of the opposite sex. When such a friend does not appear, the feeling is one of sadness and incredible loneliness.

"I suspect I'll feel this way for a long time, Amy. Lonely, I mean. I didn't feel this way after the divorce, but, then, that was my idea, my doing. I really never expected to be a widow. I always thought that went along with the problems of old age. But here I sit. I am a widow. Amy, I AM A WIDOW!"

I startled Amy, but, being as wise as she is, she encouraged me to continue. "Say it again, Pam. Say it again."

"I am a widow. I am a widow. My God, I AM A WIDOW!" I began to feel better. They say that an alcoholic cannot begin to get well until he or she stands and states openly, "I am an alcoholic." I believe the same thing is true of widowhood. I had begun to come to grips with my problem. Adopting the label was important.

Stereotypes flooded my head. The vivid images of widows I had read about or seen on television or in the movies all crystallized at once. Widows are supposed to hide romantically behind long black gauzy veils. Widows are supposed to take long restorative cruises. Widows are supposed to have enough money to lie back and devote the bulk of their energies to grief and thoughts of the lost love. Widows are supposed to be old.

I was not old. My first inclination had been to wear shorts and sandals, not a long black veil. The thought of taking a long cruise was simply amusing. I had a business to run and deadlines to meet. I had some money, but not enough to dismiss finances as a concern. Attorney Joel and accountant John had both cautioned me not to assume that my financial worries were resolved. They had pointed out that I had two young children whose schooling needed to be considered. Bill had left only a financial cushion, a cushion that needed to be protected and invested with a minimum of risk. I did not fit the stereotype of the rich widow.

"So, Amy, here I sit. I am a widow, but I can't act like one. Things are all out of whack, like I've taken my lifeline, cut it apart, and glued it back together in a ridiculous sequence."

"What can you expect? You're a life compactor, Pam. In your thirty-four years, you've managed to experience seventy years of life. It's not that you're all messed up, it's just that you move at twice the rate of us normal earthlings. So, now, you're seventy years old with two little children. It could be worse, you know. At least you don't look like you're seventy!"

I stuck my tongue out at Amy. She was teasing me, but with affection. And she was right. I had moved quickly through life and, in the process, rendered society's stereotypes meaningless. I was going to have to carve out a new role definition for myself. The standard expectations simply were not going to fit. It was good that I was aware of these expectations, though, for it was quite likely that they would cause others to make certain assumptions and to approach me on the basis of those assumptions. In addition to defining a role, it would be necessary for me to clarify to others that the existing stereotypes didn't apply.

"Amy, social situations are really going to be tough. Can't you see it? The young widow, the sexually deprived widow, the easy make."

"Sure, you'll get some of that, Pam, but it needn't frighten you. Just walk away from that kind of person."

"Yeah, that's easy enough to do. It'll be harder to deal with the guy who decides to become father protector to the poor, fragile young widow. I mean, I might even like that!"

"That's understandable. I hope you do meet such a person when you're ready. It would be nice for you to have a 'safe' male friend, if you know what I mean."

"Yeah, well, that'll take awhile. I suspect men will simply avoid my company. I've already sensed that kind of thing happening. It's as though I'm scary because I've looked at death. People don't know what to say. I make them uncomfortable, so they shy away. That's just as well. I really don't want a social life for a while."

"When you're ready, it will happen."

"Well, I'm a long way from ready, Amy. I'm still wearing my wedding ring, and I can't imagine removing it. I guess I still feel like I'm married to Bill."

"Of course you do. Don't push yourself. Stop being a life compactor. You'll know when it's time. In the meantime, you've got me to fill up your Saturday nights."

"And am I ever glad that I've got you, Amy. Saturday nights can be awful, can't they?"

As the hour approached midnight, I found I could not keep my eyes open. Amy asked if I wanted her to stay, and I said yes. I had no idea when Pete would return, and the thought of staying alone in the house at night was more than I could handle. The night has always frightened me. My imagination magnifies and distorts the least sound until I become convinced that the house is full of muggers and rapists about to do their worst. I had tried to persuade Bill to install an alarm system, but he remained unconvinced. The boat horn he had purchased in a semiserious attempt to put a stop to my requests for an expensive alarm system now seemed more inadequate than ever. I needed more than a noisemaker to take the edge off my night terror. I wanted the army and the navy but decided to settle for an alarm system wired directly to the police station.

I had made an important decision. It marked the first time I would admit that what might have been right for Bill and me as a couple was no longer right for me as an individual. I had taken the first step toward defining my own boundaries.

Lying in bed that night, and comforted by the knowledge that Amy was in the guest room on the other side of the wall, I saw the shadows returning. They were less distinct than they had ever been, but they were still in the room. Again they were comforting to me. It seemed that Bill continued to watch over me, and would do so until I had gone through all the steps of becoming a separate and distinct person in my own right. He calmed the whirlwind of my thoughts and made me feel safer and more secure. As I covered my body with a sheet, he seemed to blanket my mind with his love. I had admitted my widowhood, but I remained married. In my heart and in my mind, I continued to experience the comfort of being coupled with Bill. The shadows were my anchor. They provided the only real peace I knew.

Part II

THE SECOND WEEK

Picking Up the Pieces

5

Learning to Walk

When I awoke the next morning, my first thought was that today marked the one-week anniversary of Bill's death. I got up quickly, afraid of my own thoughts. Amy had already left for church. Pete was still asleep. After feeding the dog and the cat, I had a cup of coffee and made myself focus on the day ahead. Today was the day to set the household straight. I considered going to the grocery store, but the thought of leaving the house and venturing downtown on my own was too threatening. I didn't want to risk running into anyone I knew, not feeling capable of even carrying on a conversation with the check-out girl. No, I would ask Pete to pick up the groceries. The yard work seemed equally critical. I still had two gardens to weed, pachysandra to plant, and a yard of topsoil to spread.

Walking outside, I was confronted by a blast of heavy, hot, humid air. No matter. I looked forward to building up a sweat, and to the feeling of rough, callused hands at the end of the day. It would feel good to get dirty, really dirty. Mindless, dirty, basic work—that was all I wanted to do.

I was outdoors before ten, and was still there at two when the children came home from their weekend with Jim and Sara. Immediately they began to pitch in and help me. When I saw Melissa go to the garage to get her wagon and shovel, I smiled and cried inside at the same time. While we were working, Monica asked me if we were going to stay in the house.

"Do you want to?"

"Oh, yes, Mom. I don't want to move. I mean, I *really* don't want to move."

"I don't either, Monica, but maintaining this house requires a lot of work."

"I know, Mom, but I can help you. I'll mow the lawn and comb the dog and empty the garbage. I can paint, too, you know. We can do it, Mom."

"Yes, Monica, we can do it. Together, we can do it. We won't move, at least not for a while."

As we worked, I thought about Monica's request and the promise I had made. Yes, I owed that much to her. She needed some semblance of stability. In her eleven years, she had had to suffer through a divorce and, now, a death. I would find a way to keep the house. I had no choice.

By the time evening arrived, I was too sweaty and dirty to risk sitting down on a chair. I felt good. My muscles ached, and my hands were beginning to callus. I had become a purely physical being, my mind on "off." Wanting the feeling to linger, I walked around the yard admiring the results of my labors. Dusk brought with it a cool breeze that muted my aches. I felt healthy and comfortably exhausted.

It would have been nice to shower, change clothes, and then sit down to one of Bill's Sunday dinners. Sunday dinner had been particularly important to Bill. Occasionally he had chosen to spend the entire afternoon in the kitchen preparing a spectacular meal. But Bill was gone. If we were to have dinner, I would have to prepare it.

Entering the kitchen, I felt a surge of apathy and depression take hold of me. The chore seemed awesome. I was too tired, far too tired to organize a meal. I sat at the kitchen table and put my head down. Melissa came in and demanded her dinner. "Mom, I'm really hungry. When's dinner?"

Without raising my head, I said, "Soon, Melissa, soon."

"What are we having?"

"I don't know, Melissa. I'll figure it out in a minute. Leave me alone, please."

My child was hungry. I had to respond. Getting up, I washed my hands at the kitchen sink. I decided to make pork chops. They would defrost quickly in the microwave and took little expertise to broil. I'd get through it. I had to.

The pork chops were adequate, although the children mentioned that they missed Bill's stuffing. The rice was soggy, and the vegetables were underdone, but everyone managed to fill their stomachs. Pete and Monica teased me about my lack of culinary skills, but I didn't mind. It was an open recognition that things had changed. I had taken another small step toward asserting my individuality in the household. More important, I had managed to move around the kitchen and to use Bill's favorite pots and pans. Oh, it had hurt, but I had done it, and I was proud of myself for that.

Pete went out again after dinner, leaving me alone in the house with the children for the first time. My shower had renewed my energy, and I found it impossible to sit quietly and simply talk with them. Needing to keep busy, I washed Melissa's hair and played a few games with Monica. Not wanting to be alone, I was not at all anxious for their bedtime to come. They were my lifeline, my focus, my reason for trying to pull all the pieces together. But the beach had tired them out. By eight, neither child could stay awake. I found myself alone and sought to escape by watching television.

The escape didn't work. I became obsessed with the thought that this evening was the anniversary of Bill's death. I found myself reliving all of the events of the week before. When the clock struck eight-thirty, the time Bill had died, I panicked, and felt nauseous and dizzy. I lost my dinner. I tried to still the panic by forcing myself to go sit on the porch. The visual reminder of our last family dinner together simply made it worse. I began sobbing, and the neighbors, eating on their porch, seemed to notice. They had just moved in and didn't know me well. I didn't want them to see me that way. I went back into the house and slammed the door.

I couldn't find anything to do with myself. Going downstairs, I turned on the stereo, but the music only made me feel melancholic. I had to calm down. For the first time all week, I wished the doctor had prescribed a tranquilizer. My heart was racing. I was sweating. I was sick. I couldn't sit down. I couldn't lie down. For more than an hour, I paced the house. I looked in on the children a dozen times, wishing they would wake and need my help. But no, they continued to sleep soundly. Finally, I decided to make myself a cocktail. That was extremely unusual behavior for me. Drinking had always been a social activity. Bill and I had shared a cocktail every night after work. When he was out of town, it never even occurred to me to end the workday that way. But now I had no mate with whom to enjoy a cocktail at day's end. Alone, I had only myself for company.

A telephone call from my twenty-two-year-old cousin Barbara finally broke my panic. A student on summer vacation, she was calling from her parents' home in New Jersey. She had spent several summers with Bill and me caring for the children and, during these visits, had come to feel like a member of the immediate family. She asked if she could come visit for a week or two. She wanted to help me, but more at issue, was her own need to spend time in Bill's home and accept his death as a fact. It sounded like a good idea; she would provide the buffer I needed while I awaited Clyde.

Eventually my day in the yard took its toll. I crept into bed and waited for sleep to come. Once or twice a sound from another part of the house startled me, kindling my night terror. I was still awake when, an hour or so later, I heard the distinct sound of a key in the front door. Pete was home. I was not alone. My fears receded. I lay on my back and contemplated the shadows. They were scarcely visible. Bill's energy was elsewhere. "Perhaps he is with Ed or Cathy tonight," I thought. Sleep came without my realizing it. It seemed only minutes later that the alarm went off, signaling the arrival of Monday morning.

The day was overcast, matching my mood. Lethargic and achy, I did not want to get up. But neither could I enjoy lying in bed. It was Monday and I had to go to the office. As I shook off sleep, the whirlwind in my mind started up again. "So much to do, so much to organize. My God, I haven't done a bit of work lately. Things must really be chaotic at the office. The next thing I know, I'll lose the business. Then what? Disaster, that's all, disaster. Get up, kid. Get with it. Start walking. Move!"

As I dressed, I imagined entering the front door of the building, and having to pass by all the other offices. I knew that behind those glass doors were knowing eyes. Bill had been the president of the company. He had also been a man. People would no doubt wonder if I was capable of managing the office of president. Given the state of my emotions, I wondered myself. Hoping that looking the part would help me play the part, I decided to wear one of my best business suits, one generally reserved for meetings with clients.

I arrived at the office at about half past nine. Fortunately, I did not run into anyone in the parking lot, and there were no eyes peering at me as I walked past the doors to other firms. Opening the front door, I felt a flash of nausea and had to sit down immediately. No one said a word. Both secretaries simply sat and looked at me for a moment. Then, without a word, Jessica brought me a cup of coffee. I sat and drank it and calmed down a little before walking the twenty feet to my own office.

Sitting at my desk, I had to put my head down. I did not want to look up, knowing that if I turned my head even slightly to the left, I would be looking directly into Bill's office. To look at his empty desk was going to be just as difficult as it had been to look at his side of our bed. Meg came in and asked if there was anything she could do. I asked her to close the door between Bill's and my offices. Once she had done that, I raised my head. Meg suggested that perhaps I was pushing myself too hard, that everything could wait another day. I was very tempted to leave but didn't want to give up. Having gone through all the agony of getting there, I wanted to make the day count. I did ask Meg to tell the secretaries to hold all calls, at least for the morning. I needed time to simply get used to being in the office again, and to develop some plan of attack.

Unable to mentally focus on anything else, I began going through the piles of mail that cluttered my desk. Feeling as though only half my brain was available to me, I began throwing away junk mail and advertisements. That cut the pile in half. Scanning the remaining correspondence, I saw that most of it centered around administration of the firm: tax forms, pension forms, insurance. After opening three or four envelopes, I realized that to respond would require that I perform the function Bill had performed.

During Bill's illness, I had cursorily attended to some of these duties. John, our accountant, had made sure that tax deadlines were met, not troubling me directly with the specifics. Other administrative decisions had simply been postponed. I had assumed that, eventually, Bill would see to it that the loose ends were tied off. With only a vague idea as to where to begin, I sorted out all the administrative tasks from the pile and decided to set up a meeting with John sometime that week. I was going to have to learn, and learn fast.

The remaining correspondence was no less upsetting. There were a number of medical bills from Bill's various hospital stays. Insurance claim forms would have to be filed. I shuddered at the thought of completing the forms. In the past I had done so, asking Bill only for his signature. He could no longer sign them. I would have to do so as his executor. But the probate court had not yet officially declared me his legal executor. Not knowing precisely what to do, I put the medical bills in a file to be dealt with at a later date.

Most of the rest of the mail was composed of condolence letters from clients. They both surprised and helped me. Somehow, in my struggle to force myself back to work, I had begun to regard my business concerns as totally separate from my emotional life. On some level, I had convinced myself that in order to maintain my professional stature, I had to appear to be invulnerable and above pain. After all, the firm was in business to help client organizations resolve their people problems while creating positive attitudes and greater worker productivity. We were supposed to be the counselors, the teachers, the helpers, the strong. The letters and notes made me realize that people we had gotten to know within a business context were human and expected me to be human. I did not have to maintain a constant pretense of false courage, even with our clients.

But the letters did more than that. In addition to praising the man I had loved, they also praised me as they expressed faith in my ability to assume the reins of the business.

One letter, in particular, moved me deeply. It was from our secretary, Jessica.

Dear Pam,

This is a time, I know, when words fall short of how I feel. The firm has become a part of my life, my "second family." It is far from just a job to me. I know we all share your loss. Please do not hesitate to let me know if I can be of help in any way, in and out of business. I have always admired your strength and boundless ability to carry on since I've known you. I will miss Bill's great sense of humor and dynamism, but his spirit will never leave us. I believe he will always be standing by.

I am deeply sorry and hope I can be of help. May you always have the strength to see the light at the end of the tunnel.

Love,
Jessica

Letters from clients consistently echoed Jessica's sentiment. I began to believe what I read. "Bill was a great man. . . . You, too, are a great lady. . . . We want to help you. . . . We care about you, not just because you are good at your job but because we like you as a person."

Clients seemed convinced that I could and would cope, and cope well. My confidence in my own ability began to increase. I asked Meg to brief me on the status of various client projects over lunch.

As had happened over and over since Bill's death, I was to find my strength only to lose it unexpectedly again as I ran into an event, a place, a memory that undermined my composure. The once-simple task of deciding where to eat became a monumental emotional issue. Bill and I had been in the habit of frequenting the Orange Tree Cafe across the street from the office. An outgoing person, Bill had established a camaraderie with the hostess/owner, Julie, and Susan, one of the waitresses. The cafe was one of the few good restaurants in town. In spite of its active business, Julie always seemed genuinely pleased to see us. She noticed our absence when a project required that we be out of town. The letters from clients had reminded me that people care. I knew that the folks at the Orange Tree cared too, and that to go there for lunch was to put myself in the position of having to see my pain reflected in others' eyes. I began to understand the negative aspect of having concerned and caring friends. There was no escape from my own sorrow. The eyes of others became like mirrors, reflecting in horrifying detail the grief I was experiencing. I had a decision to make: to ignore the support others sought to give me in order to avoid the eyes or to tolerate the reflection of my pain in order to enjoy the reminder that I was not alone.

I chose the latter. We went to the cafe. The first few moments were as difficult as I had expected. Julie was openly affectionate, and distraught that she had to ask us to wait for a table. I assured her that we didn't mind waiting. Nodding sadly, she walked away. During lunch, three of the waitresses came up to the table and simply said, "I'm sorry." I could say nothing but "Thank you." Conversation was awkward. As I had perceived several times since Bill's death, it is not only difficult to be a widow, it is difficult to be a friend of a widow, or even an acquaintance of a widow. Society has not provided an easy script. Death creates an emotional intensity that defies casual conversation. Even Susan, our waitress that day, said little, letting her constant attention to our every need indicate her concern and her support. Finally, I settled down to lunch, feeling glad to be among friends.

It was a working lunch. I listened as Meg briefed me on what had transpired over the past week. I was relieved to find that I had not, in fact, lost touch with the business. We began to establish a strategy. We would focus on existing client demands and, at the same time, put the company back on an even keel financially. We discussed the ramifications of attempting to operate the firm without Bill as senior statesman, and toyed with the idea of hiring another. That was idle talk, and we both knew it. Bill was not replaceable; not as a husband and not as the head of our firm. We talked of how Meg's development and role in the firm would have to escalate, and she assured me that she regarded the escalation not as unwelcome pressure but as an opportunity. By the time our luncheon conversation ended, I began to feel that I was putting my arms around the totality of the firm and beginning to make it mine.

As we were leaving the cafe, Meg reminded me that we were scheduled to meet with a client in our office the next day and asked if I wanted her to postpone the meeting. While I was designing the program for the client, Bill was to have actually conducted the workshop. I knew the client would be concerned. I told Meg we should go ahead and have the meeting as planned.

I spent the bulk of the afternoon preparing for that meeting. That accomplished, I even found the courage to create a list of persons who might actually conduct the program for the client in Bill's stead. I did not include myself on the list, believing that the introduction of a female, any female, into that particular client situation would create unnecessary problems. I was sure the client would agree and decided to avoid even raising the issue.

I had finished all that I hoped to do by four-thirty, but was determined to remain in the office until five. I wanted to be able to say that I had put in a full day's work. Somehow, that would prove I was, indeed, coping, that I was capable of holding my world together. I made it. While leaving the office, I saw people I knew and had been so reluctant to see only that morning. But now I had a strong measure of self-respect. I returned their greetings without hesitation.

By the time I reached the driveway, I was aware of little other than my exhaustion. I greeted the children and thanked the baby-sitter exactly as I had done on so many other occasions before Bill's death. Melissa asked me if we could have pizza for dinner that night, and I readily agreed. I sensed that both children had gained a great deal of comfort and security from the fact that their mother had managed to return to work. They needed a degree of predictability, and routine, and by going out that day, I had provided it. They did not object when I said that I needed to nap before dinner.

When Monica woke me an hour later, I felt rested and regarded the prospect of going out for pizza as a treat. We had no sooner put on our shoes and found the car keys when the doorbell rang. It was cousin Barbara. I had forgotten all about her. I shuddered to think that she might have arrived to find no one at home. Standing in the doorway, she looked small and frightened. Later she was to tell me that she had spent the three-hour trip from New Jersey dwelling on Bill and the enormity of our loss. By the time she reached our driveway, she had worked herself into a panic at the prospect of witnessing our despair and grief. She had been afraid to ring the doorbell, afraid of confronting the mourners. I think Barbara's fears dissipated on seeing that the children and I were dressed, purse and keys in hand, and ready to go out. She had anticipated total chaos and saw instead an incredible degree of normalcy. Relieved, she said she would like nothing better than to join us for pizza.

Barbara and I didn't get to talk until much later in the evening. Most of our dinner conversation focused on the children, as Barbara urged them to describe their summer activities. I said little, simply watching the interaction between Barbara and Monica and Melissa. It was good to hear the children laugh again.

When we got home, Barbara went to unpack and take a shower. I put Melissa to bed and watched a little television with Monica. Pete came home, asked about my day at work, and disappeared into the sanctity of his room. Alone, I began to look at the day's mail. The pile was enormous. In addition to the junk mail that comes to anyone who does a lot of mail-order shopping, there were at least fifteen letters addressed to "Mrs. William Miller." Condolence letters. I feared and welcomed them at the same time.

I read the letter from my mother first. In three short paragraphs, she caused me to focus on love and on what I had had, as opposed to what I had lost.

Dearest Pam,

My heart is full as I think of the events of the past year and all they have meant to all of us. I think it has been both the happiest and saddest year of my life and have you and Bill to thank for the good times. [She was referring to the Christmas she and my father had spent in our home.] We are so grateful that we were able to get to know Bill and appreciate the great impact he has made on your life.

Bill was a very special person and you are indeed fortunate to have enjoyed the love of such a man. I was so touched at Christmas by his concern that you should have everything your heart desired. He even asked me whether I had noticed anything you needed and when all I could think of was black gloves, he went out and bought the most expensive ones in town. His generosity spilled over on us, partly because of his natural generosity, but mostly because it was another way of showing his great love for you.

You are very fortunate to have had him for five years, and I am sure that his having you made those same five years the happiest in his life and for that you should be very proud.

Love,
Mom

Yes, I reflected, Bill had loved me dearly. And yes, I had made him happy. I felt no guilt about my relationship with Bill. My grief was, in a sense, pure. And my pain was positive. I missed Bill as one misses a lover who is trusted. It can be enjoyable to miss someone, if the relationship is free of mistrust and suspicion and is built on a solid foundation. I was beginning to realize that grief, too, can be positive if it is grief for someone whose life you consistently affected in a positive way. Grief over the loss of someone whom you fear you disappointed or affected negatively is negative pain. Energies are focused on wishing you had done things differently rather than on enjoying the happier memories. Grief mixed with guilt brings you down; pure grief provides its own kind of joy. In her letter, Aunt Chris stated it well, and made me weep: "Remember, Pam, joy can break the heart, but who, even on the darkest day, would choose to have missed the joy?"

My father's letter helped me enormously. It marked the second time in his life he had written to me. The first was when I was getting divorced. At that time, he compared being a suburban divorcée with being an alien in a strange land, as he had been when the family emigrated to Australia. That letter had helped me put the experience of divorce into perspective. Now, he was writing to remind me that I had his unconditional positive regard, and that he had no doubt I could cope with all that was happening. His very simple and very brief statement meant so much to me that evening: "I know that you are continuing to cope."

Several of the letters focused on me and my strengths. Assurances that I would make it through this and emerge better for it were so very welcome. As I read them, I reflected on the several times during the last week when the world had seemed too large to manage, when I was overwhelmed by feelings of inadequacy. I knew that these feelings would return again and again. Being reminded that others saw strength in me was always comforting, and occasionally critical as I doubted my abilities and self-worth.

Other letters focused on Bill rather than on me. It felt good to read about his virtues as others perceived them, and to know that others would help me keep his memory alive. They made me proud not only of him but of myself for having been his wife.

I must have spent an hour or more in the privacy of my bedroom reading the letters and thinking about what they signified. They left me open, and ready to talk about all that had happened. I looked forward to sitting down at the kitchen table with Barbara.

Going in search of her, I finally found her down in the playroom, looking at the pictures on the wall. There were tears in her eyes. I put my arms around her, and she cried hard. I just let her cry. When she finally spoke, she said, "Oh, Pam, I don't think I'm going to be of much help to you. I feel so terrible, so awful. I can't even imagine what you must be feeling. I miss him so much, and I didn't even live here. How can you stand it? I just don't know how you can stand it!"

Unable to look at the pictures without falling into despair along with her, I urged that we go upstairs. I didn't want to cry, not then. I wanted to continue picking up the pieces of my life, and to retain my fragile control. Barbara didn't want to leave the room, however, choosing to experience her despair. But I had been there, and I knew that I would be there again. Leaving the room, I went to the kitchen to make a cup of coffee.

Within a half hour or so, Barbara joined me. She began with an apology. I told her there was no need to apologize, and that I understood. It seemed as though I had taken a long journey that she was just beginning. She asked me to tell her about it.

That was the first time I had been asked to tell someone about the night of Bill's death, about the days that followed, and about the spreading of his ashes. I didn't know where to begin, I didn't even know whether I wanted to begin. I might have chosen not to speak of it, but I very much wanted Barbara to understand why she found no tears in my eyes now. I feared she thought my dry eyes signified that I was not grieving. I began talking randomly, unable to sequence the events and feelings of the week.

Finally, I began to tell her of the night Bill had died. Beginning with the dinner, I went on from there. I told of watching the color drain from Bill's face and the light go from his eyes. Forcing myself to keep talking, I showed her where Bill had grasped my arm. The physical ache returned, and I began to shake. Barbara suggested that I not continue. But I wanted to continue. I wanted to tell it and, through the telling, divorce myself from the memories. I had ceased caring whether Barbara wanted to listen. She was going to listen, listen to it all. By now, my words were coming fast, very fast. I didn't want her to interrupt, or even to comment. I told her about the ride in the police car, the emergency room, telling the kids, the silent ride, the telephone calls. I described how difficult it had been for me to say the words "Bill died tonight." I said it again and again. "See, I have come a long way. I can say it. Bill is dead. Bill is dead. BILL IS DEAD." Barbara was flushed, drowning in my words and my feelings. Showing no mercy, I kept on talking. "Yes, Barbara, I can now say it. Bill is dead. I am a widow."

With that, I lost all my strength. Putting my head down on the kitchen table, I cried hard. Barbara came around the table and put her hand on my shoulder. Again she apologized for making me talk about it. But she had done me a tremendous service, and I knew it. I had described in full detail the night of Bill's death, and had somehow been cleansed as a result. There was now at least some distance between myself and that night. The story of Bill's death was one that could be told at my will, not just a nightmare that would occur of its own volition.

I was truly beginning to control the memories and pick up the pieces, the pieces of the house, the business, and, finally, myself. Looking at the clock, I realized that it was close to midnight. "Barbara, I've got to get some sleep. An important client is coming in the morning."

Barbara looked at me in utter disbelief. I realized that in the span of only seconds, I had taken her from the night of Bill's death to the present. There were worlds in between.

"You've *got* to be kidding, Pam. You're going to meet with a client? You amaze me. How can you do it?"

"Barb, it helps me to force myself, to push myself. It's that control thing of mine. If I feel things are organized, then, and only then, do I feel at all sane."

"Okay. What would you like me to do?"

"Just look around, and do whatever you feel like. Anything would help. On second thought, how about spending the day with Monica and Melissa? You could watch Monica's swim practice. Poor kid, she really has asked for so little from me. She needs some attention, some tender loving care. God knows, Melissa does too."

I handed Barbara the keys to Bill's car and then, as suddenly, changed my mind. I didn't want Barbara driving Bill's car. It, like the bedroom, had a special significance. I didn't want *anyone* to drive his car. And yet it couldn't just sit in the garage day after day. My stomach turned a little at the thought of driving it myself. I had often thought about how perfectly that BMW suited Bill's appearance and temperament. Both were like kindly bulldogs. Since the night of his death, I had consciously chosen not to drive his car. But this was another barrier I would have to cross. Deciding to take the BMW to work the next day, I handed Barbara the keys to my station wagon.

Shortly after midnight, I climbed wearily into bed. The shadows were nowhere to be seen. Bill was gone, and that frightened me. Perhaps, I thought, in telling of his death I had frightened away his presence. Maybe I had struggled too hard to distance myself from the memory of the night he died. I tried to will the shadows to return, but they would not. I went to sleep feeling sorry for myself, and very much alone.

6

Trying to Run

Feelings of apathy and loneliness pervaded my being even as I woke. The lethargy and apathy I had experienced the day before were even more intense. It took all my resolve to climb out of bed and shower.

The hot water had a positive effect on my energy level and on my outlook. I concentrated my thoughts on picking out what I would wear that day. I wanted to portray a certain message: one of professional composure, confidence, maturity. I had to make Tom, the client, comfortable while inspiring his respect for my professional ability. That, I knew, was not going to be easy. Tom and Bill had been close, both personally and professionally.

Arriving at work by nine, I headed directly for my own office. The door connecting my office with Bill's was still closed. Tom would be there by ten, which left me one hour to find the courage to open the door and get comfortable in Bill's office. I had no choice. His office also served as the conference room. Tom and I had so many papers to go over that the conference table was the only suitable meeting spot. Remembering how describing my feelings to Barbara had helped me gain a perspective, I decided to do the same thing this morning. Asking Meg to come in and talk over a cup of coffee, I shared my discomfort at having to use Bill's office. I told her I was afraid to admit Bill would *never* again sit at his desk. The expression of my feelings helped ease their intensity. Well before Tom arrived, I felt ready to open the door and walk around Bill's office.

I forced myself to sit at his desk. I had never done that before. The perspective and insight I gained was extraordinary. My own desk faced the wall. That had been my choice, my effort to minimize distractions. Bill, on the other hand, had elected to have his back to the wall. Sitting at his desk, he had looked out over a large, well-appointed conference area. His desk encouraged expansive thoughts; mine encouraged a sharp focus on the job at hand. The balance had worked extremely well.

Sitting at his desk, I began to appreciate just how dramatically my professional role had to shift. I would have to assume the responsibilities and the business perspective that went along with the president's chair and desk. I wondered whether I should literally assume Bill's office as my own. I wiggled around in the large chair and tried to feel comfortable in it. It didn't work. I felt like an intruder, an upstart, a child who has crept into Daddy's study in the middle of the night. The pain was intensifying; I was losing control. With a client expected within fifteen minutes, that would never do.

I got out of the chair and walked over to the conference table. At least that had been as much my turf as it had been Bill's. I had initiated many conferences, and this was no different, or so I tried to convince myself. I began to array papers around the table. Making ready for the meeting helped me regain the composure I had come close to losing. The papers in order, I went into the bathroom to comb my hair.

The face in the mirror shocked me more than a little. I tried putting a cold towel on my reddened eyes, but it didn't seem to help. Nor did makeup conceal the dark circles under my eyes. My face was living proof that my efforts to control my grief were continuously stressful. The person in the mirror needed a rest; she needed help. She needed to laugh and, in so doing, loosen the tautness of her muscles. Something had to be done. I tried putting on my reading glasses; they helped a lot. The lower rims covered the circles nicely, and the effect was one of studiousness and professionalism, or so I tried to convince myself.

I was back in the office only a minute or so when Jessica came in to announce that Tom had arrived. Walking into the front office, I said as calmly as I could, "Welcome, Tom." He turned around, anxiety and pain written all over his face. I continued: "It is awfully good to see you. Let's go into the conference room. Would you like some coffee?" He said nothing and simply followed me. Jessica took his silence as an indication that he wanted some coffee and, following after us, asked, "Cream, sugar, or both?"

Sitting, Tom fumbled with the lock on his briefcase. Typically a humorous man, he had nothing to say. I realized that the communication barriers were enormous, and that it was up to me to break them down. "Tom, I want you to know that there are not many clients I could have seen today. I know you felt a great deal for Bill, and that made it possible for me to find the courage to work with you today. I won't lie to you. It isn't easy for me, and I know that it must be very difficult for you. I'm grateful that you chose to come today. Getting back to work is the best thing I could do for myself, and you are helping to make that possible."

My honesty had the intended effect on Tom. He smiled and, with tears in his eyes, attempted to joke. "Oh that Miller. Always one to surprise you when you least expect it. He's been touting your abilities to me for years. I guess he's finally managed to put me in a position where I have no choice but to try you out. You're certainly a lot prettier than he was!"

Smiling, I changed the subject. "Tom, I'd like to invite Meg to join us. She has been with the firm for six months, and I think you'll find that she has a great deal to contribute."

"You're the boss, Pam. Whatever you say is fine by me."

After meeting Meg, Tom's banter came more easily. He seemed more than a little relieved at not having to deal one on one with me. As he greeted Meg, I caught a glimpse of the Tom I had known.

"I can't believe this is happening to me. Two pretty girls, and both of them are *my* consultants! If my boss could see me now, he'd flip!"

Attempting to change the subject again and get the meeting under way, I said, "Well, I guess we better show him we're up to serious work."

But Tom wasn't going to give up so easily. "I really mean it. I'm a lucky man. A blonde on my right and a brunette on my left and both of them with great minds."

I tried again, my discomfort mounting with flattery that seemed increasingly inauthentic. "Tom, I suggest we get down to work so we can enjoy a long leisurely lunch. You wouldn't want to miss the chance of having us buy you lunch, would you?"

"Absolutely not. To work, Let's get to work," Tom responded, finally giving me a chance to crawl back into the safety of my job.

I chose not to take Tom to the Orange Tree Cafe that day. I was having to play a role, a role of false gaiety and confidence, and I didn't want my friends at the cafe to be confused by it. Further, I was not certain that I could maintain my professional posture in the light of their obvious compassion. We went to a place across town where no one knew us. They would not be able to distinguish the real me from the talkative professional lady I was so desperately trying to be that day.

Tom left at about three in the afternoon, comfortable and happy with the project. It had taken every ounce of energy I had to get through the day, but I had managed. It had been well worth the effort and the strain. I had rediscovered my strength; I had also found my limitations. I had to admit to myself that I was not totally ready for direct client contact. I needed a few days to regroup. My professionalism had to come more naturally, or sooner or later I would make a critical mistake.

Returning to Bill's desk, I began thumbing through the papers that had lain on his blotter for months. They required no action; most were partially written marketing letters that could not go out under anyone else's name. I wanted to throw them away but could not bring myself to do so. They had been written in Bill's own hand, a hand that no longer existed. My mind flooded with images of his body, first in life and then in death. Visions of the awful aluminum can and the stone-sized pieces within took over my thoughts until I could neither see nor think of anything else. The handwriting before me served only as a harsh reminder that death has the ultimate control. My efforts suddenly seemed so futile, so pointless.

Laying my head down on Bill's desk, I let my tears fall. I didn't worry about ruining the fine leather on the desk, or care about getting ink smudges on my face. I didn't care about anything.

Only after a pleasant numbness began to set in did I open my eyes. In doing so, I found myself contemplating the disorganized mess on the bookcase to the right of Bill's desk.

I recalled with a sense of bitter irony how often Bill had suggested that we clean out his bookcases and use them to store a master copy of each of our projects. Somehow, his request had never been implemented, given the periodic rash of client deadlines. I wished now that I, and the others, had been more responsive to his request. And Bill had been right. We needed a better system. Hunting through eight file cabinets every time we needed to write a proposal or develop a program was ridiculous. But administration and systems had never been the focus of my concern. They had been Bill's headache; now they were mine.

The enormity of it all struck me again. I began another downward spiral. I didn't want to have to cope with office systems. I wanted only to climb into bed and hide under the covers. Courage and stamina had again vanished, leaving fear and despair in their place. Self-pity began to take over. It seemed that Bill had worked himself to death, and I was about to have to do the same thing, caught up in a monstrosity of our own making. The demanding business had to be continued if I was to keep up with the demands of a large house; the large house had to be maintained in order for me to keep up with the demands of those who lived in my household. Life appeared at that moment to be nothing but a long upward climb. To reach the summit was only to fall off the other side.

I might have continued to wallow around in despair and self-pity had not Meg come in to tell me that it was close to five o'clock and time to go home. At first, I simply looked at her. Finally, beginning to refocus, I suggested that we plan to dress in blue jeans the next day, spending the day creating master files, moving bookcases, and clearing out Bill's things. "Meg, I want to begin right away to create an office environment that is ours, really ours. It's just something I've got to do."

Meg was reluctant. "Pam, it's too soon. You'll just make yourself even more upset. Don't push yourself."

I tried to make Meg understand that revamping the office was all that I could do. "I can't pretend that nothing has changed, that Bill is going to come in one morning and finish these letters. It's not going to happen, Meg. I need to have a fresh start, both here and at home. And, on top of that, I think it will feel good, in a strange way, to finally set up the systems that Bill had asked for all along. I guess I believe that somehow he'll know we're finally cooperating with him. I need to do this, that's all, I just need to do this."

Meg posed no further arguments. Later she would tell me that the intensity in my voice and my eyes permitted no disagreement.

She was afraid to do anything but let me follow the tide of my emotions, praying that I would not drown in the process.

It was close to six o'clock by the time I left the office. As I drove home, I clung to the thought that Clyde was coming soon. He was due at any time, maybe even that very evening. I knew that I would have no warning; that the telephone would ring, and he would be on the line telling me he was downtown at the airport limousine stop.

I thought about how it would feel to have Clyde with us. Our family circle had been suddenly broken, leaving a terrible feeling of incompleteness. A mother, a stepson, and two little girls did not constitute a complete family unit. The dialectic of male-female perceptions and capacities was missing at the top of the family hierarchy. A familial role was going unfilled, and that was already creating a lot of fear and insecurity. Melissa was visibly concerned about who would function as the ultimate "boss." Monica was being too mature for her own good, obviously thinking that her mother could not cope with childlike behavior. She needed her childhood back. Clyde's presence would, at least temporarily, restore the balance.

When I got home, I found that Barbara had made dinner. The children were in a wonderfully positive frame of mind. Even Pete was at home. It was Pete, in fact, who provided the high point of our dinner conversation. He had gotten a job offer that day and was feeling very good about himself.

With pride, he told me about the salary he would be commanding, and of his plans to save, buy a car, take an apartment, and so on. I did not choose to point out to him that evening that, while his salary seemed impressive in the light of his financial past, it would not begin to cover what he hoped it would. He was overlooking certain things, such as telephone and utility bills, automobile insurance, food, clothing, and so on. I made a mental note to talk with him soon about all that, but decided that evening to simply relax and enjoy with him his feeling of success. If only Bill could have seen Pete this way. I tried to assure myself that Bill was somehow aware of what Pete was trying to do with his life. I prayed that Pete's good feelings about himself and his apparent sense of direction would continue.

By nine that night I could no longer keep my eyes open. I told Barbara I was going to bed, but that if Clyde called, I wanted to be

109

awakened. I had to be the one to pick him up, no matter what the time. But I did not really expect the call. My intuition told me that I would have to endure yet another day or two without him.

It had been an emotional day, an intensely emotional day. My sensitivities were as naked and exposed as raw nerves. I had no defenses and was unable to put distance between myself and my hurt. Bill knew, and, in the form of the shadows, he returned to calm me and to slow the racing roller coaster. As I fell asleep, I thought only about how we had all made it safely through another day.

When I awoke the next morning, my first thought was that Clyde had not called. I began to worry about him. The early-morning news was filled with concern about the path of the falling satellite, Skylab. It appeared that the satellite would fall somewhere in Western Australia. "Skylab is now expected to cast debris in a largely unpopulated area spanning the Indian Ocean to the Australian desert." That was supposed to be good news, since Western Australia is so sparsely populated. "No population mass is in direct danger." No population mass! My family, the most critical mass in the world, was in danger! I couldn't believe the irony of it all. I wondered whether Clyde's plane had been able to depart. What if a piece of the debris hit his plane? My mind began to spin. I tried to assure myself that the chance of a thing like that happening was terribly remote. Almost every hour the scientists had been changing their mind about the expected point of descent of the satellite. No, I wouldn't worry about that. I was having a difficult enough time comprehending the universe that spanned no more than the five square miles between the office and the house. To broaden my sphere of concern to the skies was impossible.

I forced myself to get up and take a shower. "Keep moving. Just keep yourself busy, and before you know it, Clyde will be here." I had breakfast with the children and dropped Monica off at swimming practice on my way to the office. Keep moving, that was the key.

When I got to the office, I found the reorganization I had initiated the day before was already in progress. Jessica and Michelle, our other secretary, had been in the office for an hour or two. There were piles of things everywhere. No office had been left intact. I was more than a little nonplussed by the confusion and suggested that we sit down at the conference table, have some coffee, and plan our attack.

Jessica assured me that she was certain she knew exactly what had to be done.

"Pam, I know exactly what I'm doing. Bill and I discussed reorganization many times. We had finally come up with a series of systems; we just never quite found the time to put them in place. Really, I know what I'm doing. Just leave it to me."

I was angry, very angry. "Jessica, I don't care about the conversations you and Bill had. He and I had a lot of conversations, too. If you'll slow down and sit down, we can decide what has to be done."

Jessica got defensive. "Pam, I was only trying to make things easier for you. You want to do it your way? Fine with me; we'll do it your way. I'll sit here and await your instructions."

Jessica's behavior made me so mad that I got up and left the office. Walking around the block, I realized that part of my reaction had been due to jealousy. Jessica's claim that she was more aware than I of Bill's plans offended me. Once again, I reminded myself that what worked for Bill and me as a couple would not necessarily work for me. That included office systems. No, I would have to take the time to explain to Jessica and to Michelle that things were going to change, that they had to change if I was to continue to function.

Returning to the office, I found that Meg had arrived and was sitting at the conference table trying to fathom Jessica's ill humor. I began with an apology to Jessica and explained to her why I needed to understand every system in the office. Since Bill was no longer running the company, it was essential that I be familiar with every operating procedure. Jessica seemed to understand, at least for the moment, and we began to create a plan.

The operating motto for the day became "When in doubt, throw it out." Bill had been a saver, in the habit of keeping every single magazine that arrived and every piece of paper that went through the typewriter. We had first drafts, second drafts, third drafts; everything had been saved. It rapidly became obvious that the first task was to sort out the necessary from the unnecessary. That accomplished, it became relatively easy to shift the remaining materials around so that they formed a coherent system. By four in the afternoon, the office was back in shape.

All that remained was to go through Bill's desk and his private files, his place for storing intimate memories, documents marking the critical events in his life, and his plans for the future of the firm. I dreaded that job. His handwriting would, I knew, heighten my sense of loss and aloneness. But until it was done, I would be unable to move freely about the office. It was the last hurdle, and the most difficult to overcome. Wanting to begin tomorrow anew, I could not bear the thought of beginning the day with that awful task. No, I had to do it today.

It was as difficult as I had feared. Everywhere I looked I found Bill's reminders to himself of people he planned to contact and concepts he wanted to research and contemplate. I found neatly sketched financial forecasts, and more half-written marketing letters. No, Bill had not finished with life. Every memo screamed out that he had been taken from life against his will. There were so many things he had planned to do, hoped to do, looked forward to doing. For the first time since his death, I felt sorry for Bill. I had lost him, but he had lost life.

My thoughts began to drift. What is life all about anyway? We struggle and work and love and play with a frenzy, unable to contemplate that it all ends someday. Death, the final result of our efforts and our hopes. It doesn't matter whether we are successful in love or in business; our successes are never great enough to change the final outcome. That can't be, it just can't be. There *must* be a heaven for those who lived fairly, for those who gave as much as they took, for Bill. Love can't be simply a biological, physical phenomenon. Love seems to have a spiritual life of its own; love is perhaps what we call the soul. Does the soul die, too? It can't be. Nothingness. Nothingness is impossible to understand. Bill *can't* have turned to nothing. He was; he must still be in some form. I can't believe that as the light went from his eyes, he simply ceased to exist. I won't believe that.

My thoughts still drifting, I began making piles. I separated personal notes that I would take home and put in the file with the rest of Bill's things, business notes and documents that I would keep and go through at a later date, notes and scratch sheets that only hinted at Bill's thoughts and were unusable by anyone else.

Eventually, his desk was empty except for calculators and bank statements. Looking through the file adjoining Bill's desk, I found mostly financial data. Suddenly I knew how his desk, his private space, would be utilized. It would become the place to store all financial and strategic data related to the company. I would use his desk only when I was performing some function that required use of that data. The bookkeeper would periodically use that desk, as would the accountant. It seemed appropriate, and I was comfortable with the decision. I would keep my own office. I left for the day ready to return in the morning and get back to work.

When I got home, Barbara told me that Brooks had called. Calling her back, I received an enthusiastic invitation for dinner. Evidently her parents were in town, and her mother had been cooking up a storm all day. I tried to tell her I was tired, but she refused to take no for an answer.

"Of course you're tired, you dummy. You should be. I hear you've already gone back to work. That is ridiculous. You didn't sleep at all last week, and now you're pushing yourself to the limit, past the limit, I would guess. Look, Rob is out of town for the week, and that gives us a great opportunity to girl talk. It's been a long time since we did that, and I need it, even if you don't. I mean, I need some sisterly advice about this pregnancy routine. So if you won't come over for yourself, then do it for me."

I told her I would think about it and call her back, but even as I hung up the phone, I knew I ought to go. I would have to get out sooner or later, and this was as safe a social situation as I would find. Given Brooks's mother's penchant for conversation, I wouldn't have to talk much. Further, since Rob was out of town, Brooks was temporarily uncoupled, and my vulnerability would not be so obvious. I had made a game of challenging myself, of pushing myself, of trying to find my limits. I felt good about the strides I had made in the household and in the office. Brooks was offering me an opportunity to begin to pick up the pieces of my social life. I called her back and said I would come. She seemed genuinely pleased.

I had barely hung up when Melissa came flying into the bedroom. Barbara had told her that I might be going out for dinner. She was outraged and challenged me with, "Mommy! You can't go out for dinner. I don't want you to go out for dinner!" The adamancy in her voice made me smile. That only infuriated her more. "It's not funny. I don't want you to go out. It's not funny." She began to cry, and I stopped smiling. She was deeply upset.

I held her on my lap until she was quiet. Rocking her, I thought about her reaction and was overwhelmed by her total dependence on me. I was having a hard enough time taking care of myself. Could I satisfy this child's needs? I was coping with Bill's death by numbing my emotions, picking up the pieces of my life in an almost robotlike fashion, running when I scarcely knew how to walk. But my child needed more than a robot who looked like a mother, who set out her clothes, packed her lunch, and made her bed. My child needed my love. She needed me to be available to her as a whole person. I had always believed that the quality of time I spent with my children was more important than the quantity. Melissa was crying out for more of my time, and I thought to myself how she sought more in quantity to make up for what had been lacking in quality.

I suggested that she might like to sleep in my bed with me that night. It had always been a special treat to be invited to sleep in the king-sized bed. Melissa had been allowed to do so only infrequently, when Bill was away on business and I had no late-night work to do. But she did not jump at the opportunity as I had expected she would. Wide-eyed, she looked at me and asked, "What side of the bed would I have, Mommy, yours or Daddy Bill's?" My avoidance of Bill's side of the bed apparently had been obvious to her. "What side would you like, Melissa?" She answered immediately, "Yours, Mommy." I said, "Okay," trying to ignore the knot in my stomach. "That's probably a good idea anyway, since I should be closer to the telephone." She didn't respond. I hadn't fooled her. She was, however, content enough with our plan to get off my lap and go back to her dolls. She would allow me to go out that night.

I was late arriving at Brooks's. Both her parents and she had already begun their cocktail hour. They had been enjoying a good conversation and were all in jovial moods. Within moments of my arrival, we got over the hurdle of acknowledging Bill's death. They expressed their sorrow. I said, "Thank you." If we had not exchanged these words, it would have been as though Bill had never existed.

The evening passed quickly. Totally engrossed in the conversation, I enjoyed myself. Brooks had been right. It helped to get away from surroundings that screamed Bill's name, exuded his presence, and reminded me of my loss. I lingered at Brooks's home as long as I could.

As soon as I got home, Barbara told me that a man named Larry Waverly had called and was anxious for me to return his call that evening. She was surprised when I told her that Larry was a business associate. Given the conversation, she had assumed he was an extremely close friend. Apparently he had kept her on the telephone for some time inquiring about me and the children. That both surprised and pleased me. I had always liked Larry and especially looked forward to business meetings with him. But a friendship had never developed, or perhaps had never been allowed to develop. I had been happily married and he had been happily single. I had always been comfortable talking with him, secure in our business relationship and the social ground rules that relationship imposed.

But now I had to call him, and I was extremely nervous. I walked around the house a few times, telling myself that my sudden attack of the jitters was nothing short of ridiculous. After all, nothing had changed between us. At least I didn't think it had. I couldn't quite understand the apparent intensity of his concern. Finally, I dismissed that as Barbara's misinterpretation and forced myself to dial Larry's number.

Barbara had been right. Larry was more than a little concerned. He asked a million questions and expressed concern that I was pushing myself too fast, too hard. He urged me to consider taking a vacation, in spite of the several important business commitments I had made to him. He asked about the children and was curious about Barbara. He seemed pleased that Clyde was coming and expressed a desire to meet him. Revealing more and more of my thoughts and fears to him, I told him that sometimes I thought I was coping too well, that when the numbness wore off, the hurt would be unbearable.

Larry seemed to understand. He talked of his brother's death, and of the emotional spiral he had experienced for months thereafter. I was eager to learn about his experience, and to thereby begin to know him on a more personal level. I believed he was attempting to build a friendship with me.

When I got off the phone, I felt both very tired and very good. It had been a very full day. I had restructured the office, enjoyed a moment of special communication with my child, rediscovered that I could survive in a social setting and that I had a new friend. Larry cared about me. An attractive single male cared about me. I was not a shriveled-up widow who had already seen the best of life.

Attractive and socially desirable, I wasn't beaten. I was up again and on the move. Life was exciting. Feelings were exciting. At that moment, I was enjoying a roller coaster ride. I was running at full tilt, unaware that I had not yet even learned to walk. I went to sleep feeling elated and very much alive again.

7

Help Arrives

While I was enjoying a temporary high, Clyde was stranded somewhere in the Middle East, trying desperately to get to me before I made a mess of my life. I had sounded just a little too confident during the telephone conversations we had had. My family knew me well enough to recognize that whenever I showed extreme strength in the face of stress, I was trying desperately to cover up a very frightened and insecure self. They recognized that I was in jeopardy of making life-changing decisions without a perspective on either myself or the consequences of my behavior. Clyde was to act as my reality base, to stop me from making decisions hastily and prematurely. As I allowed myself to think that I was unstoppable, he feared that with every passing hour I was sinking deeper and deeper into quicksand.

My elation persisted through Thursday morning. As I sat in my office, I was determined to face the world squarely and to continue imposing a sense of order on otherwise chaotic feelings. Although I still experienced pain every time I looked at Bill's desk, I was slowly getting used to it. I found I was able to take calls as long as Jessica and Michelle screened them, making sure the caller already knew of Bill's death. I did not want to be put in the position of saying, "Bill has died." By noon, I was exhausted.

Looking back, I now understand that the total exhaustion I periodically felt stemmed from the enormous amount of energy I expended in keeping my feelings and fears in check. When they broke through, I panicked. My self-image swung accordingly: I would vacillate from Miss Supreme Confidence to a trembling child experiencing an awful nightmare. I tried hard to hide the trembling child from the world. People attributed strength to me that I knew I did not have. The hours in the office seemed particularly long. The office provided no place to go and hide in order to momentarily shed the heavy mask of courage I insisted on wearing. I decided to take Friday off, telling myself that I deserved a long weekend and some time in the sun with my children.

But I would not allow myself even a weekend of leisure and inactivity. I had removed Bill's personal papers from the office and was more in control as a result. I wanted to have the same feeling about my home. I decided that Saturday would be the day to go through Bill's clothes and, with the help of his eldest son, ship his things to Kevin. Thursday night after dinner, I called Ed, and he agreed to come.

The call made me feel weak in the knees. Perhaps I was pushing too hard. I considered calling back to cancel our plans, but instead just sat at the kitchen table, staring at my coffee.

Melissa and Monica broke the spell. Melissa was delighted that I planned to take Friday off, and Monica asked if I would come down to the club and watch her swimming practice. I had not yet dared to venture down to the club. Since I had no particularly close friends among the members, I feared that many, still unaware of what had happened, would inquire about Bill's health. I asked Monica if anyone had said anything to her during the week, and she told me that a few people had asked about Bill, and that she had broken the news to them.

My child had been forced to tell relative strangers that her "Daddy Bill" had died! I couldn't believe it; the whole notion was horrifying. My child, my little girl, was having to manage feelings that I couldn't even handle. Acting as our scout, she had surveyed dangerous enemy territory in advance of our entry. I couldn't stand it. If anyone was to be the scout, it should be me, her mother. I wanted to shield her, to protect her from the pain and from the danger, but I didn't know how.

Responding to the look on my face, Monica began trying to console me. "It wasn't so bad, Mommy. It was weird, that's all. The hardest part was after I said it. Nobody said anything. They just touched my shoulder and then turned around and walked away. I think people are uncomfortable with me. It's like they think I'm different because of what happened."

"Monica, I have noticed the same thing. People who haven't experienced a death in the family, and even some people who have, are very afraid of it. They get even more frightened when someone dies and leaves a young family. I guess they think that maybe the same thing could happen to them."

Monica looked at me intently, seemingly wanting me to continue. "Honey, I'm sure that people think you are very brave to be back at swimming practice so soon. The more you act like yourself, the sooner they will forget that you have been through a very difficult time."

"Well, I wish they would hurry up and forget. They think that I don't notice them talking about me, but I do."

"Who, Monica? Who is talking about you?"

"Oh, all the mothers. They stand in a little group, and now and then, one of them points at me."

"Monica, I'm sure they're just saying that you are a very brave child."

"I don't think they're saying bad things, Mommy. I just wish they wouldn't talk about me at all. It makes me nervous. Sometimes I don't even want to go to practice because of it."

Then Monica broke down and cried. Between her sobs, she repeatedly said, "I want it to be the same as it was. I want Bill to be alive. I want him to yell at me and play games with me. I want to tell him his cooking is great, even when I don't like it. I want it to be like it was!"

It was all I could do to keep myself from crying with her. I didn't want to, not then. I believed that Monica needed a strong mother at that moment, a mother who could provide her with counsel, hope, and peace of mind. I tried. "Oh, honey, I want it to be like it was, too. Things will never be the same as they were, but we are still going to have a good life together. Really, we are."

I had the impression that Monica was not hearing me. She seemed to be miles away, lost in her own pain and her own thoughts. Then she asked me a question that completely threw me off balance. "Mommy, who do you think you will marry next?"

Marry next? With that question, we had jumped from one universe to another. From a focus on our loss and on Bill, we had traveled in a second to a future I could not fathom. Not knowing how to answer her, I stalled for time by asking, "Why do you ask, Monica?"

Her answer was pitifully honest. "Because it was so hard getting used to Bill. I mean he is so very different from Daddy." I cringed at her use of the present tense, and she must have noticed, for she pulled away from me. But she continued, "I just want to know who I'll have to get used to next."

Her question initially was amusing to me. I did not find it at all difficult to say, "I don't know. I loved Bill a great deal, and I think it may be a very long time before I find anybody else I want to marry. You won't have to get used to another stepdaddy for a long while, if ever." That seemed to console her. It triggered a series of thoughts in me, though, that were anything but consoling.

I remembered a conversation Bill and I had had several months before his death. He had begun playing a song about losing a loved one. While he sang, he looked directly into my eyes as though to say, "I am trying to tell you something, my love." I had asked him to stop. He had said, "You know, I will die before you do. I don't plan to leave you in the near future, however, and I would really like to play this song."

Looking at his wan face, and holding his colder-than-normal hand, I repeated, "Please, don't play that song. It really hurts me to hear it. I can't imagine living without you. To lose you would be to lose half of myself. I feel so much love for you that I doubt I could ever love another man because the feelings would never be as full as are my feelings for you."

His answer had been unromantic, but terribly pragmatic and honest. "That does not make me feel good at all. You have to leave me with the choice of life and death. I do not want to be responsible for your life. I want to choose to remain with you, not to feel that I must. Musts do not feel good. They are a burden, not a joy. Please don't talk that way. Love me, and need me, but not to the point that you tell me you wouldn't survive without me. That is not a sign of your love, and, furthermore, I don't even believe you. So shut up and let me play my song."

Monica broke my reverie, repeating her request that I come watch her at swimming practice the next morning. She also asked me if

Clyde would be able to join the club as a member. I promised to come watch her practice and to ask about Clyde's status at the club. I hoped they would say that he had guest privileges, given his relationship to me. After all, dues were paid per family, and we were now one less member. I knew that although making the inquiry would be difficult, Clyde would love the opportunity to swim and play tennis there. It would be worth the pain of the inquiry to be able to tell him on his arrival that he was free to use the club. After the children were in bed, Barbara and I talked of Clyde's arrival until neither of us could keep our eyes open.

That night the shadows did not appear. I was not surprised. My thoughts were on the future: on the summer and on Clyde. The shadows would have dampened my temporary enthusiasm. Perhaps Bill knew that.

Nor did Clyde call. The night passed uninterrupted.

Friday morning broke bright, clear, and dry. For the first time all week, I got out of bed eagerly, looking forward to my day off. After making a cup of coffee, I went out to the porch. Standing at the railing, I looked around and noticed that the yard was beautiful. A blue jay was busy picking nest-building treasures from the gutter over my head. The dog was lying peacefully in the shade at the base of the porch steps. The grass was lush and green, and the trees full and healthy. I took a deep breath and smiled. "Clyde is on his way. He'll be here before the day is over. And today, I'm going to play, really play."

Monica had been asking for a pair of roller skates. I spoke out loud to myself. "Okay, Monica, you'll have your skates. So will Melissa and I. We'll buy them today. Quite a trio we'll make. Disco-skating stars, all of us." I conjured up wild hairdos and fancied us in fluorescent disco suits and kneepads. Oh, I knew it would never come to that, but I did think the three of us would have a wonderful time learning to skate in the cellar or the driveway, with the portable radio providing the only ambience we needed to convince ourselves we were great disco stars.

As if to bolster my positive and enthusiastic feelings, I chose to wear a somewhat bizarre purple and pink playsuit. It was as far from widow's black as any garment could be. I was determined to shun despair, self-pity, and fear that day.

When I walked into the kitchen, Monica and Melissa were at the table having their typical breakfast of orange juice and bagels with cream cheese. I said, "You know, I think I'll make you a proper breakfast this weekend, bacon and pancakes or something nice like that." While that might have been a normal occurrence in another household, my statement came as nothing short of a major announcement. Melissa, who had known only Bill's weekend breakfasts, looked at me wide-eyed and questioned, "Do you know *how* to do that?" I laughed and said of course I knew how to do that, and planned to prove it to her.

We were at the club shortly before ten. As we parked the car, I began to feel a little nervous. Looking down at myself, I realized that my playsuit was designed to call attention to my presence. It might as well have been fluorescent. Brass bands and trumpets couldn't have announced my arrival any more blatantly. "Here she is . . . (drum roll) . . . the widow!" I wished I had worn something more sedate. Feeling like a frightened child who has wandered too far from home, I wanted to crawl into a hole and let the world pass me by.

As though she had been reading my thoughts, Monica took my hand. Looking up at me, she smiled and said, "Come on, Mommy. It'll be all right. You'll see." She tugged at my hand and I began walking toward the pool. As I followed Monica, I tried to find my courage. What would I gain by staying away? The longer I stayed away, the harder it would be. It had to be faced if I was going to feel free to enjoy the tennis courts and the swimming pool during the summer. My skin felt almost moldy from the months of weekdays in the office and weekends spent in hospital rooms. It seemed that nothing would make it feel healthy other than sun and exercise. And my children loved their days at the club. They were now my mates, my best friends, my only true loves. To lose my courage now would be to sacrifice our summer together.

As we rounded the corner and came into full view of the pool, I noticed with relief that swimming practice had begun and the attention of most of the mothers was riveted on the pool. It was easy to find a chair and join the crowd without being noticed. Once seated, I felt less visible and conspicuous. I would not have to approach anyone. And those who were likely to approach me would be people who already knew what had happened. It seemed less and less likely that I would have to struggle through telling anyone that Bill had died.

As it turned out, only two people even approached me that day. The first, a mother of a child in Monica's swim group, was also the head of the membership committee and one of the most popular women in the club. I liked Nancy, though I didn't know her well. I was actually glad when I saw her coming toward me. Somehow, in breaking the barrier with her, I would be breaking it with everyone, and I trusted that she would be gentle. My assumptions were well-founded.

"Pam, I was so sorry to hear about Bill, and I'm glad to see you here. I hope to see a lot of you this summer."

"Thank you, Nancy."

"And Monica—she really is an amazing child. She must really be a comfort to you, especially now."

"Oh, she is, Nancy. I really don't know what I would do without her. Nancy, my brother, Clyde, is going to be living with me for a while. He's coming to help me with the house and with the children. What do I have to do to arrange club privileges for him?"

"Oh, nothing, Pam. We'll just treat him as a member of the family."

"That's really nice, Nancy. But don't you want to clear that with the membership committee?"

"No, Pam. We're all aware of your situation and want to help you in any way we can. I'm sure the committee would agree with me on this. Don't give it another thought. If your brother plays tennis, he might like to join the men's tennis team. Just have him call Pete Hendrix."

"Thank you, Nancy. I'll tell him."

After she left, I remembered my concerns of the night before and felt both a little foolish and a little guilty. People were basically kind. I reminded myself to give them the benefit of the doubt a little more often. I felt more like a member of that club than I ever had in the past. Being a working mother had set me unpleasantly apart, or so I had felt. I hadn't joined the women's tennis team because I couldn't show up for midday practice. I hadn't helped with the swim meets because my time was so thoroughly committed. I hadn't appeared to help with the spring cleanup of the club grounds because Bill was in the hospital. But now, all that didn't seem to matter. The other members cared. I was one of them.

Swimming practice over, we drove to a beer and soda distributor in New York. I was determined to get some Australian beer to celebrate Clyde's arrival. In the parking lot, I attempted to close the sun roof. Something snapped, and the roof would not close. When it snapped, so did I.

I got out of the car and started randomly pulling at things. Barbara stopped me and suggested I let her have a look. As she did so, I walked away and tried to compose myself. I knew that what had happened represented nothing more than an annoyance, and yet I was panicking. The idea of having to take the car in for repair loomed as a major problem. Feeling that my day off had been ruined, I wanted to get back in the car and drive directly to the dealer and insist that it be fixed immediately. I was having enough trouble instilling a sense of order and progress into our lives; the broken sun roof represented loss of control. It represented regression, and defiance of my resolve to make our days run smoothly.

Barbara turned to me and said that although she couldn't close the roof, she didn't think it was anything serious. I yelled at her, "I have only had this car for three months. The tape deck has already been stolen once, and the sun roof was locked that time. When they took the tape deck, they took most of the front panel along with it. Oh, it's serious all right. And I don't appreciate your trying to humor me. It's not you who has to manage thousands of details each day, it's me! All you have to worry about is yourself. I don't even have time to write a letter to my parents, or have my hair cut. This is *not* just one more annoyance. It's the last straw!"

Barbara looked at me with disbelief. The storm had come from out of nowhere. One minute, I had been singing along with the car radio; the next minute, I was berating her for simply trying to calm me. I was ashamed of myself, and by way of apology I hugged her, said I was sorry, and began trying to explain my behavior. She stopped me. "It's all right. I do understand. We'll get it fixed. No, I'll get it fixed. Don't you worry about it." While I knew she could not actually get the car repaired for me, her offer was so genuinely kind that I forced myself at least to feign calmness and composure. I could not and would not let my feelings and anxieties destroy the day for everyone.

I suggested that Barbara stay in the car, leaving it to me to get the soda and the beer. She agreed. Melissa jumped up and informed me in no uncertain terms that she was going to accompany me. I gave her no argument, happy for her company. Melissa would serve as the critical prop in the play I was about to enact. Enter young mother with child ready to stock the coolers for a weekend party. See how she smiles; she anticipates a good time. See how the child helps her; what a nice child. Nothing out of the ordinary; a nice normal American mother and child.

I wanted people to believe that the play was my reality. Donning a smile, I tried to hide my fear at having to function in a retail store. This was the first time since Bill's death that I was venturing into a shop of any kind, and I felt terribly nervous.

As we entered the store, my tongue felt dry and swollen, and I feared I might not be able to speak. I wished I had more cash. I would have to write a check, a check from Bill's and my joint account. Bill would be part of the transaction, but Bill was dead. Would the cashier sense that something was wrong? I felt like a marked woman, as though I had a label affixed to my forehead that read, "Herein lies trauma, panic, death. Beware the widow."

Somehow I managed to get through the process without incident. Apparently I had played my part well. Leaving the store, I was both relieved and encouraged. I could function, after all, outside my home and my office.

After purchasing the beer, I decided that the thing to do was go directly to the dealer from whom we had bought the car and see if he could fix the sun roof. I hoped to undo the one incident that had threatened to undermine my fragile resolve to enjoy the day.

Arriving at the dealership, I spotted the man who had sold us the car and went directly to him. Bill had done most of the negotiating concerning the purchase of the car, and in the process, he and the salesman, Ralph, had developed a friendship of sorts. I did not have the energy even to pretend to be composed and decided instead to be honest about the problem I was facing, as well as its impact on me. I said simply, "Ralph, my name is Pam Miller. Bill, my husband, and I bought a station wagon from you a few months ago. Bill died only two weeks ago, and I have a problem with the car, and it's upsetting me terribly. I just don't seem to be able to deal with everyday problems yet."

Ralph was visibly shocked but retained his composure and asked, "What is the problem?" I told him, and he suggested that I sit down in the chair beside his desk. He disappeared and within a few minutes was back to say that they couldn't fix the sun roof right away because it was a new feature, and they didn't have the expertise to deal with the problem immediately. However, he handed me a set of keys and said that I could use one of their rental cars free of charge until they could get my car back in shape. For the second time that day, I appreciated that people are fundamentally kind and, if they know the awful truth, will go out of their way to make things easier for you.

Our problems temporarily resolved, I felt lighter again, happier. I decided it would be a good opportunity to head into town to purchase our roller skates. Somehow, as I made the purchase, I felt my natural child, my instinct for play and laughter, emerge as it had not in months. The skates represented a frivolous, unnecessary expense, and that is precisely what made it so healthy, so good. It is all too easy to lose the ability to play even under the best of circumstances. Confronting death brings out a child, but it is a frightened child, not a playful one. The playful child provides a perspective on life that is unique: life is not heavy, it is exciting; life is not defeating, it is invigorating. I was happy to discover, if only for a few moments, that my natural child had not died in the months of Bill's hospitalization and the days following his death.

It was dusk by the time we got home. Walking out to the porch, I looked around as I had that morning. Just as my mood had then reflected the brightness of the morning sun, so too my thoughts now reflected the coming darkness. Clyde had not arrived. I had hoped to find him at home when we returned. While my intuition told me that he would still arrive before the clock struck midnight, my belief was not firm. I felt shaky, in both body and spirit.

The ring of the telephone broke my unpleasant reverie. Certain it was Clyde, I ran into the house, almost knocking out the screen door in my haste. When I discovered that the caller was only Ed, I was severely disappointed and, without thinking, confirmed that I still intended to go through his father's clothes the next day. He promised to be at the house by eleven.

After I hung up, I had serious second thoughts about going through Bill's things. As we prepared and ate our supper, I expressed my doubts to Barbara. She urged me to do as planned. It would be an exceedingly painful task, no matter when it was done.

In a sense, I was surrounded by pain these days. Later, when joy began to creep in, I would be even more reluctant to undertake such an emotionally devastating task. It would be less traumatic now, more in keeping with our feelings and the events of our lives than it would be later. And I needed to begin thinking of myself in a new light: not as Mrs. William Miller, but as Pamela; uniquely and separately, Pamela. I was now single, no longer married. Our closet had to become my closet. Our bureau had to become mine.

Our dinner of tuna sandwiches over, I went back out to the porch. It had become my thinking place, and I had some thinking to do. Barbara was watching television with the girls. Pete had not been around all evening. I was free to let my thoughts follow their natural course.

My thoughts were at first pleasant. "I'll have a room to myself. That might be nice. It will certainly be different. I have always, or almost always, shared a room: first with Gay, then Shelley at college, then Jim, and, finally, Bill. I can turn on the television in the bedroom whenever I want. I'll feel free to spread things all over the bathroom counter, and even to leave the cap off the toothpaste if I like. The kids and I can get pizza whenever we please. For that matter, I've got a little money now, and we can begin to go to some interesting places on the weekends. Maybe we'll even hop a plane for Florida some winter weekend. Why not? We're free, aren't we?"

Yes. We were free. Free from the constant worry that Bill might at any time suffer another heart attack. Free from concern, and free from him. I had to face my true feelings. The freedoms that lay ahead were nothing in comparison with my loss. I was free, but I was alone. I had not chosen this freedom. It had been imposed on me, and it felt lousy.

I might have fallen into another round of despair had I not felt increasingly certain that Clyde was nearby. Past episodes had given me reason to trust the ESP that he and I seemed to share. I knew that he had indeed landed in the country. I could almost see him on the limousine. It came as no surprise when the telephone rang at around ten-thirty in the evening, and Clyde announced that he was downtown. I was crazy with excitement, running around the house yelling, "He's here! Clyde is here!" The children woke up and immediately raced to put on their sneakers, not worrying that they were still in nightgowns.

As we drove into the circular driveway of the downtown hotel that doubled as the limousine stop, my heart started pounding. In spite of a three-day beard, unwashed hair, and weary eyes, Clyde looked absolutely beautiful to me. Standing tall and erect, he seemed to exude health and security. His handsome tanned face represented vigor and vitality. I felt extremely fortunate to have such a brother.

He had a lot of luggage, so much that at first it seemed impossible to get it all into the car. That was a wonderful sign; I mistakenly took it as an indication that he planned to stay for a long time.

After the embraces and the greetings, an uncomfortable silence fell upon us. The children and I had shared something, Clyde was on the outside. I felt a sense of urgency about involving him and almost desperately wanted him to understand every incident and every nuance of every feeling that I had experienced. I didn't know how to begin.

I didn't have to. As I drove, Clyde filled in the silence by telling the girls every detail of his trip. We heard that he had indeed been delayed in Australia because of Skylab, and that the trouble in the Middle East had caused further delays in plane arrivals and departures. He bemoaned his layover in London, and his fatigue as he waited to clear as a standby passenger. He had been traveling for the better part of four days. He was exhausted.

Once we were home, and the kids were in bed, Clyde and I went out on the back porch to talk. Clyde denied his need to sleep, saying that while he was tired, he didn't think his internal clock would allow him to close his eyes. It was morning in Australia, and Clyde's body was reacting accordingly. I brought out the Australian beer, and we began to try to narrow the distance between us. From Clyde's rather stiff posture and downward gaze, I could tell that he felt a little awkward and somewhat threatened. I asked if something was troubling him.

"Pam, I guess I'm afraid that you want a greater commitment from me than I can make, than I want to make."

"I don't know what you mean, Clyde."

"Well, I guess it's important to me that you understand I need to have the freedom to leave whenever I feel I want to. I expect, though I'm not sure, that will be sometime in the late summer."

"Where will you go?" I asked, shaken by a discussion of his departure only hours after his long-awaited arrival.

"I'm planning to go west to graduate school. But let's not talk about that now. My plans are, as usual, very fuzzy."

"Okay. I didn't mean to make you feel locked in. You aren't, you know. I never thought you would stay forever."

"I don't feel locked in. That's not what I meant to say. I guess you just seemed a little too happy to see me. That frightened me. I don't know that I can live up to your expectations, or meet your needs."

"I don't really have a lot of expectations, Clyde. I guess I just need time to get used to running the business and the house. I need your help, particularly with the house. I mean, a lot has to be done, but more important, I need to learn how to do certain things. I wouldn't know what to do if a fuse blew. Plumbing is a total mystery to me. I've got a chain saw and not the faintest idea of how to even start it. I need your help with that kind of thing."

Clyde looked disappointed. My lie had been a little too convincing. In an attempt to diminish his anxiety, I had gone too far. I had cast him in the role of a handyman and, in the process, hurt his feelings. He needed to be needed, but in such a way that his freedom to leave was unthreatened. I tried being a little more open and honest with him.

"Clyde, above all, I need to be near you. I can be myself with you. We've been through so much together that I guess I feel it's okay to be strong or weak, rational or irrational, with you. I need you here because I need to talk and to explore my feelings without having to weigh the consequences of every word I say."

"Well, that you've got. We've always been able to talk. I know you're half crazy, you don't have to hide that from me."

"Thanks, brother. Just one more thing that I need from you. I need to feel physically secure. I mean, Pete lives here, but he's moving out soon, and anyway, he's with his girl friend most nights. I still suffer from night terror, and I need a little time to get used to being in the house alone with the children at night."

"Well, that you've got, too. I don't plan to turn into a social butterfly immediately."

The gap between us was closing, but I still sensed that Clyde could not fully understand me until I forced myself to share with him the events and feelings of the past two weeks. I asked again if he wanted to go to bed. Again he said no, he was settling in and the more we talked, the more at home he felt. Taking him at his word, I began to recite events. At first, I could not describe the feelings that had accompanied the events. Clyde helped me do that. He made me cry, and then he made me laugh, and cry again. Eventually, he shared with me his feelings for Bill, and his own reaction at learning of Bill's death. We reminisced for a while about the good times he, Bill, and I had shared.

By two in the morning, even jet lag couldn't keep Clyde awake. I, too, looked forward to sleep. It had been another long day. Once again, my emotions had run the gamut.

Seven days and seven nights had passed since I spread Bill's ashes. I had hoped to free him of the responsibilities of this world and, at the same time, to free myself of self-pity and despair. The two seemed interconnected. Bill was not yet totally free; the shadows on my ceiling spoke of his lingering presence. But the shadows appeared only when I was in need of him, when I could not face my world and my feelings without his help.

I had begun to pick up the pieces of my life, to make a coherent whole out of a fragmented puzzle. But I was impatient, impatient to put the entire puzzle back together. With Clyde by my side, I would redouble my efforts. I would begin to look to Clyde rather than to the shadows for help.

8

Waging War on the Memories

With Bill's death, I had begun a ride on an emotional roller coaster. Not a single day had passed without my swinging from elation to total despair. In an attempt to control the swings and slow down the coaster, I had tried to impose a tight control over myself and my days. Strangers thought me daring and courageous; only friends and loved ones suspected that my frantic activity was a cover-up, a pretense.

I clung to the pretense Saturday morning as I approached the task of going through Bill's belongings. By 10:00 A.M., my mind focusing only on the job to be done and fighting awareness of my feelings, I was issuing directions to Barbara.

"Barbara, I don't want Ed going through my drawers and closets. We've got to go through the house and gather all of Bill's things together. We'll put everything in the living room. He's coming at eleven, so we've got to get moving."

"Right, boss. Where should I start?" Barbara cooperatively asked.

"Down in the cellar; I store out-of-season clothes in the closet down there. You start there. I'll take the bedroom."

I opened the closet door and resolutely began to fill my arms with summer suits. The feel of Bill's jackets was more than I could handle; the mask of courage fell apart. I sat down, my arms overflowing with his garments. The smell of Bill was distinctly a part of those clothes. Memories of physical closeness with Bill flooded my brain. I pictured him in each suit, and began to cry when I envisioned him at his best, in his three-piece dark blue pinstripe. I saw him as he had been at the peak of health: sturdy, strong, and vigorous. All recollection of the frail man who had been too thin for these clothes was gone. I caressed his best sweater and pictured the warm and giving man who had been my friend. Dropping the rest of the clothes onto the floor, I put on the sweater. I felt wonderful. It seemed as though Bill was holding me once again.

Still wearing his sweater, I went back into the closet and searched for the garments that had been most special to Bill. My eye fell on the blue-and-white houndstooth jacket he had worn for our wedding five years ago. It was a fine jacket, so fine that even with almost constant summer use, it showed few signs of wear. I took it gently from the rack and held it to me. The essence of Bill was very strong. Its fibers exuded the smell of his body intermingled with the smell of his favorite shaving lotion. Feeling dizzy, I had to sit down, not noticing that I sat on a pile of clothes and sharp hangers.

Only Monica's sudden entrance broke the mood. Not wanting her to see me crying, I hurriedly composed myself and put Bill's wedding jacket aside. She tried to make light of the fact that I was wearing Bill's sweater, and pretended not to notice my tears. "Mommy, it's summer! You don't need to wear that bulky sweater today! It does look nice on you, though. I think you should keep that to wear during the winter."

Oh, sage child that she is. With those few statements, Monica rekindled my sense of purpose and resolve. Forcing a smile, I took off the sweater, vowing privately to hide it so it would not inadvertently be given away. She asked me if I needed her to do anything that day, and I reminded her that Jim and Sara would be arriving soon to take her and Melissa to the beach. I had not wanted the children around me as I disposed of Bill's belongings, and so had urged Jim to take them for the day. Looking back, I believe I made the wrong decision. It would probably have done them both good to help me deal with the more tangible aspects of the business of death. My decision had been mostly a selfish one, motivated more by the need to approach the job without interruption and challenge than by the desire to spare them unnecessary pain. The latter provided only a convenient rationalization.

As Monica fiddled with the clothes already strewn over the

bedroom floor, I noticed with alarm that it was already eleven-fifteen. Ed and Janice were, fortunately, late. I felt an urgency about getting Bill's things into the living room before they arrived. The feeling of urgency helped me overcome my desire to sit and fondle each garment. Urging Monica to get dressed, I began picking up the clothes that were scattered all over the floor.

When I got to the living room, I noticed that Barbara had already covered the sofa with piles of winter clothes. We began to pull in chairs from the dining room; that accomplished, I returned to the bedroom, and Barbara to the cellar.

The unreality of our activity struck me time and time again. Despair threatened to take over. Each time I felt my control slipping, I redoubled my activity. To further barricade my feelings, I pretended that I was simply cleaning out the closet and weeding out things that were too big, too small, or too old to keep. I set a series of objectives for each trip and tried to focus on those objectives. When my emotions threatened to break through, I made the objectives more challenging, until with each trip, I was carrying an incredible weight.

Within a half hour, we were finished. The living room was full. Bill had owned an awesome amount of clothing. Some suits I had never even seen him wear. Others were two sizes larger than I had ever known him to be; he had always intended to have many of these things tailored, but had never gotten around to doing so. His oversized suits made me sad. They screamed out that Bill had not intended to die, that he had plans for his future.

At around noon, the telephone rang. It was Ed, apologizing for being late. He and Janice had had a late night and had slept through the alarm. He said that he couldn't be at the house until one. Breathing a sigh of relief, I sat down in the middle of the living room and, for a change, allowed myself to feel.

I was surprised at how little I felt. Perhaps it was because Bill's garments lay together in a heap. One garment, by itself, had the ability to catapult me into despair; a pile of garments could not. It is not unlike the difference between learning that an acquaintance has been killed and hearing that a thousand soldiers have died on a battlefield. The single death is always more impactful than the death of many.

I began to try to make some sense out of the piles, deciding to put jackets in one place, sweaters in another, shoes in another, and so on. Barbara came in and began to help me. We exchanged no words. Soon after, Jim and Sara arrived to pick up the girls. They, too, said very little and got out of the house with unusual speed. I had come to terms in my own way with Bill's possessions; they had not. I understood their haste and was actually grateful for it. There was nothing that could be said.

Shortly before one, Clyde walked into the living room. His presence made me feel better instantly. His first comment was exceptionally brief. All he said was "Wow! Dare I ask what is happening here?" Appreciating what the scene must look like to someone who did not help create it, I smiled.

My smile broke apart as I began to explain. "These are all of Bill's things. . . ."

Seeing the expression on my face change, Clyde asked, "How can I help you? I want to help you."

"Oh, Clyde, I guess the best thing you can do for me is to stand by as I work with Ed and Janice to decide what goes where. I expect them any minute."

"I'll be right here. I think I can make things a little easier on you."

"Thanks, Clyde. Your just being here is making things easier for me. I'd like you to have something of Bill's. Is there anything here that you might like to have? I know he would want you to . . . well . . . to have something of his."

"I can't handle that right now, Pam, really, I can't— Okay?"

"Okay. I understand. Would you mind going downstairs and waking Pete? He should be here, too."

Shortly thereafter, Pete appeared sleepy-eyed and wearing only a pair of old paint-stained, torn blue jeans. After getting a cup of coffee, he came into the living room and made a space for himself on the couch. For a long time, he quietly sipped his coffee and looked around. Then he looked at me, and said, "I don't understand how you can do this." It was neither a question nor an accusation. There was only amazement in Pete's voice.

"Pete, please look over the clothes and take whatever you want."

Pete didn't respond at all. He simply sat and looked at me.

"Pete, I think that in the months to come, it will make you feel better to have a tangible memory of your dad. Would you like to have the bathrobe you and the girls gave Bill for Father's Day?"

He simply nodded in silent agreement.

"Pete, think of all the times you needed to borrow a tie and shirt for a date. Your dad really enjoyed seeing you dressed that way, you know."

Still not speaking, Pete picked up the first three ties and shirts that met his eye. With ties around his neck and shirts and bathrobe over one arm, he sat down again and sipped at his coffee.

"Pete, I don't mean to push you."

"Pam, you're not pushing me. This just makes it all so real. I mean, he's dead, he's really dead."

It was my turn to retreat into frozen silence. We had switched roles. I sat on the floor and watched as Pete put on Bill's denim jacket. Long in cut, the jacket fit Pete beautifully.

"Pete, take some socks, huh? That is, unless you really enjoy wearing two different color socks every day."

Pete smiled, though it was a feeble smile, and picked up a few pairs of his father's socks.

The sight of Pete in Bill's jacket with three ties around his neck, a bathrobe over his arm, and several pairs of socks falling from his hand was both comical and tragic. Pete caught my eye, and I could tell that he not only sensed my sadness but felt as I did. Tears came to my eyes, and to his. I said, "This is really a bitch of a thing to have to do." Pete seemed neither shocked nor displeased by what was an unusual choice of words for me. He simply nodded in agreement and left the room.

He had not been gone long when the doorbell rang. Ed and Janice entered quietly, and we passed time with casual chatter and coffee. They made no reference to our day's work, and neither did I for a long while. Only the strain of finding neutral subjects to discuss finally propelled me to suggest we begin.

We spoke little as we sorted Bill's things, deciding what belonged with whom. The silence was periodically broken by subdued mentions of experiences one or the other of us had shared with Bill. "I remember the day he bought that jacket." "He used to wear these sailing." "He really loved that ratty old sweater."

Each possession seemed sacred. In sharp contrast to my earlier haste was the time and care we gave each garment as we placed it in its appropriate pile or box. It seemed as though we were all insignificant pawns in a sacred rite. It took all day, and by the time

Bill's things were in Ed's car or in the boxes marked for shipment to Kevin, we were all emotionally exhausted. Ed and Janice left as quietly as they had entered.

Barbara had carefully stayed out of the way all day, returning the rental car and retrieving my car, and then doing a pile of errands. Only after Ed and Janice had left did she reappear. She, Clyde, and I went out to the porch to enjoy a quiet beer together. The summer evening made me sad. I was very aware that it was Saturday night. Looking first at Clyde and then at Barbara, I began to see myself as a lost soul and them as my guardians. My plight had become their purpose. But they could not keep me from drowning, at least not on that Saturday night. I was lousy company, refusing or unable to laugh or even to chat comfortably.

Clyde's eyes began to droop, and before long, blaming jet lag, he excused himself to go to bed. Barbara stayed with me for a few minutes after Clyde left. She was obviously restless. Concerned that Barbara thought she had to stay with me, I urged her to do as she pleased. She mentioned that she had been thinking of going downtown to see a movie and asked me to join her. I claimed fatigue and convinced her to leave.

With Barbara gone, Pete out on a date, and Clyde sound asleep, I became as alone in reality as I had felt while in the presence of others. There was a strange comfort in that. I felt no pressure to make talk or to hide my melancholy. I began to allow myself to really experience my loneliness, letting it sweep over me. I caught myself speaking out loud to the night air. "Bill is dead. I am a widow. I have two children to raise, and a business to run. Bill is dead. I am alone. My friends have mates. Tonight, they are together. I am alone. I am single. I have no mate. I am alone."

I opened the floodgates and let the emotions that had been locked within me do their worst. At first, it was terrifying. My stomach tightened, and my head grew dizzy. Thinking I might faint, I put my head back and closed my eyes. The deluge of feeling intensified, filling me and then bursting from me as sobs that I could not stop, could not control. Feelings and fears whirred so fast and created such a tumult that my mind stopped labeling, stopped tracking, stopped trying to understand. And then, slowly, the intensity began to diminish. Opening my eyes and lifting my head, I realized that I was still alive; I had not drowned.

No, I was alive, very much alive, with a throbbing headache to prove it. But the headache did not preoccupy me. I was consumed by my own sensitivities, experiencing aloneness to such a heightened degree that it ceased being painful. Its very depth made it somehow something to be treasured, to be celebrated.

I went into the house, turned on the stereo, and poured a glass of wine. Turning off the harsh overhead light, I sat down at the kitchen table. I had recreated Bill's and my favorite Saturday night scene: at home alone with good music and good wine, and the prospect of many hours of good talk.

The music seemed to echo my mood perfectly. Ballads of lost loves, of unrequited loves, of searching for life's meaning came pouring out of the overhead speakers. Melancholy and sadness assumed their own kind of beauty. These feelings had become my friends, not my enemies. In making them my friends, I had mastered part of my fear.

The ring of the telephone interrupted my intimate party with myself. It was Amy. "Hi, Pam. What are you doing?"

For a moment, I could not respond. It was as though the doorbell had rung when I was alone in the house and naked. I had to cover up quickly and feign delight at being interrupted.

"Oh, nothing, Amy, nothing."

"Want some company?"

"Oh, I don't know. Why? Do you want to come over?"

"Well, if you're not busy or too tired. I'd like to come over and tape a new record I got at church. And I need to get out of this house for a while. You know, the old Saturday night blues. . . ."

"Okay. Come on over. I'd like to see you, even if you're going to make me listen to church music."

With Amy on her way over, I knew that I had to pull out of the mood created by the dialogue I had been having with myself. I went downstairs and turned off the stereo. The silence was maddening. I couldn't seem to keep myself from returning to that private emotional world. Wishing that Clyde were not sleeping, I crept into his room. He was out, all right. His exhaustion had been so great that he had crawled partway under the covers fully dressed. He was snoring.

I began walking around the house in search of something to keep myself occupied, and ended up in the garage. Periodically throughout the week, I had been considering what to do about the cars. Bill's car was the finer of the two, and clearly better suited to the image I had to present as the president of the company. Mine was the newer of the two, and much better suited to my role as mother and homemaker. One was small and sporty. The other was simply functional. I felt strongly that a decision had to be made. One of my cars had to go.

I went back up to the kitchen, and got another glass of wine. Returning to the garage, I opened the front door of the BMW and took my place in the driver's seat. I tried to imagine living without it. I could not. Then I crossed the garage and, sitting in my car, tried to imagine doing without it. Again, I could not. By the time Amy's headlights came down the driveway, I had worked myself into a real state. Never one for indecision, I had become extremely impatient with the whole dilemma. I had to resolve the issue tonight. If Amy wanted to spend the evening with me, she would simply have to help me sort out all of the pros and cons until I reached a verdict.

Seeing me in the garage, Amy pulled up the sliding door and came in that way. She was amused by the sight of me sitting behind the wheel of my car with a glass of wine in my hand. "Going somewhere?" she asked.

"Crazy," I answered, "I've got to sell one of these cars, and I can't make up my mind. It's beginning to drive me crazy. What do you think?"

"As I see it, there's no choice. Clearly, you should keep Bill's car. I mean, you've been talking about having a more exciting image, and his car is clearly the more exciting of the two. It becomes you. You are just not the suburban housewife type, and that car of yours is definitely that of a suburban housewife."

"Oh, I know that's what it looks like on the outside, being beige and a station wagon, but you've never driven it. It drives like a sports car. It's really a great machine, and it doesn't cost that much less than Bill's car."

Picking up the defensiveness in my tone, Amy shrugged her shoulders and walked into the house. I had asked for her opinion, and she had given it. Instead of appreciation, all she had received was a somewhat hostile reaction.

"Hey, I'm sorry. I just believe I would feel a lot better if I could make a decision. It's like this morning, getting rid of Bill's clothes.

I've got to make this household reflect me, and me alone. To keep two cars is no different than leaving Bill's clothes in the closet. It had to become *my* closet. It has to become *my* garage. Whichever car I keep has to become *my* car."

Amy looked at my face as if to gauge the depth of my concern. Seeing nothing that alarmed her, she looked down at my glass of wine. I followed her eyes, but did not connect rapidly enough, forcing her to say, "Okay. We'll settle this once and for all. We'll spend the evening in the garage if we have to, but how about getting me a glass of wine?"

When I came back downstairs with her wine, I found Amy in the garage, looking from one car to the other. "I understand your dilemma," she said, "but I really think that you and the kids could do without the wagon. I mean, if you really need to cart stuff around town, you can borrow my car. I think Bill's car is much better for your image."

"You mean my image as president?"

"Well, sure, that is a factor. But no, I was really thinking about you as a person. You're young and attractive, and you've got a little free cash now. You're been spending your weekends in hospital rooms and your weeknights behind a desk for too many months now. It's time for you to think about you, to have some fun. Oh sure, the wagon is practical, but the BMW is fun. You've been concentrating too much on the practical and the necessary, and not giving nearly enough thought to having fun."

The idea of having fun and building a new self-image as more of a fun-loving person appealed to me. Amy had touched upon the same urges that had triggered my buying the roller skates. I did want to feel more carefree about life. But even as we discussed it, I knew that rediscovering how to play and to relax was going to be difficult.

Only hours before, I had let my emotions prevail, let them sweep over me. While I had emerged better for the experience, I did not yet trust myself or the world enough to loosen my control. Panic was still too close to the surface; I was not yet convinced that I would not drown if I stopped swimming like crazy. I had stopped once, and emerged alive. But the intensity of the experience was so great that I had to protect myself against a second occurrence.

I didn't try to express these thoughts to Amy. I didn't need to. That she already understood was evident in her comments. "You should learn to be a little more like me, and I a little more like you. I mean, I'm very good at doing absolutely nothing but flitting from one amusement to another all day. As a result, my work is rarely finished. Your work is always finished on time, or ahead of time, but you don't seem to be able to take time out. The world won't collapse, you know, if you are not constantly at your peak performance."

Not convinced that Amy was right, I decided at least to try to relax. "Maybe I don't have to make a decision about the cars right away. I mean, making the decision has assumed an urgency that doesn't really exist, does it? I feel a little like I do when I decide on a Friday night to cut the grass on Saturday morning and wake up to find that it is raining. When my life isn't going well, and I'm running scared, then not being able to do things as planned, like cutting the grass, drives me crazy. It's like that with the cars. I guess maybe I'll keep both of them for a while."

Amy appeared relieved. "I'm glad that's settled. Now, would you mind if I got some more wine, and we made that tape?"

We had barely begun when Clyde appeared in the playroom. Apparently the sound of church music coming from the upstairs speakers had surprised him enough to arouse both curiosity and concern. He knew me well enough to know that I would not have chosen that music, at least not if I was in a normal state of mind. The sight of Amy and me sitting on the floor, attempting to set the dials right, amused him. He immediately joined in, making suggestions and then taking over the responsibility himself. Amy and I turned to the jigsaw puzzle that had been sitting uncompleted on the table for weeks. Amy was soon engrossed in the challenge. Never a very apt puzzle-doer, my mind began to wander. I began to think about the cars again. Hoping that Amy and Clyde wouldn't notice, I quietly left the room and went back into the garage.

I began to favor the station wagon. I couldn't imagine ever being able to regard the BMW as *my* car. Oh, I had enjoyed driving it, but it had not been mine. It was too easy to picture Bill behind the wheel. I suddenly wanted Amy to like the station wagon, and to help me convince myself that Bill's car should be sold.

I didn't have to go into the house after her. Both she and Clyde had already noticed my absence and were standing in the doorway watching me. Looking up from the wheel, I saw that Clyde was frowning; he was clearly concerned about my state of mind. Amy cocked her head to one side and gave me a crooked, sarcastic half-smile. She said, "I don't believe you. You just can't give this up, can you?"

Amy's ploy didn't work. I felt neither cute nor funny. The business at hand was serious, very serious. I chose to ignore her attempt to tease me. "Amy, you've never actually driven my car, have you?"

"No, I guess not." She was no longer smiling.

"Well, would you please take it out for a drive?"

"Sure, sometime I'd like to do that."

"No, Amy, *now*. I'd like you to drive it now."

"Now?"

I nodded.

Shaking his head in disbelief, Clyde said, "Amy, let's go. I'll go with you."

Only as I watched them drive out of the driveway did I begin to appreciate the comical side of the situation I had created. Amy and I had managed to spend most of Saturday night in the garage of all places. It was now close to midnight, and she and Clyde were out on back country roads having a joy ride at my request. The whole thing seemed ridiculous and yet, at the same time, necessary. Clyde was very good at making me see the funny side of my behavior, and I knew he would have a grand time with this one. I almost looked forward to it.

Anticipating such a conversation, I decided to get out some cheese and crackers and peanuts while I awaited their return. I had barely done so when the car came back down the driveway. I could overhear their conversation as they got out of the car, shut the garage door, and came into the house. Clyde was saying, "It's a great car, isn't it? I mean, it really surprised me. In many ways, it handles better than the BMW."

Amy was in complete agreement, "You know, you're right. It doesn't feel at all boring when you're behind the wheel. I really enjoyed driving it. I understand Pam's dilemma, but this is all pretty crazy, don't you think? I mean, why does she have to make this decision tonight?"

By then, they were in the house and had noticed the food. Clyde did not disappoint me. "So, that was fun. What else have you got planned for our entertainment tonight? I must say, you throw an unusual party! Even the music is a surprise!" He made me laugh, and it felt good. Seeing he had struck a positive chord, Clyde continued, "You're really in an unfortunate position. You've got two fantastic cars. What a terrible problem. What I suggest is that you give both of them away and start over. I mean, you've also got two mopeds. You probably don't need a car, anyway. When a client comes to town, just lend him a helmet and you'll be all set. Just think of the money you'll save on gas. You want a new image; that should do it!" And that ended our discussion of cars for the night.

When Barbara got home from her movie, she walked in to find the three of us enjoying our wine and beer, our music and our talk. She looked puzzled at first, as well she might. Only hours before, she had left Clyde asleep and me totally noncommunicative in an emotional heap on the porch. The movie she had seen was a sad one, and she was unable to cross the bridge into our Saturday night festivities. Excusing herself, she went to bed.

Barbara's good-night triggered awareness of the time. Amy left shortly thereafter, leaving Clyde and me alone. Not wanting to break the happiness of the moment, we stayed away from heavy subjects, talking instead of great tennis matches, favorite musicians, and childhood Christmases. The evening ended on a happy note. My mind comfortably blank, I enjoyed a long night's sleep, not waking until the children returned late the next morning.

Part III

THE THIRD WEEK THROUGH THE THIRD MONTH

Bold, Brave, and Half-Crazy

9

Full Speed Ahead

Sunday morning was overcast. It was the kind of Sunday that suits long lazy hours and casual conversation, intermingled with occasional glances at the voluminous Sunday paper.

I tried, oh, how I tried, but I could not enjoy the paper. The magazine section didn't hold my interest; the crossword puzzle seemed to be impossibly difficult and not worth the effort. The travel and leisure section failed to stimulate flights of imagination. Even the book reviews could not grab my attention. Turning to the business and finance section as a last resort, I tried to force myself to study, to learn. But I remained uninterested.

Restless, I threw the paper aside and began pacing the floor. Now and again, Clyde and Barbara looked up from the paper and frowned. My pacing was disrupting their peace; their ability to relax was frustrating to me.

Giving up on them, I sought out Monica and Melissa. "Monica, do you want to take a walk?"

"No thanks, Mom. Not right now."

"Melissa, how about a game of Candy Land?"

"Maybe later, Mommy. I'm playing dolls right now. And Jenny's coming over to play soon. Okay?"

"Sure. Okay."

I tried the newspaper again, but to no avail. I had to *do* something. If I couldn't enjoy my Sunday, then at least I needed to make it count. I began to think about all the loose ends that required attention. My mind became a high-speed printer, reeling out list after list of "must dos." Paint the family room, repair and paint the back deck, finish the business management book that was already well past the publisher's deadline, repaint the cellar floor, finish weeding the gardens, get my tennis racket restrung, get the *h* key on my typewriter fixed, answer the seemingly hundreds of condolence letters that had arrived, apply a sealer to the newly paved driveway, cut the grass, fertilize the grass, shorten or lengthen or otherwise repair the enormous pile of things in my "to be sewn closet," split wood so that it is sufficiently dried out by winter, clip the dead blossoms off the bushes around the yard, get Pete's window fixed, write a letter to my parents, repair the towel rack in the children's bathroom that broke when Melissa tried to use it as a trapeze . . . and on, and on, and on.

I was hooked again, hooked by my compulsive need for organization and my inability to relax. The overcast day echoed my mood. I felt I had only one of two choices: to sink into despair or to structure my day so tightly that I had no time to feel or to dwell on life's unfairness. Only slightly aware that I was losing control even as I sought to impose a tight structure, I began to actually resent Clyde and Barbara for relaxing. And Pete was still asleep; that became nothing short of offensive. And the children; how could they be so casual about everything?

I yelled at Monica to empty the kitchen garbage, and gave Clyde and Barbara several dirty looks, as if to say, "Get with it, jerks. You're supposedly here to help me. Are you blind? Can't you see that this place is falling down around us?" Clyde had always been extremely perceptive, able to sense people's attitudes and moods even if unaccompanied by dirty looks. I'm certain he sensed that I was extremely out of sorts, for he soon left his chair and his paper and simply disappeared. Barbara announced that she was going out for a walk. The children, too, seemed to avoid my company. Their avoidance only fueled my anger.

I decided to talk openly to Clyde, only to discover that he had gone back to bed for an afternoon nap. That did it. It was up to me alone to keep this universe spinning. If I stopped, the world would surely stop. Then they would all be sorry. In dire need of a plan of action, I was totally incapable of formulating one. It would soon be

Monday, and the office would impose its own list of "must dos." The household problems had to be managed during the weekends; each day had to count. I felt abused, and deprived, and overworked, even though all I had done was sit around for hours and contemplate the work that had to be done.

Feeling almost dizzy, I wished that Dr. Wilson had given me a tranquilizer. I thought that perhaps Bill still had some Valium left; after all, it had been a standard part of his medication before his latest hospitalization. I wanted to calm down and gain enough perspective to be able to determine which of the "must dos" to tackle first.

If I had been more rational, I would have appreciated that there was no urgency involved. But rationality was not my long suit at the time; panic seemed to be more characteristic of my being. I needed help.

There was one tiny white pill remaining in a prescription vial marked "William Miller; 30 Valium: 2 mg." I was only mildly afraid of these little pills; Bill had occasionally given me half a pill when we were facing a particularly stressful situation. Well, I was certainly feeling stress now, and impetuously popped the entire pill into my mouth. "Okay, pill, do your thing." I felt like I was cheating; after all, I had gone through the two weeks since Bill's death without the help of the little white pills. But somehow the tension I was now experiencing was more difficult to tolerate. There had been a momentum about that first week, and a drama even about my return to the office. Now it was back to life as usual, but all the zest was gone, and only the chores remained. There was no drama, only work; there was no opportunity for courage or heroism, only tedium and perseverance.

Shutting my bedroom door and sitting upright in the chair, I waited for the magic to work. It did not take long. Within a half hour of self-pitying thought, I felt an uncontrollable need to sleep. I didn't want to sleep; after all, that would make me no better than the others who seemed content to waste the day. But I couldn't help it. I lay down, and by the time Melissa awoke me with a request to repair her broken doll, I felt considerably better.

"Okay, Melissa. Just give me a chance to wash my face."

She followed me into the bathroom, watching my every action. Seeing her image in the mirror, I smiled. Her eyes wide, Melissa was holding the doll by its hair with one hand. In the other, she clutched the doll's unattached leg. She brought things back into focus. My priorities were clear. Her happiness and Monica's were all that really mattered.

Melissa sat with me on my bed as I repaired her doll. It was easy to do, but Melissa thought I was very clever for making it right. Her adoration bolstered my spirits, and I began thinking of doing something special for the family for dinner. I wanted to make up for the hostility I had felt earlier in the day, and to show in some way that I cared.

Much to my surprise, Barbara and Clyde were already busy preparing dinner. Barbara was making spaghetti and Clyde was preparing a salad. Both smiled when they saw me and said nothing. Handing me a glass of wine, Clyde directed me to sit down at the kitchen table and relax. I happily did exactly as I was told. We were caring for one another, working together to build a loving environment.

Dinner that night was an extremely pleasant experience, in spite of the fact that few families would have enjoyed a hot spaghetti dinner on a hot summer evening. To set the stage, we briefly ignored the need for energy conservation and turned the air-conditioners on high. The red wine flowed freely. Monica had a long-overdue opportunity to share with us her excitement over the swim team's successes.

"I think we'll do really well in the counties, Mom. I mean, we're beating clubs we thought would whomp us. My backstroke is still lousy, but my butterfly is coming along great. I think I'll be swimming butterfly in the counties. Can you come, Mom? It's in two weeks."

"Sure, Monica. I wouldn't miss it for the world."

"I thought maybe you would have to be out of town or something."

"I'll make it a point to be there, Monica, at least for your events."

Impatient that Monica was getting all of my attention, Melissa chimed in, "Mommy, I jumped into the deep end of the pool yesterday and I wasn't even scared."

"You did what? Oh, Melissa. That scares me; I mean, you're so little to be in the deep end."

My alarm pleased her tremendously, as I knew it would. I was not actually concerned, knowing that her swim instructor was close by as she ventured into the deeper waters.

"Oh, you don't have to worry about me, Mommy. I can swim all the way across the pool."

"Maybe you can be on the swim team like Monica, Melissa."

"Yeah. Maybe next summer."

Monica, enjoying her older-sister role, encouraged her. "Oh, you should do it, Mel. Lots of little kids are on the team. I bet you could even join this summer. Then we could go to the meets together."

"No, Mon. I don't want to have to go to practice every day the way you do."

"You're crazy. Practice is fun. Well, I mean, practice is no fun, but we have a lot of fun after practice. And you could stand to lose a few pounds, you know."

"Are you saying I'm fat, Monica? I'm not fat, am I, Mommy?"

"No, Melissa, you're not fat. You didn't mean that, did you, Monica?"

"Chubby, that's what she is. She's chubby."

Melissa began to cry, unable to take any criticism from the sister she so idolized.

Pete tried to console her. "You're not chubby, either, Missy. You're cute, that's all, really cute. Isn't she, Monica?"

"Yeah, she's cute. She gets upset at the dumbest things."

Melissa, having found an ally in Pete, stuck her tongue out at Monica. Monica laughed; Melissa giggled and the crisis passed.

I thought to myself how sad it was that Bill was not with us at the dinner table. Barbara seemed to be sharing my sadness and said little besides, "I've got to be thinking about getting back home. I promised to paint two houses before the summer is out, and at this rate, I'll run out of time. I'm already out of money. Come on, Monica, let's get the dishes done."

Pete also excused himself from the table, and Melissa went off to play with her dolls. Clyde suggested that we sit and talk awhile over coffee.

"I was looking at the back deck yesterday," he began, "and I noticed that several of the boards are rotting and ought to be replaced. If you have no objection, I'll start on that tomorrow morning."

"I hadn't noticed that yet, Clyde."

"Well, you sure must have noticed a lot of other things. You were going a mile a minute earlier today. You've got to learn to relax. You've never been very good at that."

"Yeah, well, I think I'll be able to begin to relax when I feel that things are under control, when the list of 'to dos' is not quite as long."

"Like what? What is on your list?"

"Well, there is one big job. I want to paint the kitchen, the family room, and the front foyer."

"Pam, that is an incredible job. I mean, those cathedral ceilings are really difficult."

"I know it is a difficult job, but everything else in the house has been painted. Once these rooms are done, I can relax at least about the painting for a few years. I guess I would just feel better if things like that were all done before I find myself alone in this house with just the kids. But, Clyde, don't misunderstand me. I don't expect you to do the painting. I plan to hire professional painters."

"As long as I'm here, I'll do what I can, but I'll be honest with you: that is a bigger job than I had anticipated."

"Oh, there are a lot of other things you can do to help me. For one thing, you can help me seal the driveway."

"And I suppose you feel that that is urgent, too. You're really too much. Look, the driveway should not be done until fall. You've just had it repaved and it needs three months to settle."

I simply shrugged my shoulders.

"Pam, try not to get crazy again. Remember how you reacted when Bill had his first heart attack? Suddenly chores that had gone undone for months became points of real stress for you. The lists never disappear, particularly in a house of this size. It's only your attitude that changes. You'll make yourself crazy, and me along with you, if you keep this up. We'll get it all done, okay? But let's keep the panic volume low. Trust me; I'm with you, and behind you. I will not leave you until things are, in your terms, 'under control.' Now, can we please get off the subject?"

"Yes, Clyde. The subject is closed."

Grabbing one of the local papers that had been lying around most of the week, I began to scan the classified pages for painting services. One advertisement appealed. Two college boys were painting homes during the summer in order to make tuition money. I called them immediately and arranged for them to come and give an estimate the very next evening. I was quite literally unable to relax.

Walking around the house, trying to decide what to do with myself, my eyes fell upon the unanswered condolence letters stacked on the desk in the family room. In the beginning, I had responded to the notes as they arrived. But then it had become more difficult, as I found myself saying the same things over and over and getting impatient with what I regarded as unfeeling, rote responses.

I decided to try to respond to the letters that were easiest to answer, those that gave me a specific message and revealed something personal about the writer. But the majority of cards were from the Heart Association telling me that someone had made a donation. They were more difficult to acknowledge in a note, not because they were less meaningful or important but because they did not provide me with a focus for my response. They required that I reveal something of myself or of Bill. "Your gift reminded me that you care, and that helps" or perhaps, "Your gift helped do what Bill would have most wanted, to have his death trigger something good, something positive for others."

One donation had to be recognized. My former in-laws had made a contribution in Bill's memory. The senior Sandersons had never met Bill, never actually met the man who so significantly influenced the behavior and the values of their grandchildren. They had probably worried when I married Bill. There was always the chance that his role as "Daddy Bill" might undermine the affection the children felt for Jim, their natural father. Not knowing Bill, they could take no comfort in the knowledge that Bill believed that love is infinite, not finite. For the children to love him simply required that they love more; there was no need to recarve the love pie and give Jim a smaller piece so that Bill could have his share. On the contrary, Bill had encouraged Monica and Melissa to learn from and to model themselves after both the best in him and the best in Jim.

Thoughts of family life in the abstract took on a here-and-now reality as Melissa came to me sleepy-eyed and suggested that it was time for her to go to bed. I was really ashamed of myself. The child was filthy. Her hair was badly in need of washing, and her hands and face were grimmy. Picking her up, I hugged her and said that I was going to give her a bath before putting her to bed. She reached up and touched her hair, and I nodded.

"No, I want to do it in the morning."

When I refused, reminding her that I had to get up and go to work, she started crying. The pattern was typical, and I decided not to be dissuaded. The hair wash proceeded with only the usual cries of anguish, and, as usual, she was pleased with her shiny clean head when it was over.

The effort of washing Melissa's hair temporarily brought the emotional reality of Bill's death back home to me. Bending over the tub, my heart began to physically ache. Melissa looked so tiny and vulnerable sitting naked in the tub. Her wet hair accentuated her still babylike features. She and Monica were so innocent, so vulnerable. Me too, I thought. I'm older, and I'm their mother, but I feel like a baby inside. It was all I could do to stop my tears from flowing. But stop them I did, determined to act like a bold and brave grown-up person.

I put Melissa to bed. Then, remembering that I had mothered only one of my children, I went in search of Monica. I found her nestled in front of the television. Seeing me, she immediately suggested that we play a game of pool. The invitation came as a real blow. She had never before asked me to play the game with her; that had been a territory she shared with Bill. Slipping back into my shell, I suggested that I still had a lot to do, and that she should ask Barbara, Pete, or Clyde to play. She said the magic words. "Mom, you *always* have a lot to do. I want to play with *you!*"

I could not refuse. "Okay, Monica, you got it."

Monica was a solid little pool player, and I was slowly drawn into the game, leaving my preoccupations behind. Monica seemed to sense that I was beginning to honestly enjoy myself, for she encouraged me as a parent might encourage a child.

"Hey, Mom, you're not bad. Really, a little practice and you could be good."

"Sure. Then how come you're beating me?"

Then Monica brought up a question that had obviously been troubling her. "Mom, can I still have my slumber party this year?"

For the past three years, Monica had chosen to celebrate her birthday by throwing a disco-slumber party. Ten to fifteen little girls would gather in the playroom. Bill had always served as the master of ceremonies. He, Amy, and I judged the dance contests. It took all three of us to keep things moving. Pizza had to be picked up and served, and then there was the cake. Always a showman, Bill was not content with a simple verbal rendition of "Happy Birthday." While I served the cake, he sang and played the ukulele. According to Monica, her birthday party had come to be regarded by the regular attendees as one of the highlights of the summer. The show had to go on, death or no death. "Sure, Monica, go ahead and invite the kids."

Monica went to bed looking forward to her party. She had, however, triggered so many thoughts in me that I chose not to go to bed, but to stay in the playroom contemplating other family traditions. The pictures on the wall hurt me deeply, and yet I was drawn to them. Many were recent, taken within the last year. Bill looked so healthy and vibrant in them. His death seemed so unreal at that moment. I could not fathom that his body was no more, that I would *never* see him again. I tried to understand the word "never," but I could not. My mind could not grasp its significance. My heart began to ache again.

Photographs taken at an amusement park caught my eye. One of our traditions had been to take the children there every other summer. We had planned to go this summer. Bill and I had even discussed it as he lay in his hospital bed. I could not imagine going there without him. I shuddered at the thought of being unilaterally responsible for the logistics of the day and anticipated the loneliness I would feel. But, like Monica's slumber party, the tradition was important. I had to at least try.

Lying in bed that night, I thought about my day and realized that I had experienced almost every emotion, and suffered through mood swings that land some folks in institutions. I knew that my emotional health was fragile. My periodic exhaustion was a warning that my physical health was slipping. Slumber parties, trips to amusement parks, and pool games required that I stay healthy. The old saying among overworked mothers is that they aren't even allowed to get sick. Well, that saying applied doubly to me, or so I felt.

I needed my sleep. Throwing the bed pillows on the floor, I lay on my stomach in the middle of the bed and spread out my arms in an eaglelike fashion. I was challenging myself to fall asleep. It was crazy. The more determined I became, the less sleepy I felt. Eventually I got up, had a glass of milk and a cigarette, brushed my teeth again, put the pillows back on the bed, returned to my half of the bed, and huddled up in a fetallike position. Sleep finally came, but in its own time and at its own speed. Even I couldn't control that.

Monday morning dawned all too soon. Today, for the first time since Bill's death, I would have to pick up my pencil and address the various projects that were in process. Deadlines were approaching, and it had been a frighteningly long time since I had had a day that would generate an invoice. The financial legs of the firm were shaky. If we were to regain our fiscal health, I would have to work on revenue-producing projects each and every day for a long time to come. To spend any more time plotting strategy or reorganizing systems would have been a fool's game; unless we got back to the business at hand, there would soon be no firm to reorganize.

I spent the morning writing and planning a team development workshop that was to be conducted the first week in September. This was already the middle of July. The text had to be at the printer no later than the first week of August. The challenge appealed to me, and I was scarcely aware of time passing. Using all my mental energies, I was again able to put my emotions in the deep freeze.

Even during lunch with Meg, I insisted on maintaining a business focus. I think that displeased Meg, although she accepted my behavior and said nothing. She was understanding enough to let me live through my experience without taking personally my occasional abruptness and abrasiveness. She was also wise enough to know that she did not fully comprehend either the depth of my feelings or the defense mechanisms I had to apply to stay at least semisane. She was giving me time.

That afternoon, I received two calls, both of which encouraged me to push myself even harder. One was from Larry Waverly. Even as I accepted his call, I experienced a mix of anticipation and nervousness that made it difficult for me to say more than a few words.

Larry said little of a personal nature. His concerns this time were focused on business. I think my budding romantic interest might have waned at this point had he not closed with a request that I come to Chicago to see him. While the request was entirely appropriate, given our mutual business interests, his tone convinced my willing ears that his interest was at least equally personal.

I made no specific commitment to actually go see him, promising only to do my part on our projects and to keep him informed of my progress. I did promise to call when one of my Chicago accounts scheduled a trip for me.

Larry's call completely broke my focus. I had to admit to myself that I was attracted to him. At first, I tried to deny my interest—it was too soon, ridiculously soon. But I could not kid myself and finally decided to accept it as a healthy sign that someday I'd be able to develop a relationship with another man. In a way it was nice to be reminded that my feminine instincts weren't totally dead.

So I allowed myself to think about Larry. After all, I *enjoyed* thinking about him, and found myself building fantasies around him whenever I grew tired of the sad or tedious thoughts that otherwise filled my mind.

The second call was to make it possible for me to actually see Larry sooner than I had expected. It was from an important client, who, coincidentally, was also based in Chicago.

The client was calling to see how we were progressing on several projects and, more important, to urge me to put in an appearance at their Chicago office. He thought it would be a good idea for me to show people in his organization that I was carrying on. The client was right. In our business, it is critical to inspire and maintain trust and confidence. Further, our concern had to be *their* needs and their frustrations, not our own. It was necessary to destroy as soon as possible the not unrealistic assumption that I, as a very recent widow, required that others give *me* constant help and support. I agreed to come to Chicago early the following week. Not wanting to stumble over my words, I asked Michelle to call Larry and inform him of my plans.

The decision made, I felt a strange sense of excitement. For the first time in weeks, I found myself thinking about my appearance. I knew that I didn't look good. I was horribly pale for the middle of July, and my hair was shabby in both length and color. The streaks had not been attended to for months. Split ends were abundantly obvious, at least to me. I was determined to find the time later in the week to spend the necessary three hours in the beauty parlor, and to get some sun during the weekend.

Before I had a chance to call for an appointment, Monica called me. As coincidence would have it, she happened to mention during the course of our conversation that her hair had got so long that the swim coach was now forcing her to wear a bathing cap. She was finally willing to take the big step and cut her long hair.

A budding adolescent, Monica was especially proud of her hair, washing and blowing it dry with painful care each and every morning. I knew it had been difficult for her to decide to cut it and asked if she would like to make it a special day and join me at my beauty parlor. She was delighted with the idea.

After making appointments for both of us, I returned to my writing with some enthusiasm. I got so involved in my work that I scarcely noticed five o'clock come and go. By the time I left the office, it was close to six, and I felt good. I was truly back at work. I had not only had a revenue-producing day but a creative one. I felt like a functioning person, happily unaware that my demands on myself and on others were so excessive as to be half crazy.

I had totally forgotten that the painters were due at five-thirty to give me an estimate. Fortunately they were late, arriving at the house just as I did. I was not at all sorry to see the momentum continue. Things seemed to be progressing nicely in both of my worlds.

The painters' estimate jarred me a little. It was close to $1,500, more than double the price I had anticipated and felt I could afford. Much to Clyde's horror, I accepted their offer and urged them to get started as soon as possible. My underlying panic still prevailing, I was more concerned with getting the job done than with getting a fair price, or even a price that I could afford.

Clyde could not contain himself after the painters left. "Pam, you're crazy. The job isn't worth that much. You didn't even bother to get a second estimate. I thought you said money would be tight for a while!"

"I know, Clyde, but I trusted those guys, and anyway, I think other estimates would be just as high, if not higher. I mean, those two are college boys; they're not even charging union rates!"

Clyde abruptly dropped the subject and left the room. I thought he had simply given up out of sheer exasperation. I was wrong. Several hours later, Clyde told me that he had studied the job and would take it on for $400 plus the cost of the paint.

I was concerned and relieved at the same time. My sense of relief stemmed not only from the savings involved but also from the confidence I had in Clyde's abilities. My concern lay in the thought that he might be doing me a favor that he didn't really want to do. I wanted his time with me to be a positive experience for him, hoping that if it was, he would prolong his stay.

"Clyde, obviously I'm delighted with your offer. But I've got to be honest with you. I'm afraid that you'll start to resent me if you feel you're getting stuck with something."

"I thought we were past that, Pam. I mean, that's the way we operate, right? If I didn't want the job, I wouldn't have offered. It's as simple as that. Look, you know I enjoy painting, and, to be honest with you, I need the money."

"Okay then, you've got it, Clyde."

"Pam, there's something else I want to say. I feel very comfortable here. I've even begun to regard the place as home. And I'm proud of it, too. It's a great house. I'm looking forward to asking some friends over to show it off. I wouldn't want to trust *our* ceilings to anyone else!"

I reacted to Clyde's statement as does a lover when the loved one first openly declares his affection. For the moment at least, I felt neither alone nor panicked, and spent the evening enjoying what I believed were the results of my determined efforts to make my life work. Lying in bed that night, I did not search for the shadows on the ceiling. Believing that I was master of my own fate, I was content to rely on myself.

The ensuing days presented one challenge after another to my belief in my ability to cope with my life. The telephone became my adversary, as friends questioned the wisdom of my immediate return to work and forcefully suggested that I should join them for long lunches or shopping trips. Repeatedly, I said no, and worried lest I offended them. "Just let me work," I thought, "just let me work."

Accepting as few calls as conscience would allow, I kept on working. Even in the evenings, I hid in work, hoping to complete my book in time to submit it to my Chicago-based publisher the following Tuesday.

Overworked and emotionally numb, I found it hard to sleep. The shadows had deserted me. No wonder, I told myself. I had made an almost conscious decision to blunt my feelings and to become an extraordinarily task-efficient workman. In his life, Bill had intensely disliked my periodic withdrawal into my innumerable projects. He had recognized that behavior for what it was: an unwillingness or inability to cope with the emotions that were stirring inside me. When I got like that, and I had before, there was little or nothing he could do to make me emotionally available to him. It is no wonder, then, that his shadows were absent now. In life, he had not been able to break down the barriers I periodically erected. In death, it seemed he was unwilling to even try.

By Thursday evening, my regimens and emotional/intellectual balancing act had taken their toll. A bundle of nerves, I was totally unprepared for the influx of Barbara's brothers, who were due that evening for dinner and talk before driving her home.

Fortunately, by the time I got home from the office, Barbara already had dinner well under control. Even the table had been set, freeing me to lie down for an hour or so. By the time her brothers arrived, I felt like having a family party. The evening was fun, at least until it was necessary to say good-bye. It was hard to see Barbara go. She had imposed nothing on me and had given so much. She had introduced a measure of fun into each of the children's days, and order and moral support into mine. We had shared a special time, and I wanted her to remember it. Without a second thought, I suggested that Barbara take Bill's ten-speed bicycle.

Barbara reacted as though I had offered her my life, and accepted the bike with a strange blend of solemnity, ceremony, and childlike glee. "Pam, no matter where I go, I'll always keep this bicycle. I remember helping Bill pick it out. I can't believe it. You couldn't have given me anything that would make me happier. I love you. I'll keep in touch."

The house seemed strangely quiet after Barbara left. She was a very quiet person, and yet her presence had been felt by all of us. There seemed to be a significant difference between five people in the household and six. Six constituted a perpetually busy group; five represented a small family. I thought about what an odd family we were, Clyde, Pete, Monica, Melissa, and I. It amused me slightly to think that I was clearly the senior citizen, the boss, the leader, the breadwinner, the primary decision maker. At the time, the idea of filling all those roles did not particularly frighten me. It seemed odd; that's all, just odd.

The evening with the family had made me more human, more feeling, more available than I had allowed myself to be all week. That night, as I went to bed, I eagerly looked for the shadows, wanting to think about Bill and to feel his presence. It was not guidance that I sought, but a reminder of what it felt like to love and to be loved. I was not disappointed; the shadows were there, though indistinct. Lying on my back, I believe I spoke out loud. "I loved you, Bill. I truly loved you. And I miss you, but I think I'm going to be all right." The shadows did not answer, but then, I had not asked a question.

Friday was "make-over" day, and Monica and I were at the beauty parlor by nine-thirty. The mood of the place was, as always, vibrant and noisy. A party atmosphere prevailed as the stereo blasted and the hair stylists danced around their customers' chairs. His expressions of sorrow quickly out of the way, Jerry, my regular hairdresser, tried to make me comfortable by treating me no differently than he did his other customers. Songs and jokes prevailed. As he moved from one side of my chair to the other, he strutted in time to the disco music. Now and again, he backed two or three feet away from my chair to give free rein to his dancing feet.

By the time he had finished with me some three hours later, I felt like a different person. He had taken three inches off my hair, leaving it still long, but buoyant. The streaks he applied were perfect; the sun couldn't have done a better or more natural job. His associate took equal pains with Monica, and even she was pleased with the result. When we left, we both felt like we were among the most beautiful of God's creatures. The beauty parlor was a fantasy world, and we had become part of the fantasy.

Unhappily, fantasies fade, and when they are gone, reality seems especially harsh. My fantasy broke apart as the hostess showed us to our table in the restaurant. Overcome with sudden nausea, I didn't want to eat, and I didn't want to make conversation. I had an almost overwhelming desire to sleep, and to cry. Who did I think I was, anyway? Who was I trying to impress? Somehow the very act of having my hair done seemed to be a travesty, a mockery of the depth of my love for Bill and, therefore, of the depth of my loss. I felt guilty and over my head. I had no business running around like this. Only carefree women looking forward to their weekend social life go to the beauty parlor on Friday morning. I was certainly not carefree, and I looked forward to nothing.

I was glad Jackie, both friend and wife of Joel, our attorney, and her daughter were meeting us for lunch. Her comments saved me from falling into a state of remorse and self-pity. "What an improvement. You're beginning to look like yourself again." Her words were perfectly chosen. If she had said, "Wow! You look gorgeous!" my uncertainty would have escalated. To hear that my indulgence had simply begun to re-create the real me somehow made it all right, acceptable, necessary.

While the others studied the menu, I gave myself a lecture. "After all, you dummy, you should try to look your best. You've already decided not to wear widow's black. You're rebuilding your life, remember, and putting your appearance back together is certainly one of the important building blocks."

By the time our meal arrived, I no longer felt guilty about having spent the morning at the beauty parlor. Nonetheless, the morning still had an unreal quality about it, as did our luncheon. I felt like a player on a stage. Part of me was standing outside myself watching the other part of me perform. Someone stared in our direction, and certain that my widowhood showed, I immediately assumed they were staring at me. I was delighted when our luncheon ended and I could return to the safety of Bill's BMW.

I halfway considered going into the office for a few hours. Monica protested and suggested that we go shopping for a new bathing suit for her. Another public place, I thought, but I agreed to do as she wished. After all, I had planned for this to be a special day for Monica, and the day was only half over.

We went to Monica's favorite department store and spent a long while in the young junior's department. She found not only a bathing suit, but several T-shirts, a skirt, and some shorts. Then she suggested that we go look in the ladies' department. "Mom, what you need is a pair of designer jeans. I know you'll love them. And, your Levi's look awful. Come on."

Feeling confused and unhappy, I reluctantly followed Monica. Thoughts popped into my head randomly, leaving me without a clear idea of what I should and should not do. "I need a new image." "What would people say if they knew you were out looking for tight jeans so soon after Bill's death!" "It's time to begin enjoying life." "It's Monica's day; if she wants to shop, then shop." "You're out of your mind." "You're coping extremely well."

Neither my conscience, my mind, nor my heart would provide

me with a clear sense of direction. I let Monica prevail. She supervised the purchase of not only jeans, but of what she defined as the "critical accessories": a silk blouse, new shoes, and a gold belt.

I did not get a chance to contemplate my day and try to understand my reactions until I was in bed that night. Alone in the dark, without the help of the shadows, I thought about how I had spent the day. During Bill's healthy years, such a day would have brought much pleasure. But I had not enjoyed the day. I had only gone through the motions. I was still grieving all right, but I had turned my grief inward, making it a very private thing. My tears now flowed only in the privacy of my bedroom. Even then, I cried softly, for the guest room adjoined mine, and I did not want Clyde to hear.

My decision to grieve privately had not been a conscious one. It simply happened because of the kind of person I am. And yet I think it helped me. Seeing only the stronger side of me, others began to expect strength and, because of their expectations, to reinforce me in my efforts to openly master my life and my environment. Had I invited others to grieve along with me for a prolonged period of time, they might have expected and therefore encouraged my self-pity. Pretending to be strong, my self-confidence grew.

And so by the time that Tuesday arrived, I felt ready to go to Chicago and convince people in that critical client organization that I was fully functioning and ready to go back to work with a vengeance. My day began with an early lunch with Greg Jenkins, my publisher. I proudly handed him the completed manuscript; he seemed both pleased and amazed. He applauded my courage and my stamina, and thereby bolstered my confidence.

Still, I had a tough time getting through lunch. I had ordered a glass of Chablis and found that my right hand was shaking so much that I couldn't pick up the wine without embarrassment. Nor could I hold a cigarette still long enough to accept Greg's offer of a light. Predominantly a right-hander, I did not even consider trying to perform those functions with my left hand. I did not understand where the shakiness was coming from. I certainly wasn't nervous about the luncheon. There was really nothing to gain or to lose by my conversation with Greg.

Little did I know that I had just begun to experience a symptom that was to plague me for months to come, being most severe in restaurants. Perhaps that is because the attack from which Bill was never to recover occurred during dinner with a client. Restaurants were therefore fraught with tension for me. When the tension was compounded by my widow's fear of public places, the symptom emerged. It was to become uncontrollable.

Insight into the source of my symptom was to come while I was having dinner in a restaurant in Boston several months after my lunch with Greg. Suddenly over the loudspeaker would come a cry for medical help. I would try to ignore the call, a call so similar to the one that had rung out the night Bill was in trouble. But I would not be able to ignore it. In spite of my fear, I was to run up to the hostess and tell her that I was an expert at applying coronary pulmonary resuscitation and would help if I could. She was to inform me that the diner had suffered an asthma attack, had gotten medical attention, and was going to be all right. Only after that episode would the shakiness subside. Perhaps the summons in the Boston restaurant finally forced me to relive the night Bill began to die, and to stop blocking out both the memories and the fear of that night.

But lacking this understanding, I was only puzzled by the sudden emergence of the symptom during lunch with Greg. Hoping that it would not plague me throughout the afternoon, I decided not to risk even asking for a cup of coffee while with the client.

The moment had come, and I excused myself, leaving time only to make the five-minute walk to the client's office. I breathed deeply as I walked, trying to summon every ounce of courage I could. Even so, as I entered the building, I panicked. Leaving again, I walked around the block. Finally, I managed to enter the elevator and push the appropriate button.

Putting as authentic a smile on my face as I could, I nodded at the receptionists and walked directly back to the executive offices. I planned to start at the top. Fortunately June, the president's secretary, was at her desk. I had shared many luncheons and after-five cocktails with her, and did not feel the need to feign false courage. Sitting down, I lit a cigarette, my hand shaking only slightly, and shared with her my plan for the afternoon. She confirmed that her boss was in and added that while he was currently busy with several of the vice-presidents, he should break within the next ten minutes. As fortune, or misfortune, would have it, I would be able to greet most of the key people at one time. As

June rambled on, I thought to myself how bizarre was the whole situation. Part of me was stepping back and watching the other part of me perform.

I was far from an integrated, put-together person when the door to the president's office opened, and out he strolled with four of the vice-presidents. He noticed me immediately but chose to pretend that he had not. Turning his body slightly so as to avoid looking directly at me, he continued talking to the assembled group. I believe he was buying time. Finally, he turned and put a look of surprise on his face. "Why, Pam! What a pleasant surprise! What brings you to Chicago? You're looking well."

He avoided all reference to Bill's death. That meant trouble. It indicated to me that an emotional barrier, and a social barrier, existed. I could not function in my capacity as consultant to that organization if there were barriers to open communication, to interpersonal comfort and trust. The barrier had to come down.

Taking a deep breath, I walked directly up to the president and positioned myself so that it became impossible for him to avoid direct eye contact. I said, "I came today to let you know that I am eager to resume our work here. I am confident that we can do it and hope that you share my confidence. I miss Bill terribly, as I'm sure you do. Somehow his death makes me even more anxious to complete the work that he began."

After a few moments of uncomfortable silence, the president began to speak. Still looking me in the eye, he said, "The work you and Bill have been doing here is important. I am confident that by working together, we'll be able to keep it going. I am happy to see you looking so well and am glad that you came here today." With that, he walked away, but not before I noticed that his eyes were beginning to tear.

With the barriers somewhat diminished and the discomfort eased, the vice-presidents came toward me. One of them made a comment that gave me just the boost I needed. "Pam, I think you deserve a lot of credit for pulling yourself together so quickly. Bill often told me how important you are to the firm and I, personally, have not a shadow of a doubt that you can handle the work. This organization needs you."

The worst over, I proceeded to meander about the halls and various floors of the building. I had to remain perpetually alert, remembering the names of all the people with whom I had worked over the years. It was important to make each and every one of them comfortable with me again. Fortunately, given my waning energy, a lot of people were away on business trips, and I actually had to speak to only about twenty. It got easier and easier, as I began to develop a repertoire that was expansive enough to seem both flexible and spontaneous. "Hi. It's been a long time since I've seen you. How have things been going?" Then I would wait, and see if they voluntarily mentioned Bill's death. Most did, expressing their sorrow. A simple "thank you" from me was enough.

One very painful conversation occurred with an individual who was unaware of Bill's death. He actually asked about Bill's health. At first, I was unable to say anything at all. My tidy script fell apart. I wished I had never begun this charade of false courage. When I finally managed to blurt out the news, the unfortunate soul was, for a time, speechless. The apologies he finally offered seemed out of place; no words could ease our mutual discomfort.

By midafternoon, I could take no more and left, bound for the telephone and a warm reception from Larry Waverly, or so I hoped. I did not know what to expect but was certain that whatever happened, it would make me feel better. I had so convinced myself of his interest in me that I was completely unprepared for what actually happened. He did not even accept my call, having alerted his secretary to hold all calls for the remainder of the afternoon.

I was both puzzled and angered by Larry's odd behavior. At least he could have had the courtesy to tell me himself that he was busy! My anger persisted until I got to the airport. Sitting there, waiting for my flight, I began to make excuses for him, excuses that would explain his behavior while allowing me to keep my emergency fantasy intact. "He had a last-minute crisis." "His secretary forgot to put my visit on his calendar." "He didn't expect me to finish my work with the client so early in the day."

By the time I boarded the plane, I was exhausted emotionally as well as physically. I wanted to cry, to scream, to release the pressure that I felt inside. But I would not, could not. I closed my eyes and feigned sleep so that the man traveling next to me would not decide to begin a conversation. Our time in the air seemed interminably long.

Once at the airport, I decided to walk to the car instead of taking the airport bus. It was a long walk, a very long walk, but I did not think I could tolerate being in a crowded bus with more strangers who most certainly would notice my stress. Occasionally a tear fell in spite of all my efforts to stop it. When I finally saw my car, I felt as though I had found a haven in the middle of hell. Getting in and locking the doors, I put my head down on the steering wheel and let the tears come. I let the sobs come too, and then the screams. I couldn't stop. I didn't want to stop. I thought I might never stop.

But eventually I quieted down. In place of the pressure was a complete numbness that felt very much like peace. I was empty, but I had made it through the day.

As the numbness receded, I became aware of the parking lot, and of my isolation. It was dark and the night was scary. I had visions of someone breaking the windows and grabbing me by the throat. I started the car and took off, driving home in record-breaking time and thinking of nothing, feeling nothing, while I drove.

After kissing the children and listening to their tales of the day, I said good-night to Monica and suggested that Melissa and I climb into my big bed together and go to sleep at the same early hour.

It was not until twelve hours later that I awoke. The sleep had helped. The emptiness was gone, and with it, the numbness. Reflecting back on the day before, I felt extremely proud of myself. I had been bold and I had been brave.

Or so I thought. I had actually begun to believe that I was as I acted: bold, brave, utterly rational, and in full control. I had entered another phase, made hazardous by my lack of awareness of my own limitations and vulnerabilities.

10

Flying

Yes, I was becoming a unique and specially gifted person, or so I believed. My sensitivities were so finely honed by trauma that I believed myself to be unusually perceptive. And I was a quick study; so quick that I had already changed around most of the systems in the office, and they were working. The accountant said that he could already see signs of the return of financial health to the firm. Billings were at an all-time high. I was using subcontractors frequently, and using them well. I believed my innate ability to lead had emerged. Writing at twice the speed I had in the past, I had rectified the backlog in the office. And I had managed to set up routines in the household that worked so well the children seemed to be thriving.

I seemed to have an unlimited amount of energy, and thought nothing of playing a set or two of tennis after work with Clyde. As a result of the exercise and a tendency to avoid the food I cooked myself, I had lost weight and was thinner and trimmer than I had been in years. My skin had taken on a rosy tint that defied the stereotype of the widow's gray pallor. I did not feel happy, but I certainly did feel optimistic, special, and very much in control of things.

My confidence was further bolstered by Larry Waverly. He had apologized profusely for missing me the afternoon I was in Chicago. His subsequent calls were both frequent and friendly. While he never called with an entirely personal agenda, his discussion of business was always mixed with personal inquiries about me and the children. That any thoughtful, responsive person, whether male or female, would have done the same did not in the least weaken my conviction that Larry was interested in me.

I needed to believe that he was interested in and attracted to me. Such a belief allowed me to build a romantic fantasy, a space to which I could retreat from the starkness of being without a mate, alone. I had not been psychologically alone, uncoupled, since early adolescence. Now, rather than admit my essential aloneness, I created a fantasy mate.

Larry did not have to indicate an actual romantic interest in me for my fantasies to prevail. I never for an instant doubted that he could be attracted to me. I had wanted Jim, and Jim had immediately obliged. Then my heart had gone out to Bill, and again, I found that he returned my love.

Oh, I had been rejected once, but it had happened so long ago as to be only a distant memory, devoid of feeling and pain. I was thirteen years old, and in love with the best-looking boy on the block. He gave me his junior high school ring. I wore it proudly around my neck for two glorious weeks. Then, suddenly, he started paying attention to a redhead. He was a private-school boy, and she was a private-school girl. The two schools often held social events together. As a public-school girl, I was not part of these gatherings. Their interest in each other grew, and, before long, my true love asked for his ring and his pictures back. I was brokenhearted for about three days.

Rejection and unrequited love had not been a part of my adult life. I was attracted to Larry, and therefore, almost by definition, Larry would be attracted to me. I firmly believed that the fuel for my fantasy lay in mutuality of feeling. To me, that was an unchallengeable law of nature. I had a lot to learn about men, about relationships, and about rejection. But those painful lessons would come later.

But now, as my flight began, I needed the solace and comfort of a fantasy, a safe dream. That we enjoyed a business relationship provided sufficient excuse to talk with him often enough to keep my imaginary relationship alive. Geographical distance made it safe. Unknown to him, Larry was helping me to soar, to avoid the painful realities of aloneness that I was not yet ready to face.

I was equally successful at avoiding financial realities. One of the insurance checks had arrived, and, never having seen so much money at one time, I felt that I could spend and spend and still not put myself in economic jeopardy. Besides, I reasoned or rationalized as I bought one thing after another, I don't really *need* this money; after all, I am perfectly capable of making a good enough salary to support our standard of living.

It was in this frame of mind that I decided that the family should go ahead with the plans Bill and I had made to spend a week at one of the most expensive resorts on Cape Cod. I knew it would cost me a small fortune, easily several thousand dollars for six days of luxury, golf, tennis, boating, and great beaches. I felt like a grand dame as I urged Clyde to accompany us, assuring him that I had no compunctions about paying his way, since his presence was so critical to us, given the nature of the resort.

It was a family spot, or more precisely, a resort for wealthy families. They wouldn't allow just anyone to come. Bill and I had spent a weekend there the summer before and had sensed that our behavior was closely scrutinized. Apparently we had passed muster, for the hotel had put us on the waiting list for the cottage we wanted, claiming that they had to give first priority to their established guests. Presumably one of their established guests decided to become unestablished, for they let me know in the beginning of June that the cottage we had requested would be available.

Clyde agreed to do me the favor of escorting us for the week. He grinned as he agreed, saying that if all my requests were like that, he'd happily do each and every one of them. He was beginning to enjoy the things I could provide. It all seemed a bit outlandish to him, but he could offer no rational argument since he too was under the mistaken impression that I did indeed have a lot of money.

We spent hours anticipating the trip, and in the process convinced each other that we were interesting, exciting, and rather worldly people. Clyde did not discourage my soaring. On the contrary, he helped me remove the anchors.

And so it was that we headed into August with blind enthusiasm. My moments of despair became less frequent. I had found a way to stop them. Extraordinary busyness became an increasingly effective tranquilizer. I rarely sat down simply to think or to be. If I wasn't at the office, then I was working on the yard. When that failed to provide sufficient distraction, I would put the children into the car and go buy clothes, jewelry, exotic bath oils, and perfumes. I didn't have to search long for a rationalization; after all, I had been through a lot and I deserved to treat myself to small luxuries. Even when I began to question the wisdom of my ways, my friends would chime in and encourage more of the same behavior. "I'm glad to see you doing something for yourself. You deserve it. You work hard, you have a right to nice things."

I thought I was being efficient, effective, and mature. Actually, I was acting like a child, and in some ways, an irresponsible child, not even managing the insurance money well. For six weeks, the check sat hidden in a book in the bookcase. At one point, I couldn't recall where I had hidden it. The children had rearranged the books one afternoon, and the shifting of the titles confused me. The hunt for our fortune constituted a very funny evening, though we failed to see the humor of it at the time.

Monica's slumber party was scheduled for the first week of August. She and I spent many evenings the week before planning every detail. I approached it like a training design, with attention to the participants' minds as well as their feelings. There could be no consistent losers and, therefore, no consistent winners. Everyone had to feel good about something. The trickiest part of our plan centered around the placement of the fifteen sleeping bags.

Monica and her friends had reached the age when cliques prevailed. But they were not consistent in their membership. One week Laura was on the outs; the next week, Tracy was made to feel unloved and unwelcome. Much to her credit, Monica never encouraged the painful "we versus they" behavior among her friends. On more than one occasion I overheard her saying, "Leave me out of this. I'm not going to get in the middle. I don't know who is right and who is wrong. You've got to talk to her about this."

Highly sensitive to the feelings of others, and reluctant to favor any one or two persons by granting them the space of honor next to the birthday girl, Monica was distraught over the sleeping arrangements. Finally, we came up with a system for allotting floor space. We divided the playroom floor into sections by moving the furniture around. Each section was then divided into spaces. The girls would simply draw numbers from a hat and sleep in the space that corresponded to their number. Monica was finally content.

The party itself went without a flaw. Pete, Clyde, Amy, and I acted as the disco judges, eventually joining in ourselves. Amy was highly sensitive to the fact that I had grown very accustomed to running these parties with Bill and would most likely experience several painful moments as I had to repeat the tradition without him. While we never talked about it, she maintained a watchful eye, and never challenged my periodic disappearances from the scene of the festivities. She simply carried on, issuing soft directives to Pete and Clyde and keeping things moving.

Unknown to me, the girls did not go to sleep until close to five o'clock in the morning, and by then they simply began dropping where they stood. Bringing in doughnuts and juice the next morning, I found bodies scattered everywhere, with former adversaries sleeping side by side and the best of friends separated.

Amy's presence in the house was particularly critical to me the morning after the party. Fifteen mothers had come to collect their children. I did not know any of them very well. None had been in the house since Bill's death. The kitchen got crowded. I ran out of coffee, but still the mothers did not urge their children to hurry. Conversation was stilted and awkward. They were curious, curious about what it feels like inside a home that has suffered such a dramatic loss. And yet they were not familiar enough with me to ask the questions that were on their minds. I wish they had. It would have been so much easier than making casual conversation while their eyes darted from here to there and back again, as if they were trying to understand the dynamics of our family by studying the physical objects in our home.

It was well past noon when the last mother left. Amy left shortly thereafter. Monica came in and thanked me for a particularly successful party. I had done it, and done it well. I was glad about that, but even happier that it was over. It had taken its toll on me, and I had to force myself into action once again to avert the depression that I sensed lingered close by.

Finding a suitable distraction was not difficult. It took the better part of the afternoon to clean up the playroom. Still unable to sit and relax, I began hunting for things to sell in the tag sale that Amy and I had begun planning several weeks earlier.

Against the advice of John, the accountant, who sensed that my judgment was still shaky, I had decided to get rid of all presumably unnecessary possessions. Clutter troubled me, and I had begun to see it wherever I went. Things that had sat on top of the kitchen cabinets for years suddenly became junk in my eyes. Knickknacks I had once regarded as treasures began to look like unnecessary debris. I felt burdened down by possessions, even as I persisted in buying more each day.

In spite of John's advice, I decided to go ahead with the tag sale. We had tentatively set the date for a Saturday in early September, and, given our plans to go to the Cape, I knew that I was going to have to get busy pulling things out from their various hiding places and washing or repairing them as necessary. Much of the rest of the weekend and the ensuing weeknights were spent in that way.

Almost before we knew it, it was time to depart for our week in Cape Cod. The station wagon was unmercifully crowded, carrying everything from golf clubs to roller skates and surfboards. Unable to decide which of my many new things to bring, I had packed enough for a six-month stay. Not to be outdone, Melissa had done the same thing. Clyde and Monica had been characteristically more sensible.

By noon, we were ready to set out. Clyde got behind the wheel, and the two children sat in the back. As we drove out of the driveway, I thought about what a pretty picture of the typical young American family we made. An attractive man, a pretty woman, and their two rosy-cheeked children. How nice it all appeared. How strange it felt.

As we neared the Cape, I began to grow uneasy about the social logistics of the week. Checking in would present the first hurdle. The reservations were under the name of "Miller." That was not Clyde's last name. The hotel expected Bill, and because they were careful about their guests, they would be more than curious about Clyde's presence and Bill's absence. I suddenly wished that we had chosen a less intimate place for our vacation. The close personal attention paid to the guests by the staff was supposed to warrant the extravagant prices. Normally it would have been welcome. Now it seemed like a major drawback. If only Clyde were less handsome, and older looking. I feared people would assume that he was a charming male on the prowl, and that I was his keeper. Not wanting to be compromised in that way, I decided to take pains to broadcast that we were brother and sister.

I did so immediately as I approached the young, smiling girl behind the reservation desk. "Hello, I'm Pamela Miller. My family and I have a reservation for Cottage 640. My husband passed away since we made the reservation. However, Clyde Cuming, my brother, is here with me and the children."

The smile faded, and I saw on the girl's face a look of complete horror, horror not at what she had heard but at the need to depart from her friendly, hotel-imposed script. She very obviously did not know how to respond to my statement. Finally she seemed able to pick up where she had left off. "I'm sorry to hear about your husband, Mrs. Miller. I hope that you and your brother and the children will have a wonderful week with us. Please don't hesitate to ask if you need anything. As you know, Cottage 640 is down on the beach; actually, it is one of my favorites."

Safe in our cottage, our home for the week, we began to discuss who would sleep in which room. There were only two bedrooms in the cottage, each with two twin beds. I had anticipated sharing a room with Monica, and having Clyde share with Melissa. But the girls didn't want to do it that way. They both had an instant attraction to the pink bedroom. Decorated with old-fashioned, petite furniture, it looked like a room straight out of *Little Women*. Before I could say a word to the contrary, they had lugged their suitcases into that bedroom and begun to hang their things in the closet.

I looked at Clyde as if to say, "What now?" He said, "Look I don't mind sharing a room with you, as long as you leave me a drawer or two and don't wake me up at the crack of dawn every day with a preplanned list of things to do."

"Okay," I thought, "so be it." After all, why should I be modest? We were raised together and had lived a lot of life together. We had no secrets from each other. I said, "Okay, I promise."

As we unpacked, we laughed at how obvious our sleeping arrangement would be to the maids who were assigned to our cottage, and at how the rumor mill would hum with the news. The staff would make the inevitable assumptions that added zest to their otherwise boring summer routine. "Her brother; sure he is. Oh, they look a little alike, but then lovers begin to look like each other too, don't they? Chuckle . . . chuckle . . . chuckle."

With dinner hour approaching, I urged Clyde to get dressed. He was appalled to learn that it was necessary to wear a jacket and tie just to go to the dining room. Leaving him shaking his head in bewilderment, I went to find the girls, who were already out exploring the beach.

As I walked the beach in search of Melissa and Monica, I began to feel extremely sad. I could not ignore the memories of the two romantic evenings Bill and I had spent on the same beach only a year before. I didn't want to remember; such memories brought pain. But the memories were persistent; they would not be denied. I missed Bill keenly, so keenly my stomach began to ache. I began to run, and that helped. Keep moving, just keep moving. Rediscover in action the feeling of power and confidence. Run, don't walk. When you get too tired to run, then walk. Above all, don't stop, don't think, don't confront the aloneness. Will it away. Eventually the exercise muted the memories. Trying to catch my breath, I momentarily forgot my pain.

I had forgotten that my purpose in going down to the beach was to find the children. Breathing regularly again, I began looking for them. They were nowhere in sight. I went back to the cottage to find them not only there but fully dressed and, like Clyde, anxious to go to dinner. I had to hurry but that was fine with me. Haste, after all, was my secret of success.

James, the maître d', had a broad smile on his face as he watched us approach the dining room. His eyes were also smiling, seeming to signify that he did remember me. I was not surprised. As was characteristic of Bill, he had made a positive and clear impression on James. In the span of two short days, and six meals, Bill had managed to find the real person under the stuffy exterior that James presented to the world. They had laughed together and shared a few personal stories. I would guess such an interaction with a guest occurred rarely in James's life. He kept a polite distance, posturing himself as a devoted servant who is somehow regal in his own right. His habitual tuxedo gave him an air of formality and importance and defied closeness. Even the rest of the hotel staff seemed to treat him with dignity.

Because guests were forbidden to enter the dining room other than under the careful escort of James, we had to stand in line and listen to him go through his routine with three families who had arrived before us. Clyde was noticeably silent; I believe he was stunned by the rigor of the ritual. Melissa was characteristically oblivious. Social rigidity did not dampen for an instant her playful spirit. Standing beside me, she fidgeted and jumped up and down in place. It was all I could do to restrain her from running up and down the middle of the ultraformal lobby. Our turn came just in time.

As I had hoped he would, James altered his routine for us. Apparently the girl behind the desk had done her job. James had been informed about Bill's death. Apparently he had not been informed that Clyde had a name. He greeted us with, "Good evening, Mrs. Miller. It is so good to see you again. And, good evening, sir. I understand this is your first visit to Paradise. I certainly hope you enjoy it. And these must be the children about whom I've heard such wonderful things."

I thought it strange at first that James had said nothing about Bill. Taking my arm and escorting us to the table, he said so quietly that I could barely hear him, "I was so sorry to hear about your husband, Mrs. Miller. He seemed to be a truly fine man."

I thanked him, and tried to understand his reticence. Perhaps he did not feel that such things should be discussed in the presence of the children. Or, perhaps he had assumed that Clyde was the latest man in my life, and that it would be socially imappropriate to mention my previous lover in his presence.

We were not at our seats more than ten seconds before the headwaitress came over and introduced herself. She tried to mimic James's dignified manner but somehow her attempt at seeming dignified made her appear indifferent. Thinking to myself that she must be very new at this, I decided to give her the benefit of the doubt. She was obviously nonplussed when Cynthia, our assigned waitress, did not adhere to the preestablished introductory system and appear by the side of the headwaitress, her taskmaster, at the proper cue. The boss had to go and remind the errant waitress that it was time for her to be introduced to her new family.

Seeing the wine steward and the cocktail waitress descending simultaneously upon our table, I hurriedly briefed Clyde. "Clyde, let's celebrate our first night here with a really fine bottle of wine. Don't worry about the price this time around. Let's have our wine now and skip the cocktails."

Clyde accepted the wine list. His horror at the prices on the list was obvious to me but, I think, escaped the attention of the wine steward. He ordered a French dry white wine. After the steward was out of earshot, he turned on me. "Pam, you're out of your mind.

You know I picked a moderate price wine, moderate in terms of *their* price range, and it's going to cost you twenty-five dollars." I smiled and assured Clyde that I knew what I was in for, as I made the suggestion.

We turned to the menu and to the task of deciding what to eat that night. Clyde was disturbed to see that there were no prices shown on the menu and elated to find out that our daily rate did not vary according to our selections. That made his decision much easier. He determined to order the meal that would have been the most expensive had we been dining in a more typical restaurant. We both ordered shrimp cocktail, followed by vichyssoise, endive salad, and broiled lobster. The girls contented themselves with more common children's fare: fruit cocktail, fried chicken, and broccoli.

The trembling in my right hand reoccurred, but it was so slight as to be imperceptible to others. By the time I had had two glasses of wine and gotten involved in a conversation with Clyde, I forgot about my problem. It would bother me only slightly all week.

It was after nine when we left the dining room. Tired from the drive, we all looked forward to a good night's sleep and to the beginning of healthy, rigorous activity the next morning.

Arriving at our cottage, Clyde remarked how good it felt to be away from the stiff formality of the main building and safely ensconced in our more casual little cottage. Entering the bedroom in search of his blue jeans and sweat shirt, he hollered out, "My God! They've invaded my space, they've touched it, they've touched my bed!"

I understood immediately what had made him so upset. The housemaid had come in while we were at dinner and, as is the custom at Paradise, had carefully removed our clothes from our beds and neatly turned down the bedcovers.

Clyde could not find it in himself to appreciate the gesture. He felt violated and unsafe. The more he talked about it, the more upset he became. "You know, they must be watching us. Otherwise, how would they know when we went to dinner? I'm going to close all these curtains. They're probably watching us now. I don't know how much of this I can take. Yes, sir; no, sir; may I undress you, sir? That's what happens next, isn't it? Somebody is going to walk right in here and offer to undress and bathe me. I'm going for a run on the beach."

I did not hear him when he returned from his run. The cool night air soothed Monica, Melissa, and me to sleep almost instantly.

We awoke early the next morning to a bright, sun-filled day. The children were up and out exploring within minutes of awakening. Clyde and I meandered about, made some coffee, and took it out to the deck. From the deck, we could see the beach and the water, and the fishermen returning from their five A.M. foray. The scene was so beautiful that it made our sorrow seem remote.

Wanting to avoid the main dining room at least until lunch, we chose to breakfast at the more casual beach house. Clyde was hoping to avoid the maître d' or headwaitress. Not only did his wish come true, but we were hard pressed to get served at all. Apparently the waitress on duty was quite unaccustomed to having customers for the morning meal. As it was, we were the only family who had elected cold doughnuts, juice, and coffee over the elegant fare served in the main house.

By ten we were happily scattered over a large area on a very unpopulated beach. Clyde and Monica took turns watching Melissa as she played at the edge of the water. I simply lay on the sand and soaked up the delicious rays. I had no desire to move even a muscle, feeling as though the warmth of the sun was drawing all the tension out of my body. I was more relaxed than I had thought possible. My brain was devoid of thought. I was simply being, without thinking and without feeling, experiencing neither grief nor sorrow, as though I had fallen into a hypnotic state induced by the combination of the sun, the feel of the sand, and the sound of the waves. Even Melissa respected the boundaries of my trance and never tried to dispell it. I think I might have remained that way all day had not a small boy run by and accidentally kicked sand in my eyes.

Coming alive again, I joined Melissa in the water, and played a little Frisbee with Clyde and Monica. By one, we were all extremely hungry and thirsty, and began making motions to leave the beach.

As we were about to leave, the hotel lifeguard approached us and introduced himself. I found nothing unusual about his behavior, assuming that hotel etiquette was again dictating the politeness of this young blond, suntanned Adonis. Clyde, being wiser than I about the ways of young men, had a funny smirk on his face as he introduced us. "I'm Clyde Cuming. This is my sister, Pam, and her two children, Monica and Melissa."

I began to get an inkling that something was amiss when the lifeguard said, "Isn't it too bad that your husband couldn't be with you on a lovely day like this." Not thinking, I blurted out that my husband had died.

The Adonis was instantly understanding, empathetic, charming, and caring. "Oh, I am so very sorry. It must be very hard on you. Perhaps you would like some company one evening. How long do you plan to be at Paradise?"

I was so uncomfortable and felt so awkward that I could find no appropriate words to say. I simply nodded stiffly, folding up the beach towels, and picking up Melissa's scattered sand toys.

The Adonis left, but I could not help but notice that he continued to watch us intently from his guard's platform. As we walked up the path toward our cottage, he caught Monica's eye and waved. I cringed as she waved back. Running up to me, she whispered, "Mom, I think that guy likes you. And he's so cute."

Overhearing her, and seeing the stiff smile on my obviously frightened face, Clyde laughed out loud. "Well, what do you expect, you dummy? You've obviously got to learn not to go broadcasting your widowhood to every stranger that you meet. I mean, you are a really atractive gal, and when people hear that you're an available widow on top of that, I mean, you're asking for it!"

Obviously Clyde was right. His words of wisdom were not welcome, however. I was embarrassed and didn't want to be teased. I had been approached and had handled it like a jerk. I doubted that I would ever learn to master the art of repartee. Even a simple, "Thanks, but no thanks" would have been better than my deaf-and-dumb number. Feeling threatened, I suggested to Clyde that we try another beach the next day. He readily agreed. As the week wore on, I never found the courage to return to that first beach. While the other beaches were not quite as beautiful, I made up excuse after excuse, and the family didn't press me.

By week's end, we had all begun to tire of the routine and the formality and were quite ready to take our leave of Paradise. Driving home, I began to focus on the week that lay ahead. It would not be an easy one. I would have to be away from home for three days, having agreed to function as the lead trainer for a workshop in communications effectiveness. I did not look forward to it.

On that Sunday afternoon, I felt healthy and relaxed. I did not feel the least bit dramatic, nor charismatic, and wondered how I would ever find the psychological energy required to understand and work with the problems of eighteen different souls. Conducting such workshops had been Bill's forte. I had thrived in the role of workshop planner and support trainer. Now, I had to fill his talented shoes.

Fortunately, this marked the second time I had had to face this kind of challenge. The first had occurred only the week before Bill's death. Up until the last moment, Bill and I had expected that he would be released from the hospital in time to conduct the program himself. The sudden onset of phlebitis had changed all that only two days before the workshop was scheduled to begin. I was too exhausted and too numb at that point to even stop to question my ability to lead the workshop. Much to my own surprise, I had managed, and managed well. It had been a highly successful program. Running on nervous energy and nervous energy alone, I had discovered new abilities in myself. As we drove, I thought about fate. There seemed to be some kind of master plan to my life. Maybe Bill had known that he was going to die; perhaps his forcing me to fill his professional shoes before he died was but another in a long list of efforts designed to prepare me for going it alone.

By the time we reached our home, I had decided that not only could I run a successful workshop, but I actually looked forward to the challenge and to improving on my previous effort. After all, I reminded myself, you have become one of the more sensitive and emotionally aware people on earth. Couple that with your innate intelligence, and you've got a winning combination, beautifully suited to the task at hand. I was soaring again.

I had not counted on Melissa's resistance to my leaving. This would mark the first overnight business trip since Bill's death, and Monday evening she broke into tears at the sight of my packing. I didn't know what to do. Here was a problem that all the decisiveness in the world couldn't solve. I felt pulled apart, split right down the middle. There seemed to be no way to console her, to stop her tears. I wanted to get to the bottom of it, to the real fears and insecurities that I imagined were the cause of her outburst. But she would not or could not cooperate with my efforts at instant psychoanalysis. She simply kept repeating, "I just don't like it, I don't like it, I don't like it."

I thought perhaps she was afraid that I would get sick on the business trip, never to be well again, maybe never to come home again. After all, I told myself, that is what happened to Bill. And yet I had traveled since his attack and, until his death, Melissa seemed to tolerate my absence well enough. Perhaps now that Bill is gone, I reasoned silently, she's got to pin all her hopes on me. I reminded her that her Daddy Jim loved her, as did Sara. I reminded her that I was a very healthy person and certainly would not get sick while away on business. None of these reassurances seemed to touch her, for she continued to complain and began to sob.

Finally, I gave up trying to determine the source of her despair and simply picked her up and rocked her on my lap. Nestling close to me, she stuck her thumb in her mouth. I did not tell her to remove it. At that moment, crooked teeth were the least of our concerns. We remained that way for a long time, until she had quieted down. Eventually she picked up her head and asked, "Well, at least would you bring me a present?" When I told her that I would not only bring her a present, but an extra-special present, she seemed to cheer up considerably. Wanting to believe that the problem was solved, I dismissed her reaction as the result of postvacation blues. After all, in the week we were away, Melissa had gotten accustomed to having me around twenty-four hours a day. It would take a few days before she would readjust to having a working mother.

Trying to convince myself that leaving was the best thing to do, I rationalized that only if I left periodically would she learn to trust that I would return. I desperately did not want to cope with the thought that Melissa might have a deep-seated problem of an entirely different nature. I wanted to keep soaring, to keep believing I could manage and manage well.

The workshop was an unqualified success. I returned home as optimistic as I had been before the workshop. I had mastered another situation, and succeeded. I could do anything. I would do everything.

Melissa had been waiting for me at the window. As soon as she saw the car, she ran downstairs and out into the driveway. Before I was fully out of my seat, she was all over me. I picked her up, only to come very close to losing my balance. When she refused to release me, I decided that I had no choice but to hold her hand and carry one suitcase at a time into the house. Her blatant display of need and affection was overwhelming. I felt as though I had little to give, and she seemed to be a bottomless pit of need.

Reminding myself that I could handle anything, I determined to give whatever emotional energy remained to my child. She helped me unpack, and was delighted when we finally uncovered her special present, and Monica's. Wondering about Monica, I questioned Jennifer. Monica was due home any time. I knew she would not be as overtly demanding as Melissa, and reminded myself to provide her with the tender loving care that she too needed but never openly requested. Monica arrived no more than fifteen minutes after I did. Running into my bedroom, she stopped short when she saw me unpacking. "Hi, Mom. How was your trip?"

"It went very well, honey. I missed you, though."

"Yeah, I missed you too. Well, you're home now, and you can relax."

"How about giving me a welcome-home hug and kiss?"

"Sure." The intensity of her hug belied the nonchalance of her words. Monica, like myself, was perpetually wearing a mask of courage, feigning independence. But we were wise to each other and, for that reason, were able to find comfort in each other's company. Without my having to ask, Monica began picking up my dirty clothes and putting them in the hamper. She didn't stop working with me until my suitcase was entirely empty and put away.

She chose to stay home all weekend, refusing invitations from the many friends who called, saying she preferred to work with me on the tag sale. It consumed the weekend and all the evenings of the following week. The more things we put in the pile to be sold, the more things I wanted to sell. Neither the vacation nor the workshop had diminished my need to clean house, to simplify, to get rid of all unnecessary things at any cost. Clutter, confusion, and mess continued to eat away at me. They were a sign that life was uncontrollable.

I still had very strong needs to simplify my life and my environment when Pete announced that he had found an apartment and would be leaving my home. I reacted to his announcement with mixed feelings. His leaving would most certainly make my life less complicated. At the same time, I felt guilty that Bill's child was choosing to leave. Had I failed to provide him with enough warmth and nurturance? Seeking to assuage my guilt, I looked for reassurance from Pete that he truly wanted his freedom. He was convincing enough so that by the time he actually moved in early September, I could wholeheartedly support the move.

A few days later, Clyde announced that he planned to leave in mid-September. This was already September 7. His words struck me like a thunderbolt, but I took pains not to show him the full extent of my reaction. From the beginning, Clyde had expressed a concern that I would become too dependent on him. To have a dependent is to have a commitment, in his case, an unwelcome tie, an anchor. I wanted no anchors and certainly did not want to be his anchor. I understood and respected his need for freedom; it was within his grasp. To deny him that would have been potentially to weaken our relationship.

And yet I *had* become dependent on Clyde, relying on him to make me see the lighter side of life. His presence had become critical to me. Trying hard to control the panic that was building inside me, I managed to ask, "Where do you plan to go?"

"Well, I thought I'd drive out West, perhaps as far as California, and talk to various graduate schools along the way."

"Do you plan to stay out there if a school appeals to you?" I asked as calmly as I could.

"I suppose so, though I don't know. If I find a school that suits my needs and my objectives, I'll probably try to find an apartment and get a job, and actually enter the program the second semester."

"That sounds reasonable," I said, hoping against hope that he would not find such a school. "And if you don't find a program that suits you?" I asked.

"Well, then I don't know. I would like to help Dad finish the vacation house he and I have been building. I mean, I felt really bad about leaving him in the middle of that project. But I'm not sure that I'll return to Australia. I don't know. You should know better than to ask me questions that require such a definitive answer."

Smiling feebly, I said, "Right." I could neither say nor ask anything more. If I did so, I risked revealing my panic. I didn't want Clyde to know how scared I was, nor did I want to verbalize my fear, preferring to go on believing that I was invincible. I was experiencing a momentary relapse, and wanted it to pass as quickly as it had occurred. I decided to say good-night, hoping that sleep would renew my courage and my sense of invulnerability.

By the next morning, I had decided not to dwell on either Clyde's departure or the problems that I feared would beset us once he was gone. Resolving to stop relying as much on him in terms of the house, the children, and myself, I began to ask less and to share less. Oh, we continued to talk, often long into the night, but the topics were more casual or more intellectual. They were less intense, less emotional, less intimate. I was weaning myself away from Clyde, or so I thought.

At least Clyde had not become deeply involved in the business. I had built no dependency on him in that arena. Nor had I involved him in the planning of the tag sale. With the sale only a few days away, it began to demand all my spare time. The children worked along with me and eventually got so involved that they decided to use the sale as an opportunity to make a few extra dollars of their own by selling some of their less favorite toys. While the children and I worked, Clyde spent his time on his back in the garage preparing his car for the journey west.

Amy and I decided to hold the tag sale at her house. The homes were closer together there, and her garage was visible from the street. We hoped to draw more customers that way. I rather liked the idea of spending a day in the old neighborhood. I had not seen most of my former neighbors since Bill's death and looked forward to showing off, to letting them see that I had come through the storm not only intact but physically unscathed.

We had to hurry in order to hold the sale on the fifteenth of September. Amy had a lot of commitments and wanted to hold it a week later. I almost had to plead with her to hold it on the fifteenth. She finally agreed when I offered to come over the night before and help her finish preparing her things. It had to be on the fifteenth. That had been Bill's birthday. I didn't want to be anything but preoccupied and busy on that day. Even thinking about it made me uneasy, extremely uneasy.

The memories of Bill's last birthday, his fifty-first, were still vivid. The toast we had made at dinner was particularly haunting. Bill had toasted himself. "Here is to health and to life. I had thought I'd lost both. But now that I've made it to age fifty-one, I see no reason why I won't make it to at least sixty! And here's to you, Pam, who helped me through it all. To a long and happy life together!"

I had been very happy that day, believing, as Bill did, that our fight with illness and death had passed. We believed we had won. That birthday party seemed like yesterday, and yet in another way it seemed like a lifetime ago. It was a happy memory, but only a memory. I wanted to dwell on the future, not on the past, and there would be no celebrations for Bill in my future.

John tried again to dissuade me from having the sale. He remained convinced that I was incapable of deciding what I needed to keep and what I should sell. But I believed he was wrong, unable to understand that the discomfort of feeling burdened by excessive possessions had become greater to me than their material value. I really didn't care if I lost money on the deal. The point was not to make money, it was to get rid of clutter.

As John had feared, I did manage to relieve us of a good many of our possessions. Before we opened the doors to our sale, I had taken five station-wagon loads of things to Amy's house. Anything that hadn't been put to use in the previous year was arbitrarily included as a sale item. I gave no thought to the possible future usefulness of things. In spite of my large backyard, I gave away a number of outdoor torches. Why? I hadn't used them lately. A beautiful brass espresso pot that had never been used went the same way. I did not consider that my social life would change, and with it my entertaining habits. That didn't matter. Records that were perfectly good but hadn't been played recently were discarded.

Since I had given Pete the table on which the telephone answering machine rested, it had no place. That became reason enough to decide I no longer needed its help. Originally a four-hundred-dollar machine, I decided to sell it for twenty. Monica and I got into a major fight over the small black-and-white television in her room. I had decided that four televisions were at least one too many in a household of four, and soon to be three, people. Monica was determined to keep it, I was equally determined to get it out of the house. We compromised. She would allow me to get rid of one of the three portable radios if she could keep her television. I agreed.

The sale itself was enormously successful. Almost everything went. The garage was rarely without customers poking here and there, contemplating a five-dollar purchase as though it represented a total depletion of their savings. Several people wanted to bargain. Fine, no problem, that added to the fun. Amy wanted to make some real money that day, so we held her prices firm. I didn't care, so we had a heyday trying to appear to be seriously negotiating when we didn't actually have cutoff prices in mind for my things.

By six o'clock, we were exhausted from selling, playing, and negotiating and closed the garage doors to indicate the end of the sale. I suggested that we celebrate our success by spending our proceeds at a local steak house. Before we were finished, we had spent most of our money. We ordered everything in sight and a lot of the house wine. We toasted each member of the party, finding something spectacular to applaud in each child and in each other. At no time did any of us refer to Bill or to the anniversary of his birthday. By eleven o'clock, we had exhausted our appetites, as well as the patience of the waiters.

Driving home, I offered to show Amy and her girls my childhood neighborhood. Off we went, only to find that because of the hour, all the entrances were chained. No longer a resident of that rather exclusive area, I did not have a key to the lock boxes. No matter. Monica and Tommie, Amy's fifteen-year-old, jumped out of the car and held up the chain so I could drive under it. The adventure made all of us extremely giddy. From the voices, it would have been difficult to distinguish the mothers from the children. We cruised around those roads for a while before deciding to end the night with ice cream.

Getting out of the area required that we once again drive under a precariously raised chain. The second time seemed even riskier, naughtier, and, therefore, funnier than the first. Monica, Tommie, and Melinda were beside themselves with laughter; they couldn't believe their mothers were behaving in this adolescent way.

I think our behavior began to frighten Melissa. It had been a long time since she had seen her mother play, and she didn't know what to make of it. While I was mildly aware of her discomfort, I chose to ignore it, not wanting to become more sedate and thoughtful at that point. I had succeeded in turning my back on memories all day and did not want to start now when it was so close to midnight. I wanted to continue being slightly bizarre and playful until exhaustion set in, guaranteeing that I would remain unaware until the dawning of the next day.

It worked. Waking at noon on Sunday, I lay in bed contemplating the events of the day before. I had made it through the first anniversary of a special day without despair and depression. While I had not managed the memory, I had effectively run away from it. No matter. I had made it through and, in the process, created another memory.

When I got up, Clyde was packing his car and preparing to leave. I couldn't stand hanging around and watching. Suffering from a bad case of the rainy-Sunday blues, I wandered around the house, feebly attempting to get interested in something. Melissa was in even worse shape than I, and seemingly could bring herself to do nothing but sit in a chair sucking her thumb. Seeing her, Clyde mentioned that Melissa had been actively avoiding him all morning. When he had tried to kiss her, she had abruptly turned her back and walked out of the room. She was clearly angry.

I was worried about her; too many people had left her in her young life. She had experienced at least five baby-sitters. Then her stepbrother had moved out. And now Clyde, too, was going to desert her. Everyone seemed to leave her; even her father at the end of the weekend visits and holidays. Bill's desertion had been the most permanent, the most severe, the most traumatic.

It was no wonder that she was angry at Clyde. I tried to get her to talk about it, but she refused. She wouldn't talk about anything, insisting on moping around, doing nothing, and being generally bratty. My temper was rising. The day was going from bad to worse; my blues were quickly turning to mean reds. We had to do something to break the downward spiral.

I questioned my ability to withstand the pain of actually witnessing Clyde's departure and knew that Melissa should be spared that anguish. Unless Clyde objected, I would take the children out for the afternoon.

"Clyde, would it upset you if we left before you? I thought I'd take the kids to a movie."

"No, I think that's a good idea. We don't need any big good-bye scenes, anyway. I mean, since when do we really say good-bye? Who knows, I could be back very soon."

"That would be nice, Clyde. Keep in touch, would you? I mean, ESP is great, but let's help it along a little with postcards or something."

"You got it."

"Clyde, good luck. I'll miss you."

"Hey, get moving on that alarm system, would you?"

"Sure thing, first thing tomorrow. See ya."

Anxious to leave before I broke down and begged Clyde to stay, I hurried the children into the car and turned on the engine. Clyde kissed Monica; she cooperated in silence. He made one last attempt to get Melissa to respond to him, but she would not, could not. Resolutely, she turned her face away from the window, refusing to even look at him. As we drove out of the garage, I could see that Clyde had begun to cry.

We were gone for the entire afternoon, returning just in time for dinner. The house was deadly silent and felt huge. We huddled together in the kitchen, not wanting to branch out to the downstairs television room and the bedroom wing. The rain had brought in cooler weather, and we could smell or sense the coming of winter. After dinner, we remained as a group, all curled up on my king-size bed. The hours passed and I invited both children to sleep with me. We huddled together throughout the night. I slept little, uncomfortable with and frightened by my role as sole protector of my vulnerable children.

The first thing Monday morning, I called the alarm people and almost pleaded with them to install a system as soon as possible. In spite of their sympathy for my situation, they could do nothing for four weeks. Four weeks of sleepless nights, I thought. I decided to continue filling my days so full that by nightfall I would find bed welcome and sleep possible.

I threw myself with even more vigor into my business, my children, and my house. I began sanding and repainting Pete's room. The children and I saw every evening movie that was even remotely appropriate for their ages. And we spent a lot of time in department stores. My blue jean collection expanded until I had at least two pairs of each of the designer's jeans, with a full complement of what Monica regarded as appropriate accessories. The girls didn't make out badly in the process of outfitting their mom. Every time we bought something for me, we had to buy something for both of them.

As the days passed, we grew more comfortable being alone in the house. The children resumed sleeping in their own rooms, and we began using more and more of the space. Eventually we stopped jumping every time a branch scraped against the window. The dog began sleeping in the house at night, and that helped too. When the silence and our feelings of isolation became too intense, we would turn on several televisions and leave them on for a while. Noise became an ally against fear. I began to urge the children to invite friends over during the weekends, and called single women friends of mine whom I hadn't seen in years. Several who lived in New York City welcomed the opportunity of having a weekend in what they perceived as "the country." When an old friend of Bill's and mine called from Washington, D.C., and suggested that she would like to come and spend the weekend with me, I was delighted. "Come ahead," I said. "The more company the better," I thought.

Denise was not only a special friend, she was also an important client. A bright and attractive black woman, Denise had established herself in Washington as a highly influential member of the group of well-positioned civil servants interested in the preservation of human rights. She had a lot of opinions, and she expressed them beautifully. To contemplate a weekend with Denise was to look forward to a challenging and busy time. She arrived on a Friday night.

Denise, Monica, Melissa, and I spent an enjoyable night talking, playing, and getting reacquainted. We talked about Bill and discovered that he had had a similar impact on both Denise and me. In both our lives, he had been available to provide support and counsel at some critical professional turning points. I found that for the first time, I enjoyed talking about Bill, and sensed that I was beginning to be able to do so with some objectivity.

Melissa's shouts woke me at six on Saturday morning. At first, I could not comprehend what she was saying. Denise and I had talked until the early hours of the morning, and I wanted to continue sleeping. All need and desire to sleep vanished when I finally understood. "Mommy! Mommy! I can't open the bolt to the door! Clyde is back! Mommy! Clyde is back! He wants to come in. Get up, Mommy, and let Clyde in!" I bounded out of bed and raced for the door. I couldn't believe it. He had been gone for three weeks and had not called.

But it was he, all right, though much the worse for wear. Unshaven, tired, and dirty, he most certainly would have been turned away from a stranger's door. But not from our door. I felt like a child on Christmas morning, and I happily made hot coffee for us.

Melissa eagerly helped me put out doughnuts and coffee cake. She must have whispered to me a hundred times, "Clyde is back, Mommy. Clyde is back!" Her faith in humanity seemed to have been restored by his return. She gave him no choice but to hold her on his lap while we ate breakfast. He began his tale.

"Well, about four days ago, I talked to the University of Colorado. Neither they nor anyone else I spoke to on the way had exactly the program that I'm looking for. Several people urged that I check into some of the California schools. I considered driving that far, but the car seemed to be developing some trouble as I was going through the Rockies. So, I decided to give up on the academic search and to spend some time in the Grand Canyon. Well, was that ever an experience. I actually camped at the bottom of the canyon, got a real bad case of sunstroke, and had to be rescued by a passerby who happened to have a lot of cold water handy. But I want to tell you about that part of my trip at another time. I took a lot of slides and thought that once they are developed, we can spend an evening enjoying them. Anyway, I guess I just got tired of the road and homesick, so I decided to turn around and surprise you. I wanted to get back early last night, but with traffic and rain, I got held up and didn't pull into the driveway until about four this morning. Knowing how skittish you are at night, I decided I would terrify you if I knocked on your window, so I tried sleeping in the car. That didn't work out very well, which is why I finally decided to wake you up at six. So here I am. Again, I can't say for how long, or what my next move will be. But for now, I'm here, and I hope that that is all right with you."

All right with me! It was more than all right with me. It was utterly fantastic. Then I remembered that Denise was alseep in Clyde's old room. Clyde responded to this news with his usual humor.

"So, that's how it is. I go away for three weeks and you give away my room. That really makes a guy feel good. Is it rented out for the next several weekends, or will I be able to move back in?"

Not wanting him to have the last shot, I answered, "Well, Clyde, you know I lead a very active and exciting life. I mean, I just can't promise to keep your room open. There's always Pete's room. I should tell you, though, that I've torn it up and begun to repaint it, and you'd have to work on that before it would be habitable. And, of course, there's no furniture. But by now you've probably grown rather fond of your sleeping bag."

"Oh, so you got a little more independent while I was gone, did you? Okay, just as long as I know what I'm dealing with. Just give me a day or so before you stick another paintbrush in my hand, what do you say?" With that, he disappeared into Melissa's room to catch up on some long-overdue sleep.

Denise was awakened by our shouts and chatter and came into the kitchen to find out who was creating all the commotion. Not knowing just how important Clyde had been to us during the summer months, she could not fully understand our wild-eyed joy at his return. She listened, and she nodded, and then went about peeling her daily banana.

It was a lovely fall day and I suggested that since Denise was a city girl, it would do her good to spend a day doing some suburban lawn work. The lawn was badly in need of attention, and I hoped that I could cajole Denise into raking. While she did not exactly get excited about the idea, she did not object.

We spent the entire day in the yard, with our conversation breaks consuming more hours than the actual work. Now and again, Clyde came out to work or talk with us. Before we knew it, six o'clock had arrived. I had invited Meg and Grant and Amy for seven. We had planned a gala evening at a restaurant that featured one of the best country-western music groups in the area. The food was always superb, and the publike atmosphere promised to be exciting.

While I was a little apprehensive about going back to what had been Bill's favorite restaurant, I was enjoying the idea of being the one to throw the party. I wanted Denise to enjoy her stay, and I hoped to use the evening's festivities to somehow thank Amy for all the moral support she had given me.

I knew I might need Bill's help. It was extremely difficult to get a table in the music room. Doing so required either a lot of luck or some kind of pull. Bill had pull. He had struck up an unusual kind of friendship with Jean, the hostess. To Bill, Jean had seemed to be the kind of lady who should bear the name "Rose." In spite of her objections, he had persisted in calling her Rose. Finally, one evening she had asked me to provide her with a suitable retort. I suggested she call Bill "Irving," a middle name he despised. And so an affectionate banter had begun to occur between the two of them. I wasn't certain that I could actually approach "Rose" and tell her that her "Irving" had died. I was hesitant to use their private joke to secure a good table. However, I tucked the idea in the back of my mind and hoped I would not have to consider it further.

Unfortunately, the restaurant was full that evening, and they had set a table for us in the room farthest from the late-evening action. It became obvious that unless I went in search of Rose, we would have to settle for that table, and as a result probably choose to go home hours earlier than I had hoped. Feeling that Bill was with me, I decided to try to find "Rose." Bill wouldn't have hesitated for a moment to approach her; therefore, I reasoned, neither should I.

"Rose" was immediately distraught at hearing about her "Irving," and only too anxious to do whatever she could to make my evening more enjoyable. Without hesitation, she issued the directive that several of the smaller tables in the heart of the music room be joined together for our group. A few minutes later, she approached the table and spoke softly to me. "I want to tell you again how sorry I am. I am glad that you told me, and happy that I could do something to make this evening more special for you." She felt good about what I had done, and I felt good about what she had done. My guests were amazed at the power of their departed friend, as well as the courage of his still-living mate. The evening was off and running.

We had drinks before dinner, wine with dinner, and had just begun our second round of Irish coffee when a page announced that Amy was wanted on the phone. It was after one in the morning. A telephone call for Amy could mean only one thing: one of her children was in trouble. At seventeen and fifteen, both were old enough to be out with friends every Saturday night. Melinda had her own car, and Tommie was often in the cars of older friends.

Looking at me with naked terror on her face, Amy got up to go to the telephone. When she returned to the table, she was shaking, and her face was pure white. She had to sit down for a minute. After she composed herself, she told us that there had been an accident. "Tommie was at a party tonight, and a porch fell on her. She has a broken leg. She is all right, but she is in the hospital. I've got to go. Clyde, would you mind taking me back to your house so I can get my car?"

Clyde and Amy left immediately. I sat there, my mind reeling both from the news and from the Irish coffees I had been drinking so steadily and so casually. I tried to resume the role of gay hostess but could not. As the moments passed, I grew more and more worried about Amy and about Tommie. I feared that Amy was too upset to drive. Intuition told me that Tommie was suffering from something far more serious than a broken leg.

Perhaps I also knew at some level that the crisis that had befallen Tommie was to endanger my fragile emotional balance even as it wreaked havoc in Amy's life. The telephone call had stopped in midair my flight of fantasy and pseudo-confidence. A lot more than a back porch had come crashing down that night.

Part IV

THE FOURTH AND
FIFTH MONTHS

Harsh Realities

11

The Crash

The headlines in the local paper on Monday were to read FOURTEEN HURT AS PORCH COLLAPSES DURING PARTY. "Fourteen people were injured, two seriously, as a birthday party turned into near tragedy Saturday night when a porch collapsed."

Tommie had been more than seriously hurt. She lay in intensive care with a crushed pelvis, a lacerated bladder, internal bleeding, and multiple breaks in her right leg. She was in severe shock, and the doctors were visibly worried and frighteningly noncommittal in their comments.

The decision Clyde and I had made upon his return to the restaurant had been right. Taking everyone back to our house, we had asked Meg and Grant to look after Denise and, if necessary, to get her to her train the next day. We had left immediately for the hospital, arriving shortly before three in the morning. When the woman at the reception desk informed us that Tommie was in the intensive-care unit, our worst fears were confirmed.

Clyde took my hand as we walked down the hospital corridor toward the elevator that would take us up to intensive care. As the elevator climbed, I found it increasingly difficult to breathe. The very idea of entering another intensive-care or coronary-care unit was terrifying. The effects of the alcohol I had consumed were noticeably absent. In their stead was another kind of dizziness, that of unreality. I felt as though I was having a nightmare from which I would never awaken. Without Clyde to guide me, I doubt I would have found the courage to get out of the elevator when it stopped on the fourth floor.

Even though Bill had not been in that particular hospital, I knew the scenario all too well. The frightened, exhausted faces in the waiting room, the hushed silence in the halls, the superefficient, expressionless nurses. They had to be expressionless; after all, they saw too much tragedy, too much death. When the doctors walked through the halls of intensive care, they moved quickly. They did not saunter, or stroll, or cast their eyes around. Staring straight ahead and walking at a highly purposeful pace, they managed to avoid painful conversation with concerned relatives.

Clyde guided me past the main ICU waiting room to a smaller room, where we found Amy and her daughter Melinda. Ann was with them, her arm around Amy's shoulders. Ann had to be a saint. Her calm peaceful ways had helped see me through my crisis, and now, only months later, she was using those same qualities to comfort Amy. It was Ann, in fact, who had reached the hospital first. Failing to find her mother, Melinda had finally summoned Ann. When the call arrived, Ann was in the midst of serving dinner to twenty guests. Simply telling them where the food was, she raced out of the house to help a child she regarded as one of her own. Ann had been with Tommie since ten that evening.

Amy was feeling extremely guilty at not having been available to her child when she was hurt. Melinda was trying hard to convince her mother that there was no need to feel that way. "Mom, you could sit at home every Saturday night for the next ten years, and nothing would happen. So, you went out, and I forgot where you were going for a while. I mean, you really shouldn't blame yourself. I was with her, and anyway, everything is going to be okay." Ann emphasized Melinda's assurances by periodically tightening her arm around Amy's shoulders.

I felt that with my arrival, Amy's efforts to blame herself redoubled. Seeing me, she began all over again. "Oh, Pam, I feel so terrible. I mean, my child is hurt and I'm out on the town having a grand time for myself. I wonder if she will ever forgive me. What an awful thing to have to endure. How frightened and alone she must have felt. I sometimes think Ann is a better mother to my children than I am."

Turning to Ann, she said, "Oh, Ann, my children would be in really bad shape if it weren't for you. You really are a second mother to them; maybe they'd be better off if you actually were their mother." Putting her head down, she began to cry.

I sat in a chair, unable to say or do anything to console Amy. My stomach was in a tight knot, and my eyes would not focus. I wanted to run from there. I had come to offer help, but was incapable. Clyde, sensing my proximity to the cliff, stood by my side. I tried to focus my thoughts on Amy, on her pain, and on her words. I understood her feelings of guilt and failure.

I remembered my periodic dances with guilt after Bill's death. Might he have lived if I had done as he asked and picked him up from the hospital one day earlier? Arriving home late on Friday night after having conducted the workshop in his stead, I had fallen into a heap of exhaustion and could not find the energy to make the long drive on Saturday. Had Bill really understood? I brought him from the hospital on Sunday, and he died that night. Was it because he had begun to question my love for him? Had he thought that my refusal to come on Saturday indicated a loss of love? Had that made the difference in his ability to fight for life? Had I, like Amy, been unavailable at a critical moment?

I recognized that just as my reaction had been irrational, so was Amy's. Had Amy been sitting home that night, she could not have prevented the porch from separating from the house and falling on her child. Nor could she have lifted the porch, uncrushed the pelvis, or healed the leg. It is doubtful that she could have even softened the trauma of Tommie's entry into the hospital. Tommie had immediately gone into a state of shock and, even before arriving at the hospital, was largely unaware of what was happening around her. Just as I had finally convinced myself that I had not contributed to Bill's death, so Amy would have to realize that she was in no way to blame for Tommie's accident.

I wanted to share my thoughts with Amy and to help her out of the pit into which she had fallen. I started to speak to her but was interrupted by the entrance of a nurse. The nurse held a plastic bag in her hands. Written on it in big, bold, black letters were the words "Patient's belongings." At the sight of that bag, all thoughts of Tommie and Amy left my mind, as I was transported back to the hospital the night of Bill's death. My nose was filled with the smell of that emergency room, my eyes could see only the feet protruding from under the yellow curtain that blocked my husband's corpse from view. My hands once again held the bag containing Bill's belongings. I had not been able to bring myself to leave the hospital with that bag in my possession. It had seemed to be such a travesty, a mockery. I had taken my husband to the hospital; I was to leave with a lousy plastic bag filled with torn, urine-soaked clothes.

For the first time since that night, I was allowing myself to consciously remember taking Bill's ring, wallet, and watch from the bag, and putting them carefully in my purse. I had given the bag back to the nurse and asked her to dispose of it. Unable to view Bill's body, neither could I look again at the garments that had last clothed that body.

Looking at Amy clutching the bag containing her daughter's belongings, I started to cry out loud. Clyde knelt down and took my hands in his. Embarrassed, I wanted to stop crying and to be strong. This was Amy's turn to be consoled. I was unfairly detracting from her tragic drama and selfishly making myself the focus of concern.

"I'm sorry, Amy. I came here to help you, and it looks like I have become your greatest problem. I'm really sorry. I'll pull myself together."

True to form, Amy would not accept my apology. "Pam, I understand, really I do. I am so very glad you and Clyde are here. I know how hard it is for you to be here; that means so very much. And, I need you."

"I need you." That was all she had to say. Memories of the night Bill died began to fade. I wouldn't disappoint Amy. She did need me, even if only to make her feel good about herself again.

Dawn was breaking when we were finally allowed to see Tommie. Amy asked me to go with her. She was afraid of what she would see, and of her reaction. Actually seeing Tommie made us both feel enormously better. She appeared to be simply resting. The crushed pelvis was not visible to us, and the broken leg was not in itself frightening. The color of her skin shouted only health; she smiled at us, as any sleepy child might do, and said nothing. She seemed to be comforted by our presence. Amy's fears began to subside.

The definitive word from the doctors did not come until Sunday afternoon. Tommie's injuries were so diverse as to require the opinions of a number of specialists; some were optimistic, while others were cautious in their prognosis. By the end of the day, the only thing of which we were certain was that Tommie had been very lucky; had the porch fallen on her upper body, she most likely would have died. As it was, the doctors anticipated a lengthy stay in the hospital.

By Sunday night, Tommie was alert; the shock was already diminishing. She complained of pain and screamed when the nurses came to turn her. She began to recall the traumatic events of the previous night. Amy suggested that Clyde and I leave the hospital, assuring me that she was all right and would be going home herself soon. We did as she suggested. I had to leave for Chicago the next afternoon and would be gone the better part of the week. I had clothes to wash and paperwork to do.

I also had to think about Larry. I knew that I would see him sometime during the week, and I needed to decide just how much, if any, of my fantasy to reveal to him.

I had requested the impending meeting with Larry. My infatuation had bred a dangerous symptom that threatened my professionalism and my self-confidence. Like an adolescent who is experiencing her first crush, I began to come apart whenever I had occasion to talk with him. Stuttering and stammering had replaced sensible conversation.

Perhaps, just perhaps, Larry had some feeling for me. If he did, he would not have expressed it openly, given my recent widowhood. In telling him of my infatuation, I risked triggering a confession of feeling on his part. The idea was both exciting and frightening. But what if he felt nothing? Could I handle an open rejection? I thought so, hoping at least to rid myself of what was beginning to feel like a very nonprofessional, childish attachment. Perhaps in expressing my feelings, I would be able to minimize their power over me. I was no longer enjoying my fantasy. It had become an unwelcome preoccupation, something that was controlling me and hurting me. Larry's calls were infrequent, and occasionally without any personal comment or inquiry. As my fantasy grew, so did my hopes and expectations. He met none of them, and that hurt.

No, my fantasy was not my friend. It had to be addressed and destroyed.

By the time I arrived in Chicago, I felt uniquely unprepared for a conversation with Larry. I changed my mind and decided to say nothing. But then he called and asked if we could have dinner. He had some things he wanted to discuss. I had a choice: either I could behave like a raving idiot or I could tell him what was on my mind, and in so doing totally embarrass myself.

I chose to speak up. Sitting across from him in the restaurant, I summoned up my courage and began. "Larry, there is something I want to say to you. I guess . . . well . . . I don't know exactly how to put this. . . . I guess . . . well, you are very special to me."

He smiled and, I think, may have blushed a little.

"Put more bluntly, Larry, I am suffering from a kind of adolescent crush on you."

By now he was clearly blushing, but he was not smiling.

"You're what? I don't believe what I'm hearing."

It was my turn to blush. "I wasn't going to tell you about this, but I find myself unable to say anything even remotely sensible to you. I thought I'd better explain why and maybe, having said it, I'll be able to be more lucid."

Larry was looking directly at me, trying hard to comprehend what I was saying.

"Larry, I can't explain it. I've said it, and I hope my words don't mess up our relationship. Right now, I'm feeling pretty embarrassed."

"You and me both," he exclaimed, tilting back in his chair so far that I feared he would fall on the floor. "I want to tell you, this has never happened to me before in my life. I mean, I guess these things happen, but I never would have guessed in a million years. You do appreciate, don't you, that the idea of an 'us' is totally unrealistic? You know me very well from a business point of view, but you don't know me on a personal level at all. I'm really a louse, you know. And you're brilliant, I mean really brilliant. I wouldn't know what to do with you. I really can't believe this."

He put a hand on each side of his head and began to shake it, as if to wake himself from a dream.

I left Larry shortly thereafter, feeling okay about myself and what I had said. After all, I had flattered him, and he had managed to reject me not on the basis of my weaknesses or lack of appeal but because of my strengths. For the first time in weeks, I felt as if I could speak openly with Larry. I was curious whether he would call later in the week to set up a business meeting; we had not finished our work together. My curiosity was only that, however. I had no anticipation, no expectations, no concerns. I had spoken honestly, and naïvely believed that was always a safe and sure way to go.

As the days went by and Larry failed to call, my certainty began to slip, and I started feeling unpleasantly vulnerable. Larry's rejection began to loom larger in my mind than his respect for me and my capacities. By the end of the week, I desperately wished that I had said nothing. I could not resist calling him just before departing to ask him how he was feeling about our conversation. I guess I hoped that he would say something to soothe my hurt and make me feel less vulnerable.

I asked, "How are you feeling, you know, about things?" He answered immediately, "Great. I feel really great about 'things.' How about you?"

"Not so great, Larry, but I'll get over it." With that, I said good-bye and hung up, vowing silently never to say anything personal to him again, letting time dull the memories of my embarrassingly adolescent outburst.

Physical chemistry had activated my romantic instincts and my fantasies. For a while, the fantasy had permitted an escape from loneliness. But the object of my fantasy was not even my friend, much less my lover. I didn't really know Larry at all.

The plane ride back from Chicago marked one of the loneliest times in my life. I had no choice but to look at my loss directly and fully. Bill had loved me, and I him. I needed to be loved and to love, and yet I had to finally admit that a sustaining, sustainable love relationship does not happen simply because a person is lonely or in need or physically attracted to another. I had always been "in love" and didn't like living without it. I was totally unprepared for the pain of openly facing and feeling loneliness.

The romantic aspects of being a brave, bold, bright young widow had disappeared. I saw myself as a frightened, overworked, not-so-young-anymore woman with two children to raise. There was not to be an adventure around each corner, but rather a series of long, hard, lonely days. In two days, I would be thirty-five years old. I felt like fifty. In the span of a few short months, I had grown up, regressed back to adolescence, and then emerged again feeling that I was so old my life was effectively over. I needed to rest, and to have some honest, real fun. Most of all, I needed to experience firsthand the love of my family. Before the plane landed in New York City, I had made a firm decision to take the children to Australia for Christmas.

Apparently the ESP that so often occurs between Clyde and me had been working that day. When I arrived home, tired and deflated and on the verge of depression, Clyde had dinner and a nice bottle of wine waiting. The household was organized, and the children were quiet. No one pulled me or pushed me; they simply welcomed me back home. Clyde and I talked until the wee hours of the morning. He convinced me I had been lucky that Larry had not taken my declaration as an invitation for a casual sexual relationship. Clyde thought that probably would have hurt me deeply. He was right.

Bill used to tell me that I should learn to separate sex and love. Somehow the two remain intertwined to me. It is not a moral issue but an emotional one. For me, to have sex with a person is to say to that person, "You are very special to me, more special than anyone else. Because you are special, I want to share with you things I am not sharing with anyone else, my most private thoughts, my feelings, and my body." I am aware that many people regard my attitude as a throwback or, worse, as some kind of snow-white, purer than thou problem. Let them think what they will. I do not feel that I am any better or more virtuous than friends who treat sex more casually.

Had Larry taken my words as an invitation, I would probably have mistaken his response for a sign of true affection. The results would have been disastrous. Larry had been smart, and he had been kind. I had been lucky, and after a few weeks, I stopped missing my fantasy, focusing instead on my family and on Amy.

Clyde and the children made a wonderful birthday celebration for me. Clyde cooked a twenty-pound turkey and, with the help of Monica and Melissa, set a gala table. The entertainment was a showing of the slides Clyde had taken during his trip out west. Amy called, as did Ann. Jackie and Joel sent a dozen yellow roses. My parents sent a gift. I was as happy as I knew how to be.

But that feeling could not be sustained. Things began to break down on several fronts. Jennifer announced that she was close to getting her realtor's license and would be leaving us. That left me high and dry without anyone to care for the children. Without a sitter, I could not work. I wanted to work. I had to work. But finding a replacement for Jennifer was going to be extremely difficult. There were not many who would be content with a child-care job and were, at the same time, sufficiently loving, organized, and responsible to run my home in my absence.

I shuddered at the thought of having to find, train, and get to know Jennifer's replacement, and feared that Melissa would not be able to take the change of sitters in her stride. It had taken months before she had allowed herself to trust and love Jennifer. Would she react to Jennifer's departure as she had to Clyde's? Would she feel betrayed and crawl back into her shell, believing that no one loved her and that the world was unsafe? She would need a lot of consistent affection from me, and I doubted that I could give it to her. In order to take the planned five-week trip to Australia, I was going to have to work double time the weeks preceding and following the trip. Client commitments had to be met, and extra billings generated. I wondered if it would be possible to put Melissa's needs on ice until we boarded the plane. Could I then satisfy all her needs for love and attention while we were away, only to resume an active work and travel schedule immediately upon our return? I began to believe that the key to it all was Clyde, again Clyde.

Clyde and I had not discussed his life plans since his return. I had noticed that catalog from graduate schools periodically arrived. But Clyde had never given me any applications to mail from the office. He seemed willing and almost eager to take on a research job for the firm, but when I hinted that he should consider working in my field, he was anything but enthusiastic.

Given Jennifer's intention to leave, I felt I had to ask Clyde what he intended to do with his life and, consequently, with mine. He continued to be uncertain and in no way could satisfy my need to plan. We talked about the trip to Australia, and he decided that regardless of his more distant and as yet unplanned future, he would also be in Australia for Christmas. Family meant as much to Clyde as it did to me, and this trip would bring the entire family together for the first time in over ten years.

I kept pushing. "Do you plan to come back with me?"

"Pam, I'm sorry. I understand your need for answers, but I just cannot provide them. I just don't know what I'm going to do. I doubt very much, however, that I will return to the States when you do. If I get all the way over there, I will probably stay long enough to help with Dad's house. I might return in three months, but then again, it might be six. Don't count on me, Pam."

As we talked, it became increasingly clear that the answer to my own needs for stability and predictability did not lie with Clyde. The answers had to come from me. Monica, Melissa, and I had to constitute one another's constants. All that was certain was that we had each other. Others would come and go as their own changing needs dictated.

I decided to try to find a live-in housekeeper. Somehow when someone lives with you, they feel like a more permanent part of the household, more like a member of the family than a hired hand. I hoped that Melissa would learn to trust and love such a person sooner than she would if the new sitter left each evening. I also hoped to share the burden of running the house. I needed a wife, someone to either clean the house or make sure that the cleaning person came, someone to do the laundry, run the errands, and make sure the refrigerator was stocked with more than moldy leftovers. Above all, I needed a surrogate mother for my girls, someone who had the energy to play with them and the compassion to understand their fears. The right person would be able to impose a sense of order and structure without being overly strict. She would be sufficiently strong-willed to manage Melissa, and yet understanding enough to allow Monica the freedom she needed to understand her changing body, values, and needs. She had to be a fairy princess, and she had to be within my budget.

I decided that the best way to go about finding an affordable fairy princess was to tell everyone I knew that I was in search of such an individual. One thing led to another, and before long I was directed to a Scandinavian church. They knew of young women in the country who were authorized to work but had experienced difficulties locating jobs and finding compatible families with whom to live. They were certain that they could solve my problem. Understanding the urgency of my situation and the time constraints, they promised to get to work on it immediately.

It felt good to be able to announce to both Jennifer and Clyde that I had taken a major step toward diminishing my dependence on them. While I cared enough about both of them to want them to pursue their own life objectives, I felt at least a twinge of resentment at their willingness to desert me in what I perceived to be my time of need. And yet when I thought about it, I realized that I would be forever in need of the kind of household support they had, between them, provided. If they stayed around until I was unneedy, they would stagnate in the process.

Other than husbands and wives, no two adults can count on each other to be continually and actively supportive and available in time of need. That was the harsh reality I had finally to admit. I didn't like it, I didn't like it at all, but I could no longer deny it. I had to go it alone, at best with the assistance of a continually changing stream of household helpers.

12

A Child Cries for Help

My attempts to diminish my felt dependency on Clyde and on Jennifer were apparently obvious to Melissa. Minimizing her own dependency, she began to resist openly showing them affection. She withheld good-night kisses from Clyde and refused to play games with Jennifer, preferring the solitary activity of watching afternoon television. Becoming more subdued and less argumentative, she ceased demanding, and she stopped laughing.

I was not immediately aware of the change in Melissa, caught up as I was with preparing for the Australia trip and attempting to work doubly hard in the business. The first symptom that I could not ignore or overlook was her sudden total inability to board the school bus in the morning.

In the past, waiting for the school bus had been a special and pleasant experience for both of us. We would wait at the top of our driveway and talk. When the sound of the bus engine became audible, Melissa would raise up her arms for her morning hug and kiss. If either of us anticipated a difficult day, we would enjoy two kisses: one for love and one for luck. I treasured the sight of that smiling little face in the window of the bus as it pulled away. Her smile signaled to me that she was safe and happy, and freed me to go about my day with a minimum of tension at leaving her.

One dreary morning in the middle of November, that all fell apart. We had waited for the bus for about ten minutes; our talk was unusually strained and empty of meaning. We followed our loving ritual when we first heard the bus engine, but Melissa's kiss was stiff, and her hug uncomfortably prolonged and clinging. She got halfway up the steps onto the bus when suddenly she turned around, jumped down the steps, and came crying back to me.

The bus waited, the driver looking both surprised and concerned. I knelt down and asked her what was the matter. She got hysterical. "I don't want to go on the bus, Mommy. I *can't*, I *can't*. Don't make me. PL . . . EA . . . SE don't make me!" Her body was shaking. Melissa was clearly terrified. Waving the driver on, I took Melissa's hand and walked with her back into the house.

It was eight-fifteen. I had an important client coming into the office at nine-thirty. I hoped to understand and solve Melissa's problem, take her to school, and get to my own office before then. I should have known better.

Melissa could not even begin to talk about her troubles. Her sobs would not stop. I could only hold her and try to soothe her while she let out weeks and weeks of bottled-up misery and fears that had no names. She had become a baby again, an infant to whom the world seems vast and incomprehensible. As I held her, she curled into an ever tighter ball, as if to crawl back into my womb. Every fiber in my being wanted to shelter her from her pain, and yet I could not because it was coming from within her.

By nine, Melissa had exhausted herself. I tucked her into bed, telling her that Clyde would look after her and that I would come home just as soon as I could. She smiled ever so slightly and closed her eyes.

I woke Clyde and explained as best as I could what had happened. He understood instantly, for he had not been blind to the changes that had been occurring in Melissa's behavior. He assured me that he would give her his undivided attention and attempt to get her to talk about whatever it was that was troubling her. I reluctantly left for the office, thinking as I drove about Amy and her "bad mother" self-accusations the night of Tommie's accident. At that moment, I experienced my job as an adversary and my dedication to my career as a major flaw in my character. That I had no choice but to work made no difference; it was, somehow, all my fault.

The meeting with the client consumed the morning. Meg and I had no option but to take him to lunch. That, too, seemed to last forever. Meg noticed my preoccupation. Fortunately the client did not. I was home by three in the afternoon.

Melissa was huddled in front of the television. I left her there for a moment and asked Jennifer if I could speak privately with her.

"Jennifer, Melissa got hysterical this morning when I tried to put her on the bus. She just couldn't cope with it. Have you noticed any other changes in her behavior lately?"

"Now that you bring it up, I have. She doesn't seem interested in doing anything with me anymore. When I suggest we go to the playground, she just shakes her head. She used to love to do that! All she wants to do is mope around. She won't even play games with me like she used to."

Jennifer seemed to be taking Melissa's behavior as a personal rejection. She looked so sad and unloved that I hastened to say, "Jen, I think she is having a kind of delayed reaction to Bill's death. I really don't believe it has anything to do with her feelings for you."

"I don't know. This whole thing seemed to start after she found out that I was planning to leave to sell real estate."

"Sure, I suspect that's making it harder for her. Too many people Melissa loves seem to have to leave her."

"I love Melissa, Pam, I really do. I would never do anything to hurt her."

"I know that, Jen, and I'm sure Melissa does too."

"Look, I'll stay until you leave for Australia. That way, she'll be leaving me instead of my leaving her."

"Thanks, Jen, that would help both Melissa and me."

"And, it's not like I'm never going to see Melissa again. I mean, I plan to continue to come pick her up and take her on special outings."

We decided it would be helpful for Melissa to know that while Jennifer had to leave as a baby-sitter, she had no intention of letting go of the friendship that she and Melissa had established. Jennifer's assurances seemed to cheer Melissa a little, but her focus remained on me. Even Clyde had been unable to get her to talk all day. Melissa had insisted on spending her day simply waiting for her mother, her constant.

In spite of the chill in the air, we decided to go for a walk. We walked in silence for a few minutes, simply experiencing each other's company. I asked the question I had been framing all day.

"Melissa, can you tell Mommy what is troubling you?"

I knew it was going to be a long, difficult process when she answered, "It's the bus. I just hate the bus. The kids are mean to me."

"But, Melissa, you used to love taking the bus. Remember how much you looked forward to getting into the first grade so that you could ride the bus just like Monica does?"

"Well, I was wrong."

I pushed a little. "Well, then, are you telling me that if I take you off the bus and drive you to school each day, your troubles will be over?"

Melissa did not answer me for a while. She just kept on walking, with her shoulders slouched and her eyes riveted on the pavement. Finally, breaking the silence, she said, "I don't want to go to school on Friday."

"Friday? What is happening on Friday?"

"That is the day we cook a Thanksgiving dinner. I'm supposed to make corn bread. I just don't want to go that day. I can't handle it."

I could not suppress a smile at hearing her choice of words. How many times had she heard Clyde and I use the phrase "I just can't handle it." Melissa had not only used our phrase, she had used it appropriately.

I thought about Melissa's mental ability and recognized, as my parents had done, that exceptionally bright children have a great need for emotional security. When a gap is created between intellectual awareness and emotional maturity, the results can be nothing short of disastrous. Wise enough to perceive the subtleties around her, and yet emotionally too young to cope with all she saw, Melissa was struggling to keep the tide of anxiety away from her.

I understood because I had gone through the same thing as a child. I, too, had become so sick with anxiety that I finally could not cope with going to school, parties, or anything outside of my home. My symptoms had not been precipitated by anything so traumatic as a death in the family. Chronic in nature, they had persisted and intensified throughout my elementary-school years. When I was thirteen, my parents had had no choice but to seek psychotherapeutic help for me. I had to lie on a psychoanalyst's couch three times a week for one solid year before I had been able to close the gap between my mental and emotional ages and begin to function as a happy, developing adolescent.

I decided to continue asking Melissa questions, hoping to trigger thought and self-insight as the psychiatrist had done for me. In the beginning, my questions entirely missed the mark. While they might have been effective with an adult, they did not create anything but confusion in Melissa's mind. I tried stating my assumptions openly, urging her to disagree with me if she wanted to.

"Melissa, are you upset about the turkey dinner because Bill used to cook our Thanksgiving turkey? Does it make you remember him, and does that make you sad?"

"I guess so. I'm afraid that I'll cry that day in school and that the other kids will see me cry."

"Have you been crying in school, Melissa?"

"Sometimes, but I try to stop."

"What kinds of things make you cry?"

"I don't know. Mostly I can't help crying when things happen that I didn't expect."

"Like what, Melissa?"

"Well, like when we're supposed to go to the library and all of a sudden the teacher says that we're going to go outside instead."

"But you like to go outside, don't you?"

"Yes, but not when I don't expect it."

"Does your teacher surprise you very often?"

"No, but when she does, I can't handle it."

Melissa's words so vividly brought back the feelings I had had as a child that I stopped walking, knelt down, and right in the middle of the road, held my child. "Mommy understands, Melissa. I really do. And I want to tell you a story."

I shared with Melissa the fears I had experienced as a child, and told her that only through talking about it had I begun to get rid of the bad feelings that made my stomach tight and took away my appetite. Telling her that I wanted to be the one to talk with her, I suggested that we talk for a long time every day we could. I urged her to feel free to interrupt me, no matter what I was doing, if she had a need or desire to talk. She pushed me for permission to stay out of school on Friday. I promised only that I would think about it, privately planning to call Melissa's teacher that night to find out more about what had been happening at school.

After Melissa was in bed, I called her teacher, Lucie Bright. Lucie confirmed that Melissa had been having a difficult time in school. "I don't understand the change in Melissa, Mrs. Miller. Oh, I guess I do, but it's so painful to watch. Melissa used to be so outgoing, such a leader, and a clever mischief-maker. Now, she's so withdrawn. I never have to reprimand her, and she plays by herself most of the time."

"Lucie, have you found that Melissa has a more difficult time when you do unusual things, like cooking?"

"Absolutely. She seems to cling to structure and routine for dear life."

"Does she cry in school?"

"Often, I'm afraid. It's as though she feels the weight of the entire world is on her shoulders. She worries about *everything*, from being unable to finish a lesson on time, to using the wrong color crayon, to falling off the swings. She seems to spend most of her time and energy thinking of all the things that *might* go wrong. When we modify the day's schedule and don't give her plenty of time to worry about it in advance, she breaks into tears. Then she worries about having done that. Oh, Mrs. Miller, I pain for her. She is such a wonderful little girl, and I feel so helpless. Nothing I do seems to make her feel better. I wanted to call you, but I didn't want to worry you. I know this is a terribly difficult time for you."

"It is, Lucie, but right now I'm more concerned about Melissa than anything. She's doing the same thing at home that she is in school. We talked a lot today, and we plan to do a lot more of that. If need be, I'll seek professional help. I'm hoping that our time together in Australia will help. Between now and then, I guess we'll just have to do the best we can. I'd like to take Melissa off the school bus, however, That seems to get her so upset that I doubt she'll ever make it to school. I know the school discourages parents from driving their children, but do you think we could arrange it for at least a few weeks?"

Lucie assured me that she would take care of the bus problem and urged me to call her if I ever needed help or simply wanted to talk. I hung up feeling that I had a true friend and ally in Lucie. I was not alone in my concern for Melissa.

The next morning I drove Melissa to school, praying as we drove down the driveway toward her building. While I knew better, I hoped against hope that such a simple change in routine as eliminating the bus would make things right for both of us.

Her fact set in grim resolve, Melissa climbed out of the car. I waited and watched out of my rearview mirror. The other children called to her and waved at her, but Melissa did not respond. She was clearly concentrating all her energies on finding the courage to enter the school building. She did not turn around. Paining for her, for my baby, I wanted to protect her from hurt. That I could not tore me apart inside. It was difficult, very difficult, to drive away.

That night, I congratulated Melissa on her courage, and told her I understood it had been difficult for her to go to school, and that I thought she had shown a lot of bravery. I wanted her to talk but could not get her to focus on anything other than attempting to get my permission to stay out of school the day of the Thanksgiving dinner.

I feared that in letting her stay out of school, I would encourage her to displace all her anxiety onto the school experience. Having suffered myself from school phobia, I did not want to contribute to the same in my child. Once that displacement was made, I knew all her energy would go into avoiding school rather than into trying to understand what was making her so unhappy. Regardless, I wanted her to explore her feelings with me, and Friday had become a major obstacle. Finally, I gave in and assured her that she did not have to go to school that day and could come spend the day helping me in the office instead. For the first time in weeks, I saw a genuine smile on her face.

Melissa continued to persevere, forcing herself each morning to go into the school building. We talked each night. By the end of the week, we had together labeled her problem as her "worry jar." The symbolism helped. Each night, she and I, or sometimes she, Clyde, and I, would talk until Melissa reported that her worry jar was empty, at least for the moment.

We began to be able to track the kinds of events that rapidly filled her jar. The biggest source of stress was absence from her mother; the second was unpredictability in her own life. These fears had to dissipate if we were to continue to live, and if she was to grow and develop. We had to get to the underlying causes. It was to take months.

Now and again over the next several weeks, Melissa was unable to summon the courage necessary to actually enter the school building. On these occasions, I drove her there only to have to turn around and bring her home. I never tried to force her to go to school, believing that coercion had no place in the trauma she was experiencing. I had to have her complete trust if I was to help her discover the source of her anxiety.

Fortunately, having Melissa at home on these days did not create too much of a problem. Clyde was often there doing a research project for the firm. On days he had to leave the house, Jennifer was put on alert, asked to be ready to come to the house at 9:00 A.M. if necessary. With everybody pulling together, I was generally able to go to the office. While I could not work double time to generate billing sufficient to cover our five-week vacation, I was able to keep up the momentum of the firm. It at least posed no insurmountable problems.

It was during this period that the business of death began to require attention. The Internal Revenue Service raised a question about the distribution of Bill's pension funds. Apparently I had inadvertently cashed a small check from a previous plan and, in so doing, made it necessary to take all the pension monies before the end of the year. According to my alarmed accountant, John, this presented a significant tax problem. I let John fret over my tax problems. I simply could not be bothered, unwilling to create a worry jar of my own when Melissa's required my constant attention.

I could not ignore or delegate, however, the demands of the banker who functioned as co-executor of Bill's estate. He needed all papers relating to Bill's obligations and assets. That meant going through boxes in the cellar and through the file cabinets to search out all checks Bill had signed, all bills on which he was named as payee or co-payee, and many other documents.

There is nothing like going through several years' worth of checks to bring your life back into focus. I chose a rainy Saturday when Jim had the children to re-expose myself to Bill's and my years together. I will never forget the pain of that day. The work itself, if approached as an unemotional project, would have consumed no more than three or four hours. But I could not approach it that way.

Each check that bore Bill's signature sent a stab through my heart. Many of the bills represented payments on behalf of the life we had hoped to build in the future. In going through the checks, it was impossible not to notice that none of Bill's expenditures had been for himself. He had been an outgoing, assertive, unselfish man who had truly loved his second family and, particularly, his second wife. The checks themselves told his story.

Throughout the day, I had to stop, overcome with memories and needing to relive scenes from our life together. The check to the gardener made me visualize the evenings we had spent walking the yard together, deciding what had to be done this year and what could wait. The checks to the local hardware store conjured up scenes of our typical Saturdays.

The co-executor was pleased with my work. Everything was in order and organized. I had done my part; the rest was up to the bank. I was free to return to the business of living.

It wasn't long before Thanksgiving was upon us. Another holiday; how I hated it. I felt uniquely unthankful and alone even while in the midst of Amy, Melinda, Clyde, Pete, Pete's girl friend, and my children. Clyde had tried so hard. He had gotten up early and prepared the turkey. But, notwithstanding the feast before us, we could offer no special thanks at the end of the standard predinner prayer. Bill was conspicuously absent, as was Tommie. The conversation itself was somewhat stilted as Pete and I tried unsuccessfully to pretend away the gap that had begun to exist between us. There was no hostility, simply an appreciation that we were no longer "family," and that even friendship was not coming naturally. Bill had been the tie that bound us. He was gone. We shared little more than our last name. It seemed we had no cause for celebration.

We spent much of Thanksgiving weekend shopping for clothes for our trip to Australia. Even that brought its own measure of pain. The stores had all begun decorating for Christmas, and everywhere we turned there were early signs of the holiday that had represented a very special time in Bill's and my life together. Each year, Bill had eagerly worked with the girls as they painted ornaments for the Christmas tree. Enjoying his second family, Bill had happily embraced the role of Santa Claus. He had often told me that Monica and Melissa made Christmas special for him. It was as though their youth, hope, and excitement on that day had renewed his vigor.

This year, we had painted no ornaments and purchased no gifts. Even had we not been going to Australia, I doubt very much that I could have maintained many of our traditions. I did not feel like Santa Claus. My Santa Claus had died. But Melissa was still a believer and Monica was still a child who deserved the magic of the day. I was glad that we were going to be in Australia for Christmas. When Christmas falls in the heart of the summer, everything gets scaled down. Oh, there would be magic, but it would be less awesome, simpler. Instead of a ten-foot tree, we would decorate a three-foot tree. Turkey salad in the backyard would replace a multicourse hot meal in the dining room. Gift opening would take only an hour or two. The magic of the day would be provided more by the sun and the surf than by the tinsel and colored lights.

But Santa Claus had to make an appearance sometime. He could not do so in Australia without creating the problem of getting new toys back to the United States. It seemed best to suggest that Melissa write a letter to Santa asking him to come early and to bring trip money instead of toys.

On Sunday morning of Thanksgiving weekend, Melissa woke me excitedly. "Mommy, Santa Claus came last night! Do you believe it! It is not even Christmas and he already came! Quick. Get up!" With that, she ran from my room, bound for Monica's room. Within minutes, she had succeeded in getting both of us up and out into the living room.

In spite of Monica's wisdom, she was clearly delighted with the surprise. Sitting on top of a long-desired electronic music game was an envelope for her, another for Melissa, and a third for me. Each contained one hundred dollars, and a note that read, "You have been so good this year that I decided to bring you an extra-special treat. Use this money to buy whatever pleases you during your trip. I'll be visiting you on Christmas Eve in Australia, but I won't be bringing a lot of toys because you couldn't bring them back with you. Have a wonderful time. Love, Santa."

Santa's visit, combined with a long weekend and a break from school, had brought back signs of the old Melissa, the spontaneous, unworried, smiling child. By Sunday afternoon, however, her anxiety was in full bloom once again. She was immobilized by it, finding it impossible to get involved in games or even to watch television. For a long time, she simply sat in a chair and watched me reading the Sunday paper. Putting down the paper, I decided to try to get her to talk.

"Your worry jar is full right now, isn't it, Melis?" She nodded.

"What is it filled with?"

215

"I just don't think I can go back to school. Everything is all crazy right now. We're celebrating Hanukkah this week, and I'm not sure what's happening."

I found it difficult to be a patient and understanding listener. Overcome myself by the memories the holidays triggered, I was also feeling anxious. And my mind was preoccupied with the myriad of details that had to be attended to within the next two weeks, prior to our departure. Business commitments were going to command twelve hours a day; I had a three-day workshop to run. Somewhere in between, it would be necessary to make provisions for the cat and the dog, get traveler's checks, give keys to the neighbors, teach a neighbor how to turn off the alarm if it were triggered, find someone to water the plants, alert the police department, get the mail stopped, and on and on and on. I wanted Melissa's problems to disappear, at least for the next two weeks.

There was undoubtedly an edge to my voice as I suggested she only had two weeks, ten days, of school between now and the start of our trip. I reminded her she was going to miss a lot of school while we were away, and couldn't afford to miss any additional days. I was firm as I told her she had to find her courage.

Needless to say, I handled it poorly. All I managed to do was add to her concern. The lid blew right off the top of her worry jar. She began to sob and ran to her room, locking herself in and the world out.

I broke down. The pressure was too much. She needed help. I needed help. I called Clyde, and through my tears told him that I couldn't take it, that Melissa's problems were breaking my back. He listened and he sympathized, and offered to do whatever he could to help. But he was leaving in nine days, forced to fly before the rest of us in order to be eligible for budget fare. Given my business commitments, the children and I had no choice but to travel during the expensive period known more commonly as peak season.

Clyde suggested that I take a nap. He volunteered to make dinner, and to try to get Melissa to unlock her door and talk with him. I did as he suggested, happy to lean on Clyde as long as he was there.

When I awoke, Melissa was working with Clyde on dinner preparations. He had given her the task of washing and breaking up the lettuce for the salad. They were talking. Wanting to be part of the conversation, and yet not wanting to interrupt, I entered the kitchen quietly and sat down at the table. Clyde brought me into the conversation immediately as he urged Melissa to tell me about the plan they had created.

She began. "Well, you see, Mommy, this is what we're going to do. When I can't find my courage, and don't go to school, then the day is a zero. I put a zero on the calendar. When I do go to school, and I don't cry and I have a good day, then I put a ten on the calendar. If I go to school, but I have a bad day and I cry, then I write down a five or maybe a six, depending on how bad it was. Zeros are bad. I'm going to try to not have any zeros, but it's going to be hard."

Standing behind Melissa, Clyde winked at me. I felt as if he had worked a small miracle. Melissa's problem was far from solved, but her attitude was positive, and her resolve firm. I couldn't ask for more. I congratulated Melissa on what sounded like an excellent plan. During the week to come, she was to have two zeros, two tens, and one five.

I ran around all week, rarely letting myself get out of fourth gear. Using Melissa's analogy, I experienced a week that never rose above a five in terms of pleasure and joy. It was sheer hard work, but by week's end, it began to look as though I would indeed get everything done. Due to an internal crisis of its own, the client organization had canceled the workshop for the following week. Had it not done so, I suspect Melissa would have fallen apart and I right along with her.

Jim and Sara had planned to take both Monica and Melissa for the entire weekend preceding our departure. It would be the last time for six weeks that they would be together. Their plans included an early Christmas celebration with Jim's family. The weekend was extremely important to Jim. He was upset at the prospect of not being able to spend Christmas day with the children and was doing his best to salvage at least a little of that special feeling in advance of the actual day. Neither of us could have predicted that Melissa herself would abort his plan.

Jim and Sara arrived on Friday night, smiling and laughing and eager for the weekend. Monica shared their excitement. Melissa, however, did not. Her typical mode of greeting Jim was racing to be the first at the door, flinging it open, and jumping enthusiastically into his arms. This time, when the doorbell rang, she continued to sit where she was, looking down at her lap. When Jim tried to pick her up and give her his typical bear hug, she resisted, pulled away, and came to me. That had never happened before.

The smile on Jim's face fell away to be replaced by a combination of utter confusion and hurt. I felt his pain and tried to indicate to him through my gestures that I did not understand Melissa's behavior any better than he did. I asked Melissa, "What's the matter, honey?"

Clinging to me and refusing to look at her father, she whispered, but loudly enough so that Jim heard her, "I don't want to go, I just don't want to go. I don't want to sleep at my grandmother's. I want to stay home. That's all, I just want to stay home with you."

In an equally low voice, I tried to convince her to go. "Melissa, this isn't like school. You're going to have a Christmas celebration. I'm sure there will even be presents for you. And it is going to be such a long time until you see your dad and Sara again. I think you'd be making a big mistake if you didn't go. Mommy is going to be home doing boring chores. You wouldn't have anything fun to do if you stayed at home."

"But I don't *want* to go. Everybody is going to talk to me, and kiss me, and make me embarrassed. I don't want to go, Mommy."

Jim had heard enough. Hardly able to hold back his tears, he said, "Melissa, I would never force you to come with me. I want you to come, but only if you want to."

A sensitive child, Melissa undoubtedly saw the hurt on her daddy's face and heard the pain in his voice. That made her feel not only anxious but guilty. The combination was too much, and she began to sob. Understanding that she could play no part in this sad little drama, Sara left the room in search of Monica. I suggested to Jim that he sit down and hold Melissa for a while. He did so, but he was stiff and uncertain. He had been hurt, deeply hurt, by Melissa's rejection.

In time, he began to relax, and as he did so, Melissa snuggled closer to him and began to speak with him. "Daddy, if I go to the party with you, can I come home to sleep?"

"Of course, Melissa. But why don't you bring your suitcase anyway, just in case you change your mind later."

Jim had made a tactical error. Melissa was threatened, suspecting that she might be trapped into staying away from home that night.

218

"No. I'm not bringing my suitcase. I'm not staying. Anyway, I don't want to go at all."

Jim tried to correct his error. "Melissa, okay, no suitcase. We'll just go to the party and then I'll bring you home. Okay?"

Melissa only nodded, and with reluctance left with her dad. Concern had replaced their earlier joy. They looked more like a group bound for a funeral than for a family Christmas party.

Melissa had hurt her father. She had also destroyed the evening for Clyde and me. We had planned to take advantage of the children's absence by going out to a very special restaurant and toasting the times, both good and bad, we had shared during his five-month stay. We wanted to say farewell to the pain and wish each other luck in the future. It was to have been a significant celebration for both of us. We needed to mark the end of another episode of life that we had experienced together. But it was not to be. It was already eight, and Jim planned to have Melissa back home by ten. Both the time and our tempers were too short to permit the kind of open and feeling exchange that we wanted and needed.

By nine-thirty, Clyde was so restless that he decided to go downtown to a bar he enjoyed. That left me with nothing to do but to think gloomy thoughts and wait for my troubled child to return home.

Left by myself, my thoughts got me into trouble. I began to focus on my aloneness, dwelling on the absence of advances from men and requests for dates. I could no longer dismiss my social isolation as a function of my recent widowhood, and began to blame it instead on my assertiveness. Undoubtedly, men preferred passive, weaker women. But I had to be strong and purposeful if I was to run the firm and our home. I knew that I would feel like a traitor if I pretended in social situations to be more passive, more stereotypically feminine.

Besides, hadn't Bill enjoyed my strength? Hadn't he, in fact, encouraged me to be all that I could be? My strength had not been a threat to him, but a complement. His maleness was solid, not fragile. His sense of self-esteem was dependent not on my passivity but on an awareness of his own strengths. But how many men were like Bill? Few, I thought. I doubted that my aloneness would ever be relieved. I would never be part of a dynamic, happy pair again.

I had reached a state of angry despair by the time Jim brought Melissa home. He was right on time. She had held him to his word.

Melissa immediately went to bed. Jim's attitude toward me was hostile, as though I had won something at his expense. Melissa felt safer with me than with him; that seemed to make him the loser. Trying to talk with him, I suggested that he not take Melissa's behavior personally, that he not allow it to hurt him. I had told him of Melissa's difficulties earlier but not in great detail. Now I described it all, and added my belief that it had something to do with Bill's death. I reminded him that she had not openly grieved or even cried after Bill's death, and shared with him my hypothesis that Melissa had repressed her feelings, so they were now controlling her. Jim's hostility only seemed to increase as I talked. It compounded his hurt to think that Bill, either in life or in death, could have had such a profound effect on his little girl. Talk was getting us nowhere. Jim left, saying that Melissa had agreed to have lunch with him the next day and that he would be back shortly before noon on Saturday.

A good night's sleep and the tender loving care of Sara and Monica did Jim a world of good. He called Saturday morning, ready and willing to talk about Melissa's troubles. He no longer had the need to lay blame; nor did he feel like a loser. We were friends again, facing a common unknown enemy. Our only disagreement was over how to handle Melissa's problem.

Jim was pessimistic and urged me to seek professional help immediately. Protesting, I claimed I had reason to believe that Melissa and I could overcome the problem by talking often and at length. After all, we had already made a lot of progress in understanding the contents of her worry jar and in developing the zero-to-ten code. By the end of our conversation, Jim seemed to agree with the way I planned to handle Melissa.

As we entered the next week, the anticipation of our trip sustained all of us through some very trying moments. Clyde's departure was pleasant; after all, we would be seeing him again in only little more than week. Melissa managed at least to go to school every day, although her tears were frequent and she never scored above a seven. She worried herself sick all week about whether or not her teacher would remember to pull together her lessons for the trip. Assured that Lucie had in fact done so, Melissa then became annoyingly preoccupied with concern that I would not show up for my appointment to actually collect the schoolwork. I finally got so tired of her pestering that I sat her down and talked with her about trust.

"Melissa, I have promised you that I will be at your school at one on Friday afternoon to collect your schoolwork. Have I ever broken a real promise to you?"

"Well, only when you said you'd take me to the movies and then you didn't."

"When did that happen, Melissa?"

"Last summer. Remember, Monica was staying overnight at Bev's and I had nothing to do."

"I remember, Melissa. Do you remember how sick Mommy felt that night?"

"Yes."

"Well, there was no way I could keep that promise. Can you think of any other times when I've told you I'd do something and then disappointed you?"

"Well, sometimes you say we *might* do something, and then we don't."

"That's right. But I'm not saying I *might* go to your school on Friday. I'm saying that I *will* be there. That makes it a promise."

"Okay."

"Melissa. Sometimes I feel that you don't trust me. Trust is when you really believe that I will do my best to live up to my promises to you."

"Oh, I do trust you, Mommy."

"Well, then, how about showing me that you do by letting me take over some of the things in your worry jar."

"Like what?"

"Well, like stop thinking about Friday, and also let me worry about getting us ready for our trip. You seem to have put things like packing in your worry jar, too."

Melissa began to smile. I continued, "So, if you will trust your mommy to handle these kinds of things, then your own worry jar won't be so full. Okay?"

"Okay, Mommy."

As she ran off, I noticed there was a bounce in her step. Her depression seemed to have lifted a little, and we had both learned some important things about each other. From that point on, Melissa seemed to be better able to focus on the day at hand, concerning herself less with possible disasters that tomorrow might bring. At six years old, her anxiety and propensity for borrowing the worries of the world was so great that she had to be taught the lesson "One step at a time." I, too, had had to learn that lesson.

As we headed for the airport, I had the feeling my wounds were beginning to heal. I had finally learned enough to pace myself, to walk instead of run when the emotional terrain got rocky. I looked forward to the five weeks in Australia as a time to step back, slow down, and gain a perspective that would make the rest of my widow's journey less traumatic and volatile.

Part V

THE FIFTH THROUGH
THE ELEVENTH MONTH

In Search of Self

13

Regrouping: The Widow's R and R

The first leg of our journey was pleasant. Melissa and Monica were enchanted with the concept of movies and meals in the air. Neither grew bored or restless. We were tired but in good spirits when the plane touched down in Los Angeles. It was 11:30 P.M. New York time. Kevin was at the gate.

Still savoring my newfound friendship with Bill's youngest brother, I had called Kevin and arranged to spend our twenty-four-hour layover at his home. Understanding and knowing the Millers had been of little importance to me during Bill's life. After his death, I felt a strong need to gain some insight into the family whose name I now bore.

At my urging, Kevin had attempted to plan a day for all of us at Disneyland. Monica and Melissa were beside themselves with joy at the prospect of seeing that famous wonderland known to them only through television. Entering the age of hero worship, Monica was also fascinated with the idea of spending a whole day amid movie stars. She had been fantasizing for weeks about seeing her movie idols in person, and about being discovered as the great child actress that she believed herself to be.

Needless to say, Monica was not "discovered" during our layover. Nor did the children get to go to Disneyland. As fate would have it, we were there on a Tuesday, the one day out of the week when the park is closed. But their disappointment was short-lived.

The children all got along very well with one another, so well, in fact, that they were quickly able to content themselves with games around the house. Not willing to dismiss Monica's fantasies, Kevin suggested that we all go to another amusement park. The day was spectacularly warm and sunny, and before long Kevin and I were enjoying the rides in the park as much as the children. Kevin was so delighted with the motorcycle ride that he stood in line three times, refusing to let the rest of us move on. I became equally obnoxious over the bumper cars. By nightfall, only Kevin's wife, who had had to go to work that day, retained any kind of an adult orientation.

We were rowdy and jovial right through dinner, vowing to get together on one coast or the other at least several times a year. Boarding the plane for the next leg of our journey, I felt tired and dirty, but happy. I had managed to play all day, unpreoccupied by work and sadness. And I truly felt like a valued member of the Miller family.

The seat assignments we were given in Los Angeles were to remain unchanged all the way through to Sydney, Australia. Our eighteen hours in the air was to be broken only by brief refueling stops in Honolulu and Auckland, New Zealand. I had made that journey once before and knew what a physically debilitating experience it can be. One prays for a partially empty plane and the opportunity to grab a string of empty seats. Somehow, sleeping in a single seat, semi-upright with neck crooked and legs cramped, leads to short tempers, upset stomachs, tense muscles, and general discomfort.

As our plane began to climb high over the Pacific Ocean, I became concerned not with the seats themselves but with their location: in the nonsmoking section of the plane! By the time we had arrived at the Los Angeles airport, only single and double seats had remained in the smoking section. I had tried to convince myself that eighteen hours of forced nicotine deprivation was a good thing, an appropriate way to begin a trip designed to restore peace to my mind and health to my body.

Now that we had actually taken off, I was finding it hard to be quite so rational. My body was shouting for its dose of tar and nicotine. Claustrophobic, I tried closing my eyes, but my sense of confinement simply intensified. Finally, able to take it no longer, I asked Monica to watch Melissa and went in search of an empty seat in the smoking section. None were available in our part of the plane, and I was reluctant at that point to venture out of visual range of my children. I checked two or three times during the course of the next hour, and eventually one of the passengers traveling in the smoking section with his family noticed and apparently understood my plight.

He spoke very little English and had to introduce himself by way of a business card. I did the same in return. Standing, he gestured as if to light and puff on an invisible cigarette. In response to my nod, he motioned for me to take his seat next to his wife and child. He took the nonsmoking seat directly across the aisle.

While I puffed away, satisfying my craving, he attempted to tell me about himself. A citizen of Hungary, he was a famous "artista." He and his family, which also included his father and mother, were on a worldwide tour and planned to be in Perth during the last week of my visit there. I could not comprehend exactly what kind of artista he was but assumed, for no particular reason, that he was a famous painter. I imagined walking into a gallery in downtown Perth and finding his paintings displayed. He mentioned something about a "service," which, I guessed, was his way of describing a gallery opening.

I borrowed his seat on several occasions during the long flight to Sydney. Each time, we communicated as best as we could. Before we parted in Australia, he had invited Monica, Melissa, and me to his home in Hungary. I, in turn, had urged them to stay with us next time their travels brought them to the New York area.

As I enjoyed our traveling companions, so Monica and Melissa began to feel increasingly comfortable in their airborne home. Monica settled into her schoolwork, determined to get her lessons out of the way before we arrived in Australia. Her perseverance was astounding. The child had to be exhausted, and yet she continued to study.

Monica was efficient; Melissa was creative. Her creativity stood her in good stead during our journey. When I returned from a trip to the bathroom, I discovered that Melissa had solved her sleeping problem. Having begged, borrowed, or stolen at least six of the plane's blankets, she then put our three tray-tables down and draped the blankets over the trays, creating a woolen tent. The remaining blankets served as the floor of the tent. My trench coat became her sleeping bag. Her own coat served as her pillow. Neatly placed in her tent were her dolls, coloring books, crayons, and reading books. Safe in her curious little world, she could stretch out and sleep in perfect comfort.

Monica and I were forced to make certain sacrifices in the interest of Melissa's creativity and comfort, but neither of us minded. Sitting on our legs seemed preferable to enduring the moans and groans that were certain to occur if Melissa became overtired and restless.

Before long, Monica and I discovered a way to keep our legs from cramping. By putting down the arms between the three seats and sitting with our backs to the outer arm of each of our own seats, we were able to stretch out our legs. By periodically alternating our positions, with her legs on top of mine and then vice versa, we were even able to maintain our circulation.

All the creativity in the world could not have made the trip bearable, however. By the time we landed in Sydney, Monica and I were so exhausted that the sofas in the airport lounge looked like the most inviting beds we had ever seen.

Our layover in Sydney came very close to being thirty-six hours rather than the planned seven. I had forgotten that Sydney has two airports, one for international flights and the other for domestic. Although it seemed peculiar that the Ansett counter was unmanned, I did nothing about it until one hour before flight time. Only then did I pick up the green phone that sat on the counter. The person at the other end became frantic when I described the reason for my confusion. We were, indeed, in jeopardy of missing our flight. Another was not scheduled until the evening of the next day.

The voice suggested that I gather together our luggage and race for the bus that ran between the airports. Well, retrieving all that luggage from the airport locker and dragging it to the bus stop was no small feat. It took three trips, and we missed the bus. Picking up the green phone again, I began to plead for help. Fortunately, the individual on the other end was extremely responsive and sympathetic to our situation and arranged for another bus to come back specifically for us.

We made the flight with only three minutes to spare. I was a wreck. Monica was exhausted, and Melissa was threateningly close to a temper tantrum. In order to make the plane, I had had to keep prodding and pushing her along. The more I pushed, the more she slowed down. My cajolings and urgings turned into hollers and demands. She resisted, and I insisted. Finally, I had had no choice but to spank her, grab her hand, and forcibly drag her around the airport. She was nothing short of belligerent as we boarded our flight to Perth.

Sheer physical exhaustion saved us from insanity. Within an hour or so, both children were fast asleep. Beyond sleep myself, I passed the hours in a state of semiconsciousness. When the plane landed at 11:00 P.M. Perth·time, we looked like homeless refugees who had not had the benefit of a bath or shower or change of clothes in weeks. We felt almost as bad as we looked.

Only a family could love such a trio, and love us they did. We saw them as soon as we reached the steps of the plane. I felt saved, literally saved from some undefined horrible fate. They were there in full force: Gay and Dick and their two little towheaded boys, Clyde and Joy and, of course, Mom and Dad. Mom was crying. Dad was smiling a wonderfully big, broad smile. The little boys were jumping up and down, proudly waving the welcome signs they had taken such pains to make. Gay was reaching out her hands to me, even though fifty yards still separated us. Dick was busy restraining his boys from running out to meet us. Clyde was looking sympathetic and knowing; after all, only days before, he had endured the same grueling flight.

The energy of their combined love reached out and seemed to grab us even as we began the walk toward them. It frightened Melissa, who began clinging to my leg, slowing my walk. Taking her hand, I half pulled and half pushed her along. Monica, too, seemed to be a little intimidated by the enormity of the feeling that was passing between all of us. She also hung back for a little, and began looking everywhere but at the faces we were approaching.

Suddenly they surrounded us, grabbing each one of us in turn and hugging us tightly as if to dispel the pain they knew we had experienced during the last five months. Each hug contained its own expression of love. My father's strong pat on the back said, "Courage; you have courage; you can make it." My mother's soft, lingering embrace said, "I am your mother; it pains me when you feel pain; I want to protect you as I did when you were a child. I want to kiss the pain and hurt away." Gay's hug was tentative and uncertain, though loving. She treated me as one does a fragile object that might break apart if held too firmly. Dick's peck on the cheek was just enough to say, "I am reserved and restrained, but know that I, too, love you." Clyde uttered a simple, "Hi, there!" In that single phrase he let it be known that he and I shared a special and unique relationship, that we had experienced a lot of life together, and required no reunion.

Joy waited until last. I had not seen her in six and a half years. All the others had visited the States at least once during that period. It took only a moment together for the years to disappear, however. As I was to learn over the weeks to come, Joy and I had a lot in common. Both ambitious and independent, neither of us were content to lead a life comprised primarily of husband, home, and children. We both valued challenge over security and excitement over predictability. Finally, we shared a belief that anything is possible. She hugged me and said in a whisper, "I am so glad that you have come."

We stayed up until the early hours of the morning drinking champagne and talking. I did not need to dwell on Bill's death, nor on the difficult times that had followed. Clyde had done a thorough job of sharing with them all the events of the past five months. It was a festive evening, without a trace of sadness. Before we went to bed, my father, who is fond of playing captain and organizing the logistics of everyone's day, wanted to know about my hopes and plans for my visit.

"Our wants are simple, Dad. Sun, rest, and time with all of you is what this trip is about."

My answer triggered something in Gay, and, looking directly at our mother, she said, "See I told you so, Mom. Pam doesn't want you to organize a bunch of parties. She wants to keep it simple; we are enough entertainment for her."

Mom looked at me, as if seeking confirmation, and I enthusiastically provided just that. "Mom, Gay is right. I have been pushing myself very hard, and what I want most of all is a life without complications and without social musts. Even the very idea of having to make idle chatter at a cocktail party bothers me. Please, don't do anything special for us. Give us sunshine, a bed, and your time, and we will be extremely happy people."

My mother, as literal a thinker as I, assumed from my words that I was uninterested in leaving Perth. Looking at my father, she said,

"See, Jack, I told you Pam wouldn't want to go down south for a week. She wants to stay here. You heard her."

With that, my father looked at me, not for confirmation but for denial of what my mother had said. I had no problem providing what he wanted. "If you mean driving down south to the Porongorups to see the house that Dad is building, then I very much want to go. I've been hearing about that property and that house for six years, and I'm not about to miss seeing it. In fact, I just might lend a hand in its construction. I mean, everybody has got to earn their right to stay in it, don't they?" Dad smiled, and Mom gave up her case.

As long as we were talking about plans and logistics, I decided to mention that the first thing the next morning, I wanted someone to take me downtown to pick up a rental car. On the way over I had decided that, regardless of the expense, I had to have my own means of transportation. At the moment, Mom, Dad, and Clyde shared a car. Joy had to borrow it whenever her motorcycle didn't suit her purpose. Determined to visit the beach each and every day, I did not want to be dependent on their schedules and, consequently, on their ability to transport us.

Going to bed that night, I felt as though I had come home. I was completely safe, secure, and well loved. There was no despair in this home, only tenderness and happiness. It was summer, and everything was in full bloom. The warmth in the air complemented the warmth that existed between us. The contrast to the bleak New York winter, and the loneliness within our home, was enormous.

The next morning, Clyde drove me to the car rental agency and I became the proud temporary owner of a bright red compact car. I barely made it back home in one piece. Driving a strange car on the left side of the road was, at first, a terrifying experience. Everything seemed to be backward. Under-bridge crossings, of which there were several, were the most hazardous. Believing that my left shoulder approximated the edge of the car, I barely allowed enough room for the three feet or so of automobile that, in fact, remained beyond that shoulder.

Apparently God was looking after us, for by eleven, Monica, Melissa, and I were on the beach. I had almost forgotten what a soothing effect the sun and the surf can have. And there is no sun and no surf quite like that found in Australia. Looking at the Indian

Ocean stretching out before us and watching the surf pound on the beach, I began thinking about all that had happened in my life. The setting provoked in me a feeling of calmness and a new perspective. I was probably as deeply religious at that moment as I have ever been in my life. I had no need to control life's events, believing fully that there had been a reason for everything that had happened. Perhaps it was the uncontrollable nature of the surf that triggered my sudden burst of faith.

Somewhere in my being, I knew that Bill's time to die had come, that he had seen his best years, and that had he been allowed to live longer, he would have suffered as he watched himself lose vitality and, ultimately, self-respect. I believed, too, that I would again be fully challenged and fulfilled in my own life. Sitting there getting a massive sunburn, I felt bold and courageous, but at the same time I was neither frenetic nor half-crazy.

Returning from the beach, we showered, put on pretty sundresses, and spent the afternoon in talk first with one family member and then another. During the summer, many Australians slow down by two. They are expert at the art of relaxation and don't believe in pushing themselves too hard during the warm season of the year. My family had learned the art. Highly efficient when they set out to do something, they were totally relaxed when they decided that the work for the day should end. Generally they made this decision by midafternoon. Consequently, we did not lack companionship.

That afternoon, as was to be true of most of our afternoons, we let the Australian wine flow freely. Purchased by the five-liter spigot box, the wine was both inexpensive and superb. Our talk flowed as easily as the wine. I began to reunderstand my family: their values, their hopes, and their dreams. I liked and respected what I heard.

One afternoon it dawned on me that these people had become far more than family. They were my best friends. I could think of no one else with whom I would rather spend my time. They seemed to feel the same way. Joy and Clyde began minimizing their social commitments to friends in order to spend time with me and my children. Gay, Dick, and their children began coming to Mom and Dad's home almost every night for what was to become the traditional backyard barbecue.

Our brief visit with Kevin and his family had encouraged me to think of myself as a "Miller." Now, my maiden name became more meaningful to me than my married name. I was rediscovering my roots, my history, the source of my values, beliefs, and aspirations. I was a Cuming through and through, and I was proud of it.

The many hours we spent as a total family group talking about life, its meaning, and its alternatives were having a positive impact on me, helping me redefine myself as a separate and capable person. We represented a diverse group, both in interest and aspiration. My father, the engineer, could not fully comprehend the interest that Gay, Clyde, and I all had in the "soft science" of psychology. We talked about that on more than one occasion, each time gaining additional respect for the discipline pursued by the other. Clyde, the counselor by trade and social worker by instinct, challenged Dick's and my interests in running a small business. Gay, the almost full-time mother, was intrigued by and yet skeptical of balancing the world of work and the world of home.

The differences that existed among us were the source of unending exploration, not of conflict. The biggest value difference that set me apart from the rest was what Clyde had labeled my "love for things." I was clearly the owner of the most possessions, the biggest house, the most jewelry, and the most expansive wardrobe. Stated differently, I was more American and less Australian than the rest of them. The single crisis of our visit occurred, in fact, because of my penchant for owning valuable things.

One night, I was pounding ground meat into hamburger patties in preparation for our traditional barbecue. Not wanting to get the meat into the crevices of my opal engagement ring, I took it off and placed it on the kitchen counter. Of all my possessions, my engagement ring was the one of which I was most proud. It was not only beautiful and valuable but also extremely symbolic and meaningful. Becuase of both its worth and its sentiment, it was irreplaceable.

I did not think of the ring again until around three in the morning. Abruptly sitting upright in bed, I realized that it was no longer on my finger. After a few moments of panic, I remembered what I had done with it. Retrieving it, however, was not going to be easy. The house was dark, and after stumbling around for a while, I still couldn't locate the light switch or the doorknob. Not wanting to wake the family, I decided to go back to sleep, confident that I could retrieve the ring early in the morning.

My body was growing accustomed to Australian time, and I slept later than usual the next morning. By the time I got to the kitchen, my father had been up for hours doing things around the yard. My mother was busy puttering around the kitchen. I said nothing about the ring, not wanting to alarm anyone. I simply began looking, picking up this and that, but to no avail. Finally I had no choice but to explain my behavior. "Mom, yesterday, when I was making hamburger patties, I took off my engagement ring and put it on the ledge of the counter. I forgot to pick it up when I was finished. Have you seen it?"

I was immediately sorry I had said anything. Losing things, anything, drives Mom completely crazy. When, as children, we misplaced a mitten, or a hat, or a pair of eyeglasses, she would spin around the house, pulling out drawers and dumping out their contents, tearing things from closets, and moving furniture. If the missing object was in the house, she inevitably found it. In the process, however, the entire place was literally turned upside down and inside out. The more valuable the lost object, the faster she spun and the wilder she became.

My query about the ring triggered the same behavior. Before the morning was over, every single kitchen drawer had been dumped out and sorted. All pots and pans had been removed. The refrigerator was emptied of its contents. The remaining, uncooked ground meat was manually sifted. She demanded that my father move the refrigerator away from the wall and check behind it. Then, suspecting the ring might have fallen on the floor and been kicked, she urged that we scour the rooms that surrounded the kitchen. Nothing. She was getting more and more upset. I was getting progressively less upset about the ring and more anxious about the intensity of her reaction, given her history of chronic hypertension. Telling her that I had a few ideas about where to look, I suggested that she relax.

Suspecting the ring might have been thrown accidentally into the garbage, I ran out to the backyard. My heart sank as I lifted the lids of the cans only to discover that they had already been emptied and the garbage taken to the dump, or the "tip" as they say in Australia.

Moments later, Mom was back in the kitchen. She had suddenly remembered that the night before she had helped to make a salad, using the very space on the counter where I had placed the ring.

"Honey, I hope I'm not responsible for this. I mean, I'm sure I'm not. I *was* cleaning lettuce on that counter, though. But I would have seen the ring. Don't you think I would have? I mean, I couldn't have thrown it out with the lettuce wrappings, could I?"

She was getting upset again, beginning to blame herself as well as driving herself crazy over my loss. "Yes, Mom, I agree. I'm sure you didn't throw it out. It probably got brushed off the counter before you even began cleaning the lettuce. You really weren't in the kitchen very long anyway."

"Pam, have you checked your room? Sometimes we put things away and are not even aware that we're doing so."

"No, that's a good idea, though. I'll go and do that."

There was the remote possibility that she was right. With the help of Monica and Melissa, we began going through everything in the bedroom we shared. While we did manage to find an earring that Monica had lost and Melissa's missing barrettes, there was no sign of the ring.

By now the entire household was actively involved in the search. Clyde suggested that perhaps the ring had been kicked into the backyard. He and my father began a careful search of the grass. As they were searching, the yardman came to cut the lawn. I saw my father talking with him, and realized that he had been told of the loss and asked to be on the lookout for the ring as he cut. When he had finished, Clyde and my father actually sifted all the grass cuttings that had been deposited at the rear of the lawn.

They could all visualize the ring for which they searched. More than six years earlier, Bill had wired money to my father and asked him to purchase the best two black opals he could find. He had done so, and Joy had brought them to the United States for us. Bill and I had then chosen settings and had them made into rings. Bill's had served as his wedding ring. Shortly after his death, I had had his ring made into a pendant. Since the day I picked it up at the jewelers, I had *never* removed it from my neck. It had become my amulet, my protection against evil.

As the search wound down, and it began to become obvious that the ring was not going to be found, I started to think about the meaning of the two stones. Had I lost the pendant, I suspect that I would have gone directly to the tip, stopped the bulldozers, and begun sifting through the acres of sand. My own engagement ring meant far less to me than did Bill's stone. Still believing that a master plan governed much of our lives, I began to reflect on the symbolism of the loss. After all, the marriage was over. Perhaps the loss of the ring had been intended to propel me forward in life. I had to give up my marriage to Bill's memory if I was to build any kind of meaningful relationship with another man.

Glancing down at my left hand, I studied my wedding ring. Perhaps it was time to remove that also. After all, I was not a married woman; the ring belied my singleness. I twisted it around a few times and smiled as I recalled the evenings we had spent designing it. The edges on either side were jagged; it looked like a two-sided king's crown. The design signified life's ups and downs and our intention to experience both the highs and the lows together.

I slowly took the ring off my finger. My hand felt naked. Wiggling my fingers around, I tried to get used to the feeling. Stretching out my hand, I studied its nakedness. The ring was not going to be removed so easily. The Australian sun had tanned my hand as thoroughly as the rest of my body. The place where the ring had been was so vividly white in contrast that it almost looked as though I had not removed it at all.

That too seemed strangely appropriate. The white area would slowly disappear, just as my past would slowly give way to my future. I put the ring away. The marriage was over, and its symbols removed from my sight.

Having accepted the loss of my engagement ring, I urged my mother to do the same. She could not. She felt responsible for what had happened. I tried to explain to her that, after all, it was only a "thing" and was not worth the stress and tension it was creating within her. My father wholeheartedly agreed, and complimented me on my maturity and ability to put the loss into perspective. The compliment felt good. While my mother began to speak of the ring less often, I know that to this day she is still searching for it.

The crisis of the ring put into perspective, we began preparing for Christmas day. As the day neared, my father's concerns mounted. He had shared a Christmas with Bill and me, and knew we had tended to spend a lot of money on gifts and a lot of time on the festivities of the day.

Taking me aside one evening, he urged me to be a frugal Santa Claus. Apparently my mother had given some indication that she intended to depart from their more simple Australian Christmas in order to provide the expensive, lavish Christmas she thought the children and I expected. My father did not want to reintroduce the lavish Christmas. He had managed to change that tradition when the family emigrated to Australia. He was visibly relieved when I told him that Santa Claus had given the children money before we left the States, and that they did not expect much more than a stocking.

His relief was so great that when I suggested that I would like to decorate a three-foot live tree, as opposed to his six-inch artificial tree, he readily agreed. He added, however, that he thought we should cut branches off the trees in the backyard and wire them together rather than spend money on a store-bought tree.

Willing to at least give his idea a try, I began scouring the backyard for appropriate branches. Pretty soon, my father joined me. I cannot remember ever having laughed so hard with my father. Evergreens are not exactly in abundance in Western Australia. Having to work with semitropical bushes, our efforts to simulate a Christmas tree were totally unsuccessful. The product of our efforts was nothing short of bizarre.

I was actually tempted to use the peculiar tree we had made until I saw that it upset Melissa. When she saw it, she began to cry. "Mommy, you and Grandfather are making fun of Christmas." As she ran into the house and slammed the door, we knew we had to give up our tree as an idea that had failed. My mother and I raced down to the shopping center just minutes before closing and bought a bedraggled evergreen that looked a little more like the traditional Christmas tree.

Melissa was delighted with it and happily spent the day before Christmas working with Monica and their cousins to make ornaments. Their attention never wavered as they applied glitter, crayon, and ribbon to Styrofoam balls. By the end of the day, the children were extremely proud of "their" tree. I believe they derived more pleasure from that shabby little bush than they ever had from the lavish, perfectly formed giant trees that had adorned our home on the other side of the world.

Similarly, Monica and Melissa seemed to gain a new understanding of the meaning of Christmas day. The mountain of gifts that had typically confronted them Christmas morning had led to cries of glee, but to little appreciation of the thought behind each individual gift. Further, when faced with too many treats at once, they had tended to rush and to pay little attention as others opened their gifts. With only a few things for each person, they learned to savor each gift and to take a real interest in things that were given to others in the room. I think they began to understand and to experience the joy of giving as opposed to the fun of receiving. They did not feel cheated.

And I learned a valuable lesson. I did not have to go on pushing myself to the point of exhaustion to continue to provide the children with all the things they had got accustomed to in the past. On the contrary, our traditions could change, and in the changing, both the children and I would benefit.

Alternatives; yes, I had alternatives. That became increasingly obvious to me as our stay in Australia progressed. The rest of my family had opted for a life-style that was markedly different in some important respects from the one they had pursued during their years in the United States. They were all thriving, happy, and healthy. Instead of donning a three-piece suit and commuting to the frenetic city each day, my father put on a pair of knee socks and Bermuda shorts and strolled over to the university to lecture. Rather than spending her weekends running around from one crowded store to another, my mother read and relaxed. She had no choice: the shops in Western Australia religiously close up tight at noon on Saturday. Instead of trying to conduct business after staying out until 3:00 A.M. at a Christmas party, Dick simply closed his shop for the holiday week. This was, after all, a widespread custom in their part of the world.

They urged me to consider embracing their life-style. Each morning, my father avidly went through the real estate section of the paper, circling properties that represented both good investments and sites on which to build a future home. Tempted, I spent several days actually looking for a site. I stopped doing so only when it became obvious that in order to make an investment of that nature in Australia, I was going to have to spend most of my time dealing with banks and brokers. That was work; I didn't want to work.

Even after I stopped looking at sites, I continued to notice "For Sale" signs. The Australian way of life, compounded by the tender loving care of my family, had renewed both my body and my spirit, and I was reluctant to give that up. The environment had brought back the old Melissa. She laughed and played with total abandon. Her worry jar was consistently empty, and every day was a ten plus. Even while working on her school lessons, Melissa maintained an optimistic, cheery demeanor. Monica, too, was blooming. Having mastered the art of raft surfing, she spent hours each day in the waves. Her skin tone was beautiful; her mood matched her appearance. Gone was the self-consciousness of early adolescence that had begun to plague her.

The alternative way of life offered in Australia became even more attractive as a result of our visit to the Porongorups, a heavily forested mountain range and the site of my father's planned three-bedroom home.

To accommodate all eleven of us, Gay and Dick had reserved an A-frame chalet. It would hold eight, and the three remaining would sleep in the three-man tent my father had erected at the building site. If we were a tightly knit family while in Perth, living together in such close quarters in the Southwest made us even closer.

Things that had remained undisclosed or hidden over the years came out into the open. Gay declared that she was sick and tired of being regarded as the passive weakling. She challenged my occasional pushiness and insisted that her children begin to respect her rights. We talked of life and of love, of family and its meaning. We stopped pretending that we were unaware of Dad's increasing loss of hearing, freeing him to discuss his hopes and fears openly. We pledged mutual support to one another.

Talk was easy and fulfilling. We also experienced some wonderful silent periods together. The most special of these silent times occurred at a beach outside the town of Albany.

After waking up one morning, we decided to go in force to the beach. Clyde, Joy, Monica, Melissa, and I piled into my rented car. Mom and Dad joined Dick and his family. An hour later, we entered a massive reserve and began to follow the signs to the beach area. As mile after mile slipped away, the road became increasingly precarious. Pavement gave way to bauxite, roadways turned into trails barely wide enough for travel by car. Both cars were covered with a film of reddish bauxite powder. It seemed the beach would never appear.

Suddenly the road came to an abrupt stop. We were three feet from a cliff, with only a small crudely built wooden fence separating the cars from the drop. At the bottom of the cliff, the Indian Ocean pounded the rocks; to our right stretched an enormous expanse of beautiful beach.

Given Albany's sparse population since the decline of whaling, its only industry, and the difficult trek across the reserve, there were never more than ten people on the beach. It was effectively ours. But, typical of my family, they were not content until they had explored all available options. Joy, Clyde, Monica, and Melissa took off, climbing up the steep rocks that came right to the water's edge.

When, after a half hour, they had not returned, I went in search, but could find no trace of them. It was as though they had vanished. The Australian bush seemed to have swallowed them whole. As much concerned as amazed, I asked my father to join me in my search. He was amused at my concern, more comfortable than I with Australian nature. Taking me by the hand, he helped me up the giant rocks. We walked and climbed for a full half hour before, rounding a bend high up on the rocks, we saw below us a scene that would inspire a poet to greatness.

Monica and Melissa were swimming in calm, pure blue water that was so clear even from the hilltop I could see tiny fish swimming about under the surface. Joy and Clyde were stretched out on pure white sand that looked like fine baby powder. Rocks taller than the ones we had climbed made a giant semicircle around the beach, keeping back the heavy surf and protecting the sand from the wind. It was the kind of natural miracle that inspires tribes of men to build altars and worship mysterious powers.

Leaving my father standing atop the rocks, I climbed down to join the others. We were to remain there in total peace and silence for the rest of the afternoon. Wanting to stay there forever, I determined to come back the next day and each day that we were down South. I could not get enough of the place, or of the feelings it inspired in me. My attachment to the site was so great that for several days after that first experience, I studied the Albany newspaper in search of a home that would permit us access to that beach. Yes, I even considered living in that dying, uninspiring Southwest Australian town just in order to be able to swim in that water and feel that sand.

The power of the beach lay not just in its beauty but in what it symbolized. It reminded me of the basics of life and brought my priorities into focus. Work and money were but means to ends. Compulsive organization was not the key to my sanity; health, love, and peace of mind became my life objectives.

New Year's Eve was suddenly upon us. I looked forward to saying good-bye to 1979. It had been a year of illness, suffering, and pain. Believing that I had grown because of it, I was eager and ready to put my new perspective to work making 1980 the wonderful year I sensed it could be. My optimism was clouded only by the knowledge that in eight short days, Monica, Melissa, and I would have to leave Australia and our family behind us.

I had volunteered to make lasagna for our dinner. That was no mean feat in the tiny kitchen. The pots and pans were as miniature as the chalet itself, and in order to feed eleven, I had to repeat the entire process three times. The others chipped in and made salads, desserts, and hors d'oeuvres, and by eight we were ready for a grand banquet. Dick had gone into Albany that afternoon and purchased a five-liter container of our favorite wine. The champagne we had brought from Perth was perfectly chilled.

We talked of happy times that had been and that were to come. By 2:00 A.M. everyone except Joy and I had celebrated themselves to sleep. Joy and I shared a wine-and-weather-induced euphoria that would not permit sleep. Choosing to cling to the happiness of the moment, we decided to stay up all night. By alternating glasses of wine with cups of coffee, we maintained both our euphoria and our wakefulness. As dawn broke, we decided to take a sunrise walk in the mountains.

Naturally fearless and curious, Joy led me down the most secluded of the mountain paths. We saw whole families of kangaroos running in the wild. To a suburbanite from the outskirts of New York City, the sight of kangaroos in the wild was mind-boggling. I had the sensation of having been transported into an unreal land of fairies and goblins. I was soon exhausted and barely able to keep up with my agile youngest sister.

"Hey, Joy, slow down. I'm tired. Let's stop."

"How about going back to the chalet and sneaking a little more of last night's lasagna? I'm starving."

"Okay. You eat, and I'll rest. I mean we've done it, haven't we? We did manage to stay up all night."

But Joy, my teacher in the fine art of unadulterated play, was not yet through with me. "How about sleeping for a couple of hours and then celebrating the first day of the New Year by climbing Devil's Slide?"

Having no idea that this was the most difficult climb in the Porongorups, I enthusiastically agreed before dropping off to sleep next to my mother on the floor of the chalet.

Four hours later, Joy and I were climbing. In the beginning, it was easy. We meandered up dirt trails that got progressively narrower but were so flat we could easily stand upright and climb without tilting our bodies forward. Our only concern during that phase of the climb was that we might inadvertently step on a snake. Since snakes can be particularly venomous in that part of the world, I took Joy's advice and watched very carefully as we walked. We were lucky. No snakes appeared to undermine our courage and spoil our climb.

After about forty-five minutes of walking, the mountain began to challenge us. The dirt trails left off, and we were forced onto sheer rock. It wasn't long before I understood why the trail was known as "Devil's Slide." At one hundred meters, the route up the mountain became hazardously steep. Amazed that this was a public trail, I questioned Joy about it.

Her answer should not have surprised me. "Oh, Pam, we didn't want to do this the tourist way, the easy way. We left the actual trail a long time ago. We're on our own, forging a new way up the mountain."

"Terrific, Joy. I should have known. Leave it to you to seek the greatest adventure. Okay, well, I guess there's no turning back now."

And there was, indeed, no turning back. Looking down to determine whether I had any option but to follow Joy, I practically scared myself right off the face of the mountain. Five hundred meters can feel like ten thousand when the only thing you can see over the ledge is a sheer rock vertical slide. I called to Joy, "We're going to have to find a different way down, scout. There's no way I can handle going down that thing." From her perch twenty meters or so above me, Joy simply smiled and snapped the shutter of her camera.

Her calm and cool attitude provided just the challenge I needed. I was determined not to let the twelve-year difference in our ages make me appear any less fit than she. I practically ran to catch up with her. We progressed another hundred meters or so on all fours. Again she got well ahead of me. She had reached another ledge, another resting point, and called down to me to turn around and look at the scene stretching out so far beneath us. I made the critical mistake of doing as she had suggested.

The height instantly made me dizzy and sick to my stomach. Believing that I was about to faint, I lay down on the sheer slope of the rock, placed my cheek against the stone, closed my eyes, and held on. The rocks seemed to be moving. It was an awful feeling. I sensed that the only way to stop the sensation of movement was to open my eyes and fix on a stable object. But I could not open my eyes, to do so would have been to focus again on the height and to reexperience my initial surge of fear.

Joy began to tease me. "What's the matter? You tired, mate? Come on now, another twenty meters or so, and you'll be right. Give it a fair go, hey?" I did not respond; I could scarcely comprehend her words.

Her teasing continued, but a touch of concern had entered her voice. "Pam, this is a silly time to decide to take a nap. Come on, now. The sleeping is much better up here. If you don't get up and move your bod, I'll take another photo of you."

And still I could not respond, though I had begun to hear her. Her words were providing me with a focus, something on which to concentrate. The rocks stopped moving. I could feel the stone scraping my cheek. Raising my head ever so slightly, I looked up at her. "Joy, I'm really frightened. I mean, frightened like never before. I can't move anything. I'm frozen. I can't go up and I can't go down. I'm not kidding, really, I'm not."

"Calm down, Pam. Let's just talk a little. Stay where you are. I mean, we're in no hurry, are we? Just look up at me again. Don't look sideways or down. Just look up at me."

I tried, but it was several minutes before I could do as she suggested. Once our eyes met, she continued, "Now, just keep looking at me. Get up slowly, but keep both your hands and your feet on the rocks." Again, I could not respond immediately. Only after I had managed to get up on all fours did she continue. "Okay, now one step at a time. But keep looking at me. That's it. Good. One step at a time."

I began to gain momentum, and my steps became more rapid.

Finally, when Joy was within five meters or so of me, I began to move very rapidly. I reached her. I had made it. Sitting down on the ledge, I broke out in a cold sweat. She held my hand for a while, until I calmed down. Pretty soon, I dared to look around. I saw what she had seen. It was beautiful: majestic, with vibrant colors distinguishing vineyards from farms, planting land from grazing land and land lying fallow. In the distance rose the peaks of the Stirling mountain range. Interspersed here and there were deep blue bodies of water. The terrain was only occasionally broken by winding reddish-colored bauxite roads. But the stillness and the beauty were undisturbed. We could sight no cars and no people.

We sat there in silence for a long time. I had overcome the greatest fear experience of my life, and my sense of mastery was enormous. Having come so close to giving in to my fear, I now needed some time to get used to both the fear and to my victory.

After an hour or so, I wanted to continue climbing. We were about three-quarters of the way up the mountain. My fear was under control, to reach the top was within our grasp. Joy was reluctant at first. She finally confessed that I had scared her. Only after I repeatedly reassured her that my fear was gone would she agree to lead me to the top.

Rather than continuing up the rock slide, we began to crisscross the mountain. In doing so, we elected to cut through dense bushes and thorns in order to avoid a repeat of the experience I had had. In that way, we slowly made our way to the crest.

This time, Joy was as pleased with herself as I was with myself. She admitted that, in spite of her adventurous spirit, even she had never undertaken such a difficult climb. Dropping all pretense, we talked of many things. And we played. I photographed her and she me. We picked the few flowers that were within reach and heartily laughed at anything worth even a casual smile.

I suspect we might have remained there for hours, but the day was drawing to an obvious close and we wanted to be back at the chalet before nightfall. On top of that, we had decided to take the longer and less frightening route down the mountain.

We had been gone about eight hours. The family, who had delayed dinner, had grown concerned about our safety. I tried to explain how special and important the day had been, but my words could not do justice to the day. I do not believe that any of them, other than Joy, really could appreciate what occurred on the mountain. That didn't matter. They didn't have to understand. They were content that my visit in their country was having such a positive effect on me.

My father, who I sensed had been watching me closely throughout the visit, said, "You know, you look like a different person from the woman we met the night of your arrival."

"Oh, Dad, I am a different person. I feel so healthy, and thanks to all of you, I've got a different perspective on things."

It was true. Australia had been good for me. Good for us. But something was stopping me from remaining there. My father knew what that something was. It was he, in fact, who first verbalized the reasons why I not only had to return to the States, but had to remain there for the foreseeable future.

Sitting in the backyard late one evening, he said, "I have been watching you closely. You have matured a lot during the last year. You have the ability and the drive to accomplish whatever you set out to do. But the opportunities are not here, in terms of either your profession or your books. You have got to go back to the States in order to realize your potential. Maybe someday, when you're ready to settle down and have achieved what you need to achieve, you'll consider returning here. I very much hope so. But for now, you don't belong here. You know that as well as I do."

I knew that he was right. While I did not have the same degree of confidence in my ability as he did, at the same time I appreciated that the slower and more leisurely Australian pace would, in time, begin to drive me crazy. Strongly motivated to achieve, I needed to be in a work environment that encouraged self-discipline and provided continually changing stimulants for thought. Yes, I belonged in the United States.

But I was going back as a significantly different person. I had learned something about myself and about my values and priorities, and appreciated that I did not have to struggle continuously to retain control over things, events, and people. It was possible for me to relax, to play, and to enjoy life as it came. Having reexperienced the love of a family, I knew that I wanted to love and be loved again. Finally, I had come to understand that it is not where you live but who you are that makes you happy or sad, fulfilled or unfulfilled.

The day before we were scheduled to depart, my mother

announced that she had a special surprise for us. She had purchased five tickets to the Monte Carlo International Circus, the circus made up of the best performers in the world. It was her birthday gift to Melissa, who would turn seven the day after our return to the States, and to Joy, who would celebrate her twenty-fourth birthday later that month. The five tickets were for Clyde, Joy, Melissa, Monica, and me.

Monica and Melissa were delighted. While I thought the gesture was awfully kind, it seemed a bit odd to me to spend my last afternoon not with my parents but at the circus. But my mother is wise; by keeping us occupied that last day, she helped us all avoid painful hours of bemoaning our imminent departure.

Arriving at the circus, we found that Mom had bought the best seats in the house, right up against the ring. The various performers were to come so close to us we could almost reach out and touch them.

The show was superb but managed to capture only part of my attention. My mind was filled with thoughts about preparing to leave. I was only partly seeing the performers when suddenly my attention was riveted to the group directly in front of us. My Hungarian "artista" was inside the ring, not more than ten feet ahead of me! Next to him, bedecked in a graceful acrobat's costume, was his wife. To his right, dressed in a funny, baggy clown costume, was none other than his petite, hyperactive "pa pa."

Not believing my own eyes, I grabbed the program from Clyde and hurriedly looked up the listing. Sure enough, it was the very same family. My friend was performing not only with his wife and his father but, in addition, with his brother and his brother's wife. The program said that they were widely regarded as the world's most talented clowns and acrobats. I had to laugh out loud at myself for assuming that the word *artista* represented only the fine arts. So that is what he had meant when he referred to the "service"; of course, he had been attempting to say "circus"! Not able to restrain myself, I reached across and tapped Monica's shoulder. She leaned toward me, and I toward her, and poor Clyde was squashed in the process. He was bewildered at my sudden excitement and then even more mystified when my words, of which he could only catch fragments, triggered equal excitement in Monica.

After their act, I let my mind wander and only vaguely focused on the lion tamer and the aerialists. We had traveled halfway around the world with the Hungarians only to then find them in Perth. The world seemed small and manageable. It made the journey we faced the next day seem somehow less awesome, and the break with family less final.

We were home by five, and were instantly occupied with preparations for the last of our backyard barbecues. Everybody seemed determined to make the last night happy and gay. There was only minimal reference to our departure. I promised to return each and every Christmas, knowing this couldn't and wouldn't happen. It couldn't happen because of money, the children's schooling, and the business. And it wouldn't happen because, sooner or later, I would reestablish a life momentum and routine that I wouldn't want to break. Someday, I thought to myself, there will be another man in my life, and our energies will focus on each other at Christmas. That's just the way it is. But I didn't need to express those thoughts that night. We all knew it, and yet talked of Christmases to come and contemplated how nice it would be if, during our next visit to the Southwest, we could all stay in the house that Dad was building.

Nor did I share the fears that were increasing within me as every hour passed. I had begun to realize that my reentry into the world I had left would be both demanding and lonely. I would have to reopen a house that was undoubtedly cold. I wondered whether the pipes had frozen and burst during our absence, and anticipated the worst. Five weeks' worth of mail would have to be sorted. The cat and dog would have to be retrieved almost immediately. The business would not tolerate any kind of easy transition back into the world of work. Melissa had been playful and contented during our vacation, but now she had to return to school. I had no reason to believe that her earlier fears, anxieties, and worries would not return at the same time. Jennifer was willing to come back and baby-sit for a short time only; I had no idea whether or not the church had succeeded in arranging for a housekeeper. Most of all, I feared living alone in that large house with only the two children.

Clyde had left for Australia only five days before our departure. I had been too busy and excited during those five days to even notice that the girls and I were living alone. It was all I could do to restrain myself from begging him to come back with us. It was so difficult to avoid making such a request that I actually avoided private conversation with him that last night.

We drank a lot of wine. I was glad in a way. My father always got very warm and philosophical when he had had a sufficient amount of his beloved Australian Rhine. Taking me aside, he bolstered my ego with talk of the great things he expected me to accomplish. He prophesied I would manage incredible feats that would make all of them proud. He mused out loud about how important it was that I take the time to write and to share what he regarded as my mature and unique perspective on life. He never once questioned my ability to cope. His belief in me was so great and meant so much that I vowed I would not crumble and show the full extent of my fears the next morning at the airport.

Our plane was scheduled to leave at noon. By ten-thirty, the entire family was at the airport. That hour and a half was extremely difficult and awkward for all of us. My mother kept excusing herself to go to the ladies' room and each time she returned, I could tell that she had been weeping. She said very little, periodically reaching out and touching my arm. She did not understand why I had to leave behind the warm protection she was so anxious to provide.

Like my mother, Gay said little in words but a great deal in gestures. Now and again, she would come up and brush my cheek with her hand and then turn away. Her big hazel eyes were consistently moist, though she stopped short of tears. When she did speak, just before we walked down the ramp to the departure area, she said only, "I'm so glad that you came. It has meant a lot to me. I feel close to you and stronger because of our conversations."

Letting Gay express the sentiment for both of them, Dick gave me a strong hug and eased the tension by continuing the pretense that the children and I would be back within the year. "We love you, and we'll see you soon."

Only Joy and I could say good-bye without pain. She picked those final moments to tell me of her decision to come to the States to pursue her architecture career.

"Hey, mate, how would you feel about my coming over there to work and get my master's?"

"How would I feel? I'd feel great!"

"I figure it's my turn, after all, to spend some time in that great house of yours I've heard so much about."

"When would you do this? I mean, the sooner the better as far as I'm concerned."

"Soon. In three months or so. I've got some projects to finish up and my portfolio to put together, and then I'll be off."

"Super, Joy. I can't wait."

I felt like I had had a last-minute reprieve from having to sever completely the psychological umbilical cord that had been nurturing us for the past several weeks.

Joy's announcement made it easier for me to endure the intense pain of saying good-bye to Clyde, my mother, and my father. My mother was first. Her sadness was so visibly deep and my fear so close to the surface that neither of us could say much. I began. "I love you, Mom. I'll miss you so much."

"Oh, dear, I love you too. And the girls; take good care of them."

Our embrace spoke of the rest, of the hurt, of the need, and of the very deep bond that existed between us.

Looking around for my father, I could find no trace of him. Panicked lest he miss my departure, my mother started calling out for him. Dick calmed her down, pointing out that he and Clyde had made their way down the ramp, prepared to say their good-byes where regulations and ropes insisted on a separation of passengers and visitors.

My father's hug was so intense he practically squeezed the wind out of me. I thought I saw a tear in his eye, but he maintained his normal reserve and turned away before the tear dropped.

Appropriately, Clyde was last. Thus far, he had walked the widow's walk by my side. Believing that the most treacherous part of the path was behind me, he was forcing me to go the rest of the way alone. His eyes showed that he had both confidence in my ability to manage and concern that he would not be there the next time I tripped. I tried to thank him for all he had done, but my words were painfully inadequate. He clung to me too long; I began to crumble, and admitted my fear. "Clyde, this is incredibly hard; I'm really so very frightened. I feel like I'm about to board a plane that's going to drop us right off the edge of the world."

Clyde tried to console me for the last time. "I know that you are frightened; if you weren't, I'd worry about your sanity. You have every reason in the world to be frightened. But remember that good-byes between us have always been temporary. And we've always got that ESP between us. If you're in trouble, I'll know it, and I'll respond if I can. I expect the same from you, by the way. And who knows what I'll end up doing? It just may be that you'll see me sooner than you think."

I couldn't take any more. Taking Melissa by the hand and motioning to Monica, I entered the corridor that led to the plane. We did not look back, not even once. To look back would have been to risk turning back. Only after we were seated on the plane did I dare to look again at the family. They had gathered on the observation deck and were waving frantically, unable to see us but trusting that we could see them. I hoped for all our sakes that the plane would not remain on the ground too long. As long as it sat, we had the option of getting off. I knew I could not resist for long.

Fortunately, our takeoff was almost immediate. We had been almost the last to board, and within minutes the plane was moving away from the terminal. The family receded into the distance, and finally it was possible to pick them out only because of their continued frantic waving. We were on our way home.

14

On Our Feet Again

It was early morning when the pilot announced that we would be landing momentarily in New York. Looking out the window, I felt a surge of excitement at seeing the New York skyline come into view. This had to be the greatest city in the world. I thought, "Ah, yes, this *is* where it happens. This is where I'm going to *make* it happen." Neither the patches of dirty gray snow lying here and there nor the bleakness of the overcast morning could dampen my enthusiasm.

Jim and Sara were at the gate. Jim could not wait to hold his children. Sara kept her distance, as is her custom, letting him consume all of their attention. I, too, stood apart. It was his turn, and it was their turn. A small tug in my heart reminded me that had it not been for Jim and Sara, no one would have met our plane at that hour unless I had specifically asked someone to do so as a favor to me. There was no special love in my life whose excitement at our reunion would parallel my own.

No, my reunion would be with my home and my career. My excitement would have to come from self-made successes and from play activities that I planned, initiated, and financed. I did not regard any of that with despair or fear. It had simply become a fact of life.

I was grateful, though, to Jim and Sara for providing the children with the feeling that they had left one loving environment only to enter another. They eagerly began to tell them of our experiences. I said little as we drove home.

We were actually in the house by ten in the morning. As we had predicted, it was freezing cold. Leaving the mounds of luggage in the front hall, we huddled in the kitchen for a while, trying to borrow warmth from one another while we waited for the heat to rise. Jim and Sara did not stay long.

Eventually Monica and Melissa began to tire of the kitchen, and, dragging suitcases behind, they disappeared into their own bedrooms. I understood their need to renest and left them in peace for a while. Their behavior was typical, occurring each time they had been away from home longer than a weekend.

I, too, had a need to renest, but it was going to take longer. As is my habit, I began with the mail. Meg had done her best to minimize the shock of having to face five weeks of mail. It was excessive, with holiday greetings and year-end tax notifications added to the normally abundant pile of bills, news magazines, and catalogs befitting the shop-at-home superconsumer.

In spite of Meg's efforts, the piles were still overwhelming. I had a strong urge to simply leave them where they were, go to my room, climb into bed, and pull the covers over my head. I might well have done just that had I not scheduled a return to the office the next day. I knew that there I would face a similar buildup. This was Tuesday. I set myself an objective: to get everything back under control by Friday so I could resume the life of leisure over the weekend. For the next two hours, suitcases and coats still strewn all over the front hall, I sat at the kitchen table separating junk mail from nonjunk mail, paying the bills, reading the letters, and thumbing through several weeks of *Time* magazine. A lot had happened in the world during our absence. The Soviet invasion of Afghanistan loomed as a threat to the free world, economic predictions were dismal, inflation was skyrocketing. It appeared that the holiday season had brought nothing but grief to the world at large. I had reentered the hub of the world, and it was a mess. The relaxed Australian way of life already seemed remote.

Reaching the bottom of the pile of correspondence, I found a long note from Meg. After welcoming us back, she indicated that like it or not, I had to take immediate action on several fronts. Apparently, my young housekeeper had arrived in the area two days prior to our return only to find no trace of the family she had hoped to join. At this moment, she was waiting at the home of an acquaintance of a friend of a friend. Meg urged me to contact her immediately, as she sensed the girl was more than a little nervous at being so displaced.

While I was delighted that my baby-sitter problems were potentially solved, I wondered where I would find the energy to actually go to get her and then, more difficult still, to begin to make her feel comfortable in a home in which I was not yet comfortable. The demands on me seemed to be increasing in intensity with every hour that passed. "One step at a time, Pam, take one step at a time," I said out loud to myself before picking up the telephone to call Christina.

Christina turned out to be an angel. I knew almost immediately that she, the children, and I would get along very well. She was pretty, but not preoccupied with her prettiness. Her big, wide brown eyes were full of warmth and curiosity. Standing tall and erect, she seemed to have enough self-confidence to squarely face the demands of our world. She was young enough to bring enthusiasm to our home, and yet seemingly poised and mature enough to provide the children with guidance.

But in spite of Christina's reassuring presence, it was difficult for the children to adjust to being home. Both were experiencing a touch of "vacationitis" and spoke of their dread of resuming the schoolday routine. Monica knew that she was behind in her work, since the teachers had been unable to give her post-Christmas-break assignments. She had a week's worth of work to catch up on already.

The next morning, however, Monica left the house bound for the school bus stop with little more than an occasional moan and groan. There was a twinkle in her eye and a bounce to her step. I sensed that her reluctance to plunge back into schoolwork was counterbalanced by excitement at seeing her friends again and by the thought of being, for at least a few days, the center of attention as she shared her unusual adventures.

While Melissa was too young to get behind in formal assignments, she had begun to fill her worry jar with similar concerns. "Mommy, what if the class is doing something that I don't understand?" "What if the class is going on an outing and I don't know about it?" "What if my teacher is mad at me because I didn't finish all my phonics lessons?" While I tried to put her concerns to rest by responding to each question in turn, I knew that they were symptomatic of a general fear of going back into the school environment that had so threatened her before our departure. Unhappily, there was no trace of enthusiasm in Melissa's voice as she prepared to go to school, and the tautness of her facial muscles showed that all her energies were going into finding the courage necessary to do what Mommy had said must be done that day.

I drove her to school the first few days and tried to talk of pleasant superficial things with the hope of distracting her from her worry jar. Arriving at the school each morning, we exchanged many kisses and even more hugs. She counted them one by one. I whispered to her that I hoped she would have a "ten" day. She never commented. It tore me apart each day to watch my baby get out of the car and, with stony expression, march resolutely down the path to her building.

Like Melissa, I felt anxious and distraught, and questioned my ability to cope. The winter flu developing inside me did nothing to help. Fortunately, Christina persisted in asking me one small question after another about the workings of the house, and before long, she had it humming. Meg, too, was patient and persistent, drawing me slowly and steadily back into the business. By Friday, I was in bed with a high fever, but our life had regained a momentum of its own.

Melissa struggled valiantly throughout the month of January. By mid-February, she was again allowing herself to smile, to laugh, and to play. She chose Saint Valentine's Day to reveal the source of her despair and to share the insight that had cured her.

Valentine's Day was painful for me. For the first time in twenty years, I found myself without a beau with whom I could exchange a loving greeting. I resented my coupled friends and pretty much stayed to myself. Only my children made me feel better. They were on winter break from school and were leaving the next day for a vacation with Jim and Sara. Sensing that I was going through a lonely period, they took special pains to make me Valentine's gifts. They were prettily wrapped and arrayed on my bed when I got home from the office on Valentine's night.

Monica's gift focused on my health and her concerns about my smoking. She had taken a giant piece of poster paper and outlined a heart in cigarettes. Inside the heart she had carefully inscribed, "Mommy, I love you so very much, and want to keep on loving you. I need you. My gift to you is to ask that you keep your cigarettes to six a day. Love, Monica."

She could not have delivered a more loving message. I hugged her for a long time, as Melissa grew increasingly impatient for me to open her gift. I could tell from the wrapping that it was a picture of some kind. Melissa loved to draw pictures of animals and houses, and my office walls were covered with her artistic endeavors. This, I expected, was another such illustration. I was totally unprepared for its content.

Opening the pretty red wrapping, the first thing I noticed was a house. There was nothing unusual about that. Inside the house were three stick figures. The hair on their heads indicated that they were females. They were of dramatically different heights: one, tall; the next, moderate; and the last, very short. Again, there was nothing unusual about that. Melissa often drew stick figures to represent herself, Monica, and me. But then, looking closer, I noticed that there were tears coming from the eyes of the tallest figure and of the middle-sized figure. The eyes of the tiniest figure were conspicuously dry. That puzzled me, and I looked to the carefully and painfully printed letters on the top of the page for an explanation. It read, "Dear Mommy. I cry when people are dying. I do not cry when they are dead. I love you very much. Love, Melissa."

The full impact of her statement did not dawn on me immediately. Before I was to realize fully what she was trying to tell me, I would thank her somewhat superficially and give both girls my gifts to them. Only after dinner, when I sat quietly mulling over the events of the day, was I to begin fully to appreciate Melissa's message. Calling her to me, I said, "Melissa, it's okay, you know. It's okay that you did not cry when Bill died. I know that you loved him. He knew that you loved him. He still knows that, from his place in heaven. This has been bothering you for a long time, hasn't it?"

She simply nodded.

"Do you want to talk about it some more?"

"No. I want to watch television." She was smiling.

"You seem to be feeling pretty happy."

"Yeah, Mom. Come on, Mom. I don't want to talk now."

"Okay. Okay. I get the message."

Melissa was clearly freed from something. I sensed that she had finally gotten to the bottom of her problem and that her nameless anxieties would from then on lose their power to ruin her days.

She began to report that more and more of her days were tens.

Soon she was expressing a desire to have friends over in the afternoon. Occasionally, she would even venture across the street to play with a neighbor's child. Melissa had regained her former spunky, self-confident manner. She expressed the desire to spend more weekends in New York City with her father and Sara. Jim happily obliged, delighted that his youngest was back on her feet again and desirous of spending time in his home.

Freer than I had been in a long time, I wanted to get out and see other people and be seen on a more frequent basis. I began accepting every invitation that came my way, and happily, there were many. Apparently, sufficient time had passed that when people gave dinner parties they considered me fair game to round out an otherwise uneven number of guests. Society, in effect, was declaring that it was socially acceptable for me to stop the mourning process.

15

Proms and Fantasies

I was ready, ready to stop grieving. Tiring of the widow's role, I often thought about how nice it would be to have the attention of a man. I was not yet thinking of sexual attention, but of social attention. My sexual urges had been muted a long time ago; during Bill's last illness he had neither the strength nor the desire for sex. Almost a year had passed since I had slept with a man. I did not miss it yet; I simply did not think about it, or perhaps did not let myself think about it.

Bill had been dead eight months, long enough to make me miss male companionship. Wanting to feel pretty and desirable again, I needed to be treated not just as a special person but as a special lady. I wanted to have a chance to wear the new clothes that Monica and I had so painstakingly chosen. In short, I wanted to be courted.

At first, I tried to ignore thoughts of dates and courtships, assuming they were at best inappropriate and at worst immoral. After all, I had not yet been widowed a year, and something in my upbringing told me that for the first year after a husband's death, the wife still belongs to him. My mind and heart were supposed to be filled with thoughts of him, of Bill, and of the times we had shared. I was supposed to be mourning, not seeking love; to be grieving, not wondering about the availability of the men I met.

My conscience was totally untroubled by my earlier fantasy flirtation with Larry Waverly. I understood that for what it was, an attempt to avoid having to make the widow's journey alone. But my thoughts now were different. As reflections of real needs, they were potentially dangerous. The rational side of my being knew that I was in jeopardy, and vulnerable to the advances of the least likely candidate for my affection.

Fortunately, I did not know just how to go about meeting men. Given my romantic belief that love must happen naturally and of its own accord, I had an aversion to singles bars and to being "fixed up" by friends. Further, I believed that love cannot exist to any meaningful degree without friendship and that friendship had to come first. So it had been with both Jim and Bill. But my male friends were not available. Only in my fantasies was I other than alone.

I tried to hide my needs and longings from others. As a professional who worked primarily with men, I could not afford to be sending out subtle signals and messages indicating my availability. Conscious or unconscious, such messages confound communications and destroy client relationships. I watched myself carefully in all professional situations. I thought I watched myself equally carefully with friends and with the children, but apparently I was mistaken.

Monica's behavior indicated that she was terribly conscious of my need for male attention. Each time I went to a friend's house for dinner or to a movie with Amy, Monica queried me upon my return, "Did you meet any nice guys, Mom?" Time after time, I would simply smile and reply no, I had not. Finally, exasperated with my apparent inability to stimulate a more satisfying social life, Monica decided to take matters into her own hands. She began asking her friends about their divorced fathers. Not stopping there, she advertised my widowhood to all eligibles or friends of eligibles. Her behavior was never so blatant as to be embarrassing; it simply amused me.

"Hello, you must be Monica Sanderson."

"Yes, I am. My mother, Pam, is a widow."

Or: "Happy to meet you, Monica. . . . And what does your daddy do?"

"Well, my stepfather died last summer. My mother is a consultant. She is also a widow."

One evening Monica, in collusion with her dearest friend, Beverly, actually succeeded in cajoling an unattached male into our home. Though to this day they deny both collusion and intent, the smile on their faces that evening convinced me his presence in my kitchen was far from coincidental.

For weeks, Bev and Monica had been talking in the privacy of Monica's bedroom about getting Jack, Bev's father, and me together. I had some notion of their schemes and, now and again, confronted them with my suspicions. "Could it be the two of you are talking about me and a certain man in Bev's life?"

"I don't know what you're talking about, Mom. What man in Bev's life?"

"Her father, perhaps."

Bev would begin to giggle, and Monica would join her.

"I don't know what I'm going to do with the two of you."

"Why don't you sign up for a paddle tennis court on Sunday mornings, Mom? It would be good for you."

"Somehow, Monica, I don't believe you and Bev have been worrying about either my paddle tennis game or my health. But, as a matter of fact, Brooks and I have taken a court every Sunday morning at eleven."

My announcement triggered another giggling spree, and I asked, "Bev, does your dad play at Fairbanks on Sunday mornings?"

Giggle . . . giggle . . . giggle.

It became a game, an entertaining game for all. The more we joked about it, the less likely it was that I would ever contemplate Jack as a lover, fantasy or otherwise. After all, he had become the object of a child's game and, as such, could not become anything more in my mind.

That all changed very quickly one Monday evening. Bev and Monica were working on a project for school, and I asked Bev to stay for dinner. She called her father and asked him to pick her up at seven-thirty. Of course the project was not finished by that time. When Jack arrived, the girls were still working frantically at the kitchen table. Jack had no choice but to stand there and wait for them. For my part, I felt I had to stop packing for my business trip scheduled the next day and help him pass the time.

Conversation between the two of us was immediately effortless. Within a few minutes, we discovered that we had a lot of mutual interests. As we talked, each of us leaning against opposing kitchen counters, I could not help but notice that he was an extremely attractive man, in a rugged kind of way. His brown eyes were warm and sensitive, his gestures thoughtful, and his shoulders broad. Before long, we both stopped urging the children to finish their task. We simply kept talking, exploring, and learning about each other. The children showed enormous restraint, suppressing all giggles and convincingly pretending long after the project was finished that a few critical details remained to be done.

By the time Jack left, the object of the children's game had assumed a form, a shape, and an appeal that would subsequently make me take the game a lot more seriously. During the course of our conversation, I had promised to introduce Jack to Debbie, a friend who shared his professional interests. I liked Jack enough to want to make my promise more than an idle one.

Sensing my newfound awareness of her friend's father, Monica pounced on me. "Mommy, you liked him, didn't you? I mean, I *know* you liked him. You just talked and talked and talked. Bev and I were finished a long time before they left, and you didn't even notice. Oh, I've got to call Bev. She's going to be *so* excited."

Embarrassed by Monica's enthusiasm and a little threatened by her perceptiveness, I wanted to restrain her. In something close to a harsh voice, I insisted that it was late and she had to go to bed. I resumed my packing, and within a few minutes had quite thoroughly refocused my attention on mentally preparing for the impending series of business meetings.

The meetings went well, uninterrupted by thoughts of Jack or of faceless fantasy lovers. I was fine when I worked. I was even happy.

But, focus or no focus, my social/sexual self continued to assert its needs and to demand attention. When the opportunity presented itself to fulfill my promise to introduce Jack to my friends, I jumped at it.

Debbie had been asking me to have dinner with her and her husband, Peter, for months. When she called not long after my conversation with Jack, I suggested, without giving it a second thought, that they come to my home for dinner two weeks from Saturday.

I hung up, thinking I had reached a turning point. For the first time in my single life, I was in a position of calling a man and asking him to come to dinner. I was a nervous wreck. Sitting in my bedroom one evening, I could not initially summon the courage to finish dialing Jack's number, and hung up several times before the ringing began. When I finally allowed the call to go through, I sat in terror that I would be unable to actually speak when he answered. My relief knew no bounds when the call was answered not by Jack in person but by a recording of his voice. The recording urged me to leave a message after the beep. Unable to do so, I hung up. First, I had to frame my message and recompose myself.

I felt ridiculous. After all, I reminded myself, you're not actually asking Jack for a date: This is as much a business meeting as anything else. Rationalizing, I told myself that I had absolutely no reason to be nervous. After all, I was only doing him a professional favor. That we were both single and of the opposite sex was irrelevant. That had nothing to do with anything. Jack was just a friend. Not even that; he was barely an acquaintance. I dialed again, preparing to identify myself and ask that Jack return my call either that night or at the office the next morning.

No good. I couldn't do it. I couldn't even introduce myself as the caller. I wasn't even sure Jack knew my last name, or if he did, which last name he would recognize. Because of his daughter's friendship with Monica, he knew the Sanderson name. He may or may not have been aware of the Miller name. It was extremely unlikely that he would recognize me by my maiden name, my professional name, the name that I found myself using with increasing frequency: the Cuming name. I hung up again.

Finally, I tired of my own ridiculous behavior. Dialing for the sixth or seventh time, I managed to blurt out, "Hello, Jack. This is Pam Miller, Monica's mother. I would appreciate it if you would call me back either tonight or at the office tomorrow. The number at the office is . . ."

I had taken the first step, putting the ball in his court. I hoped against hope that he would return the call in the morning. I was always more composed at the office than at home. Somehow, making the invitation from the office would make it seem more casual, more professional, and less like a date.

My assumption that I could be calm, cool, and collected if Jack called me at the office was entirely unfounded. When Michelle buzzed me and announced that Jack was on the phone, I panicked. I could not take the call for a moment or two. Before I did so, I took a deep breath and a gulp of lukewarm coffee. No client call in the world could have made me so nervous. Finally, I started muddling through it.

"Hello, Jack. Thank you for returning my call. I have spoken with Debbie and Peter, the people I mentioned might be of some help to you. Well, they are coming to dinner two weeks from Saturday, and I thought that maybe you would like to come also."

Jack was silent for what seemed like an eternity. "That's very nice of you. I would love to come. What time?" I hadn't thought of that. Again, my head started spinning. I must have sounded like a jerk as I said, "What time suits you, Jack?" After a bit of bumbling around, we decided that he would come at seven.

My nerves were so frazzled by the call that I found it impossible to return to the work that was scattered about my desk. Picturing the dinner party, I romanticized every detail. I would set the most beautiful table Jack had ever seen. I would be amusing, scintillating, and gorgeous. Sitting opposite me at the far end of the table, Jack would at first be intrigued, and then anxious for Debbie and Peter to leave so that he could focus on getting to know me. He would suggest that he stay after they left to help me clean up the dishes. I would demurely tell him that he needn't, but he would politely, softly, and firmly insist.

My one encounter with Jack prior to the dinner simply encouraged my fantasies. Knowing that Jack regularly played paddle tennis on Sunday mornings, I went early for my match, deciding to sit and watch him play. He noticed me immediately. It pleased me when he missed a shot, as I was certain that my presence accounted entirely for his blunder. Every good shot was, I assumed, equally stimulated by my presence. The look in his eyes as he glanced in my direction while leaving the court convinced me that he cared, and cared deeply. Any lingering sense of reality vanished as he elected to sit and watch me play.

The problem with fantasies is that they can skew your perception of reality, or make reality a disappointment. In my case, they were to do both, creating a great deal of unhappiness. By the time the day of the dinner party arrived, I had woven enough fantasies around Jack to be effectively unable to appreciate that I scarcely knew who he was and that, in fact, we had no relationship, romantic or otherwise.

Jim picked up Monica and Melissa early on Saturday morning, leaving me free to spend the entire day shopping, polishing, doing my hair, and dressing. I was ecstatically happy, acting and feeling like a little girl on the morning of her birthday party. I blasted the stereo and sang as I worked. All the chores finished by noon, I decided to drive over to Amy's house and borrow back the guitar I had given her. Bev had told me that her father played the guitar, and I thought he might feel like picking it up at some point during the evening.

Bouncing into Amy's house, I sat down at her kitchen table and proceeded to tell her how excited I was about the evening ahead. For the first time since Bill's death, I felt ready and eager to begin really living again. I think I surprised her more than a little, but she was not displeased with what she saw. "I don't know quite what's come over you, but I'm glad to see it. You look like a sixteen-year-old!"

Amy shared my buoyant mood. Tommie had recovered more rapidly than expected, and was home from the hospital. Life's troubles seemed to be a thing of the past.

Like adolescents, we talked about what I should wear that evening, dismissing one outfit as too formal, another as too casual, a third as too conservative, and a fourth as too revealing. It was a game, a wonderful game, and the hours passed quickly. With a start, I realized that it was three, and that Debbie and Peter would be arriving in an hour. They had agreed to come early to help me prepare dinner. If I didn't hurry, I would not have time even to change, much less to pay attention to the fine details of my grooming.

Fortunately, Debbie and Peter were late, arriving shortly after five o'clock. By then, I was as well groomed as I could be. At seven-fifteen, the doorbell rang. With great trepidation, I answered it. There stood the object of my fantasies, holding two bottles of wine and visibly nervous.

"Hello, Jack. It's good to see you."

"Hi. Thank you. It's good to see you, too. I, uh, I brought some wine. I hope it suits the dinner you're planning."

The wine was in a brown bag, and I had no idea as to its color, but nonetheless hastened to say, "Oh, that's wonderful. It's perfect."

Jack's moustache moved a little, indicating, I guess, the beginnings of a smile at my blunder.

Realizing I was still holding the door ajar, and that Jack continued to stand out in the cold, I felt rather silly. "Please, come in, Jack. I don't know what I was thinking."

He entered a bit reluctantly, still clinging to the wine.

"Can I take your coat? Debbie and Peter are in the kitchen."

I was glad to see that Jack was as nervous as I; after all, if he wasn't interested in me, he'd have no reason to be anxious about the evening. Somehow, his anxieties calmed mine as I focused on trying to make him comfortable. That was not difficult. Debbie is a great talker, and there was not even a moment of awkward silence after the introduction.

Nor was there a minute of silence all evening. Debbie and Jack did, indeed, have a great many common professional interests, and could not find enough hours in the evening to discuss all of them. Peter and I, meanwhile, always comfortable with one another, bounced from topic to topic, enjoying ourselves immensely at the other end of the table.

All through the conversations, I was highly aware of Jack and sensed that he was equally aware of me. As I had hoped, when Debbie and Peter made a motion to leave, Jack held back. Instead of leaving with them, he helped me walk them outside to their car. As though he had been reading my fantasies, he then offered to help with the dishes. Almost according to script, I urged him to just sit and talk with me while I worked. But he would have no part of that. The next thing I knew, he had rolled up his sleeves and was up to his elbows in dirty dishwater.

We talked as we worked, but our conversation was awkward and strangely superficial, given the anticipation in the air.

"I liked your friends. How did you get to know Debbie?"

"Well, we went to the same college, but I didn't know her then. We met when our two firms successfully made a joint bid on a training project for a pharmaceutical firm."

"She certainly can talk."

"Oh, yes, Debbie is never at a loss for words. Did that bother you?"

"No, I found her conversation to be very interesting."

And so it went, as we struggled to find casual topics until the dishes were done. That a more serious subject awaited was obvious to both of us.

Finally, we went into the living room. Within minutes, Jack was holding me. It felt good, very, very good. My fantasies paled into insignificance beside the wonder of the reality of his touch. One thing might well have led to another that evening, until we found ourselves in bed together. That would have been unfortunate, marking the end of a relationship even before it had begun. We were acting on sheer physical attraction, not knowing enough about each other to have any real feelings of affection. Perhaps Jack sensed that I was confused, not ready or able to distinguish between physical attraction and emotional love. Or perhaps it was I who applied the brakes, out of fear if nothing else.

At any rate, we began to talk. I wanted Jack to understand that I was not in the habit of jumping into bed with every man who crossed my path.

"Jack, I feel a lot for you right now, and it's important because it's the first time since Bill's death."

"But you don't even know me."

The bitterness of reality struck home. "No, I guess I don't. I'm a great one for building a total personality given only a few small clues. Anyway, with you, I'm really fond of the personality I've created."

"That convinces me you have no idea of who I am. I really question my ability or even willingness to get into another relationship at this point."

"Why, Jack?"

"Oh, I don't know, I guess it has a lot to do with the divorce. Oh, I am seeing someone now, don't misunderstand me, but it's . . . well . . . it's not really a commitment kind of thing."

I said that I understood, though in reality I did not. Relationships and commitments went hand in hand as far as I was concerned. All I had heard, really heard, was that Jack, the object of my true-love fantasies, was seeing someone else.

As bizarre as it sounds, I was jealous. That's right, jealous. That I didn't even really know Jack, that this was our first evening together, made no difference. Because of my fantasies, I felt I had a claim to his affection.

I said nothing of that, however. Instead, I began to distance, getting up from the sofa and moving to another chair. We continued to talk.

"Pam, you seem to be a real romanticist, and an awfully intense one at that. I sense that what I've said troubles you, and yet it shouldn't. You and are in different places; we probably always were. I mean, you're clearly ambitious; I can see that just looking around at this house. I'm, well, I don't know what I am. We're different, that's all."

"Perhaps we are, Jack, though I've never thought that differences are necessarily a problem between people."

"Maybe not. I guess the important difference is that it takes me a long time, a very long time, to get to know someone, and to trust a relationship enough to invest any real feeling in it. You seem to be quite the opposite, at least right now. But then, you've been through so much pain. I don't want to hurt you. I really don't, and I sense that I could."

I simply nodded. Jack was very perceptive, telling me things about myself that couldn't be denied, in spite of my efforts to do so.

He continued. "I'd like to get to know you. Perhaps we can do some things together with the children. How does that sound to you?"

"Okay, Jack, I guess that sounds fine."

Somehow, in our talk, Jack had managed to bring reality to bear on our evening. He had been kind, but I was not to feel grateful to him until much later. I didn't welcome reality. It did not jibe with my fantasy of a sudden discovery of true, long-lasting, dedicated love.

Jack left at about two in the morning, leaving me fatigued but unable to sleep. After pacing the house for a while, I put away the last of the dishes and poured myself a glass of wine. I felt an enormous need to sort out my thoughts but could not find a place to begin. I had to understand something, but what I did not know. The elation of the day had disappeared, leaving self-doubt and disillusionment in its stead. I was embarrassed but could not say why. I felt rejected, and yet Jack had neither done or said anything to trigger that feeling. Mostly, I felt alone; my fantasy had deserted me. Perhaps that is why I could not go to sleep. My fantasy had become my sleeping pill, and the vial was now empty. I had nothing with which to occupy my thoughts.

The next morning, I seriously considered canceling my paddle tennis date with Brooks. I was exhausted, and afraid of running into Jack. The evening had left me in a bad way, and I suspected it had been hard on him, too. I was afraid of looking into his eyes and seeing the desire to avoid me, or to undo our evening. Only my pride spurred me on that morning. To fail to show up would be to let Jack know that he had upset me. That would be to let him in on yet another of my psychological secrets. I had to distance myself from Jack, and the way to begin was by indicating that I was largely unaffected by the events of our evening together. Putting on my paddle clothes, I arrived at the court precisely on time.

Much to my amazement, Jack sat and watched our game for the better part of the hour. When I switched sides, he shifted seats. He was clearly studying me. Brooks noticed, too; it was impossible not to notice. Finally, she stopped playing and approached me.

"What's with you and Jack? I mean, Pam, it's obvious that something is going on. He looks at you like you and he are having a full-blown love affair. Come on, confess. You can't hide anything from me, you know. You're sleeping together, aren't you? Come on, I know you are."

"Brooks, it's both a long story and a short story. No, we are not having an affair. Yes, there is something between us, but I'm not sure just what it is. Whatever it is, it's not likely to turn into anything more, at least after last night, and I can't stand here and talk about it with you. I'm so tired, and so psychologically drained, that I can hardly stand. If I don't keep on running, I'll surely fall down. So, hit the ball, would you. As soon as he leaves, I want to leave, too."

Plastering a smile on my face and willing my legs to run, I resumed play. It took every ounce of strength I had remaining to keep going. Finally, looking at the observer's deck, I noticed that Jack had gone. I motioned to Brooks that I had to quit playing. Reluctantly, she went along. She quizzed me all the way to the parking lot. I would tell her very little. Shaking her head, she left saying only that, given the look on Jack's face and my obvious struggle, the end of our story was not yet at hand. The more vehemently I protested that she was wrong, the more convinced she became that she was witnessing the beginning of another chapter in my life.

She was not altogether wrong. Jack did call again several weeks later and invite the children and me to go roller skating. Again, I found myself in a high-pitched state of excitement over the prospect of such an unusual "date." Again, anticipation of the date triggered my fantasies, and again they were disappointed. Oh, the evening was fun. It was more than fun. I laughed harder than I had in a long time. But the evening could not match my imaginings; such would not have been possible. Neither was I as distraught as I had been the first time around. I had begun to learn about relationships, and to be able to distinguish fantasy and reality. Jack and I are now able to enjoy each other's company. We have managed to build a special friendship.

The friendship was important, but not enough to satisfy my longings. And so when, in the early spring, a tall, blond, eligible bachelor asked me to dinner, I was ecstatic. My fantasies bloomed again.

Our relationship lasted only a few months, ending as abruptly and quickly as it began. I had not sufficiently learned my lesson, and persisted in confusing the fantasy of sudden true love with real life. Asking too much, too soon, I denied both of us the opportunity to really get to know each other.

Oh, he was not faultless. Unlike Jack, he found the pace exciting and even intensified it as he showered me with calls, perfume, and fine wines. He treated me like a princess, and I enjoyed playing the part. I thought for a blissful few weeks that my fantasies had come true. But no. Reality soon intruded as I discovered that his affectionate displays would be sporadic and whimsical. The very intensity of my romantic feelings threatened his need for freedom and spontaneity. We both suffered as a result.

I suspect that all widows are, to one degree or another, in danger of looking for too much, too soon from the first several men who enter their lives after the death of their husbands. The loss itself creates an intensity of feeling and of need that stimulates a retreat into fantasy. Anyone expressing concern and a romantic interest at the same time can so easily be given a key part in the widow's fantasy. But fantasies have a way of bursting.

That was fine with me. I was finally ready to enjoy the real me, functioning, and functioning well, in the real world. My romantic fantasies had triggered as much pain as pleasure. Only as I left them behind did I begin to experience a sense of psychological stability that I had not known since Bill's death. It had taken almost a year.

Part VI

ONE YEAR HAS PASSED

Journey's End

16

Me, Myself, and I

On the shingles to the right of the front door of our home is a three-by-five-inch rectangular space that is visibly darker than the rest of the house. In the corners of the darkened space are four small holes indicating that something once hung there. The discoloration was produced by a small brass plaque which read, "The Millers." It had been a wedding gift from Brooks and Rob. One Saturday afternoon in the early summer, I removed it. I had needed to remove it. This was no longer the Miller home. It was the home of Pamela Cuming and Monica and Melissa Sanderson. No one bearing the Miller name resided in the house. All that was left of the Millers was the love for Bill that resided and would continue to reside in our hearts. But the man was dead, and the people who had made up his family were no longer comfortable living under the banner of his name.

Even as I write this, I am in the midst of the seemingly endless hassle of changing all my records and charge cards. Each day I force myself to confront at least one bureaucrat with my name-change request. Without exception, they assume that the reason for the request is divorce. When they notice that the address is unchanged, they inevitably comment, "Oh, so you got the house, did you? And the kids with it?"

My pain might be less if I let such questions go unanswered, but I cannot. To do so would be to let the bureaucrats believe that the love Bill and I had shared had died, that the relationship had grown sour.

It had not. Having been divorced once, I knew the difference. Bill had died even while our love was strong. I could not let their assumptions go unchallenged.

"My husband and I were not divorced. He died." Then I would wait for their inevitable stumbling, their silence, and their obvious disapproval.

"Your husband *died*, and you're giving up his name?"

"That's right. I have always worked and written under my maiden name. While my husband was alive, there was a reason to bear the confusion of two names. Now that he is gone, I find it even more difficult and more unnecessary to continue to carry two names. This is going to simplify my life."

In spite of assurances to the contrary, I knew they did not understand. I sensed that they felt the least I could do was to continue to keep Bill's memory alive by bearing his name. But perhaps they did not actually disapprove; I may have been projecting my own disapproval onto them.

The Miller children, Ed, Cathy, and Pete, would disapprove, I feared, and this added to my discomfort as I contemplated a name change. The decision was so difficult to make, in fact, that it took me a full month after announcing my intent to Monica and Melissa to actually contact the lawyers and set the legal machinery in motion. During the three or four weeks it took for Joel and his partner, Roy, to get the request on the court calendar, I changed my mind several times. On at least three occasions, I asked Michelle to get Roy on the telephone so I might stop the legal process before it was too late. But each time, on hearing Roy's voice, I made up some feeble excuse for calling and let his efforts continue.

My parents were delighted when they heard of the impending change. They seemed to think that I was taking the step not just for myself but for them as well. They had always been proud of me, and pleased that I had chosen to write under their name. In her enthusiasm, my mother seemed to be saying, "Yes, dear. You are coming back into the fold that is the Cuming family. It is only appropriate for you to bear the name that we bear."

While it felt good to make them happy, I was not changing my name for them, nor was I resuming their name as a symbol of reentry into the family. After all, I had never left the family. Why was I going through all of this? What was impelling me to incur the bureaucratic hassle, the expense, and the guilt? I asked myself that question dozens of times. There seemed to be no clear, clean, simple answer. A number of things were motivating my behavior, some of them noble and others not so noble.

Perhaps the most compelling of motivations was that I had been the second Mrs. Miller. The oldest child in my family, I had never gotten used to hand-me-downs; in some ways, I felt like I had a hand-me-down name. The name Pamela Cuming was not a hand-me-down name; to my knowledge, it had never belonged to anyone else.

There was more to it than that, however. My lifeline had been broken by two major crises: the first had been the divorce from Jim and the second, Bill's death. With each crisis, I had been forced to create a new identity; first as "divorcée," and then as "widow." And yet even as I worked through the crisis and found a way to stand on my own two feet, my name had belied my efforts to create an independent identity. It had been Pamela Sanderson who had married William Miller. Somehow, Pamela Cuming kept getting lost in life's shuffle. I could not stand the thought that at some future date, Pamela Miller would meet another man whose name she would choose to adopt. Somehow, if that happened, Pamela Cuming would be forever and irretrievably lost.

I could not let that happen. No, I had experienced too many significant life changes and with each change, my sense of self, of basic self, had been threatened. It was now time to go back to basics and to reintroduce to the world a person who was whole in her own right, who had been given a name at birth, who brought certain assets and certain liabilities into the world, and who would someday die a separate and individual death.

If nothing else, I had learned that coupling is temporary. Relationships can die, and people can die. In the end, we are each of us alone. To take someone else's name feels good at the time it is done; it provides a feeling of closeness and enables us to believe that the coupling is forever. But it had been Pamela Cuming who married Jim Sanderson, and it had been Pamela Cuming who married William Miller, and it was Pamela Cuming who suffered when he died.

I was telling the bureaucrats that the motivation for my name change was life simplifcation. That really was the least of it. The confusion was not that bad, after all. The worst of it occurred in hotels. Clients would make the reservation under the name of Pamela Cuming, but it was a credit card issued to Pamela Miller that paid the bill. Occasionally, this would provoke the hotel to question my identity. But that happened only rarely, and was more amusing than anything else.

No, the motivation behind the name change was far more significant and complex than that. I desperately needed a feeling of continuity, something that did not change as my relationship changed. The only constant in my life was me. Even my children had come from an impermanent relationship and as a result, they bore a different name.

There were times when I considered instituting a name change in their behalf, but my motivation was selfish. To do so would have hurt not only Jim but eventually the children as well. Jim is very proud of his children, and it means a lot to him to have them bear his name. More important, they too have a right to a continuity in their lives. They were born Monica and Melissa Sanderson, and regardless of marriages, they will die the same two people. I have no right to arbitrarily force on them a new name and, in its wake, a shift in self-concept.

Regaining a sense of continuity in life was important enough to me to endure the expense, the red tape, and even the scene in court. Appearing in court was extremely painful. Roy had told me to meet him at ten-thirty. I was early and he was late. For nearly twenty minutes, I paced the marble-covered massive entrance to the court, feeling small, insignificant, and scared.

Perhaps Roy sensed this, for he took pains to be kindly, supportive, and soft-spoken. Without my saying a single word, he reassured me that this was something I had to do. Taking my arm, he led me into the courtroom itself.

The actual ceremony was, like a wedding ceremony, brief but impactful and essentially unalterable. The judge asked me to confirm that I had been using the name Cuming over the years, and that many already knew me by that name. He queried me about debts, seeking reassurance under oath that the notivation for my change of name was neither to default on payments nor to defraud others.

Attempting to spare me pain, Roy answered as many of the

judge's questions on my behalf as he could, turning to me only when my speaking would be likely to prompt a favorable ruling on our motion. The judge was most interested in the children and the impact of the name change on them. I had to repeatedly assure him that the change would only simplify their lives.

He ruled in our favor, making the formal pronouncement that, henceforth, I would be known legally as Pamela Cuming. As the gavel hit the bench, I felt no elation, only numbness. It was over. I had gotten my way, and yet I was not happy about it. In the span of ten minutes in that courtroom, Pamela C. Miller had ceased to exist. She was no more.

Meg and I had lunch that day and toasted my name change. The guilt had begun to recede. I knew in my heart that I had done what had to be done. Bill was dead. I was alive, and the resumption of my own name provided a feeling of stability that would help me not only to cope, but to actually enjoy living. I had taken a giant step in the direction of asserting my individuality; I was beginning to trust my ability to go it alone—to run the business, the household—and to create a healthy and stimulating environment for my children.

Even as I appreciated that I was capable of doing it alone, I had to admit that I did not *want* to do so. I do not understand people who claim that they live alone out of choice and preference. Neither do I understand people who are afraid of getting involved, of loving and being loved. I suspect that they do not know that a life without love is bleached out, devoid of both the highs and the lows that make living a vivid, dynamic experience.

I am a winner. I lost a man I loved, but I am still a winner. I loved someone deeply, and my loss was intensely painful. But I would not have done it differently. I am sorry, deeply sorry, that Bill had to die. But I am joyful that I knew him, and that I loved him. The joy far outweighs the sorrow. If it did not, I would probably be sorely tempted to refuse to get deeply involved again. I will not so refuse. On the contrary, I hope very much that someone enters my life whom I can love. I may lose again. That is a risk that I will have to take. But if I can learn from the loss and gain in self-insight and in the understanding that I have of people and of living, then even if I lose the relationship, I will not have lost as a person.

Oh, I have my bad moments when everything seems pointless and flat or impossibly difficult. But these minidepressions occur less and less often, and when they do, I can recognize them for what they are. More resilient than I used to be, I no longer cling to despair or to anger. It would be a severe exaggeration to say that I am now serene; I have not and probably never will find that kind of continual peace within myself. But neither am I tightly strung and defensive.

I very much believe that people can do with their lives almost anything they want to do. Fate wields some severe blows now and again, as it did when Bill died, but even when fate is that harsh, there are options.

In my case, to follow the path of least resistance would have been to crawl into a cocoon and wait for life to pass me by. My other option was to summon all available energy, make use of all offered assistance, and proceed to turn our lives into something positive. The activity was sometimes frenetic and other times methodical. But at least it was activity rather than a passive acceptance of fate.

The children and I are going to return to the site of the spreading of Bill's ashes on the anniversary of his death. We plan to take a picnic lunch, climb the rocks, and wade in the brook that carried Bill to the sea only a year ago. As we contemplate the day, we anticipate joy and happiness. We may cry, but the tears will not be the bitter tears of loss and regret but the tears of deeply felt emotion and awareness of life. I do not believe that we will feel Bill's presence. He is gone, he is free.

We, too, are free, free from grief and the kind of pain that drags you down. We are not, and hopefully will never be, free from the memory of Bill and what he represented. Each of us, in her own way, has overcome grief and despair and learned to live more fully by acting in accordance with the statements Bill made during our marriage:

Live your life as though you have only one life to live. Give your love as though you have only one love to give.

Remember, you must be responsible for you—your life, your love, your clarity.

*　　*　　*

I am not sorry that I had to walk the widow's walk, nor do I regret that my children had to endure it along with me. We are all better for having had the experience. Our minds, bodies, and hearts are finely tuned as a result of the demands that were placed on us. We are ready and eager to set out again on whatever path opens itself to us.